words and beautifully illuminating pictures. What a wonderful resource for both the lay reader and the seminary student!

Havilah Dharamraj, PhD
Professor of Old Testament,
South Asia Institute of Advanced Christian Studies, Bangalore

With a careful attention to their literary form and setting, and placing them in their cultural context, Dr. Peter Ho opens up the books of Habakkuk and Zephaniah. Although these prophetic books are among the lesser-known parts of the Old Testament, Dr. Ho's expert guidance will help readers to understand them both as an ancient text and as the living word of God that continues to speak today.

David G. Firth, PhD
Old Testament Tutor,
ty College, Bristol, UK

Christians often embrace a simple theological framework that suggests that if we obey the rules, we will be rewarded, but if we fail to obey, we will suffer the consequences. However, as Dr. Peter Ho points out, this retributive principle does not always work in real life and we, like the prophets Habakkuk and Zephaniah, struggle when justice is perverted and God seems to be silent. Dr. Ho shows how the books of Habakkuk and Zephaniah help us catch a glimpse of God's answer to the prophets' struggles. God challenges his people to persevere in living by faith and to live faithfully, trusting that God's justice will always prevail.

Dr. Ho has analyzed the books of Habakkuk and Zephaniah with masterful biblical scholarship through an artistic lens. His commentary offers many applications for the modern world, with specific reference to the Asian context. He pays particular attention to the poetic nature of the two books and analyzes, in great detail, their literary elegance and careful syntax. The spectacular description of God as the Divine Warrior, going into battle and defeating his enemies, is worthy of attention. I highly recommend this book to all readers, especially pastors, ministers of the word, and seminary students.

Patrick Fung, PhD
Global Ambassador,
OMF International

Peter Ho aims to "demystify" Habakkuk and Zephaniah, who can seem rather imposing prophets. He helps us to follow Habakkuk's wrestling with the question of how theology relates to reality, and he shows how the God of Zephaniah not only acts in judgment but commits himself to the total rejuvenation of his people. What significant prophets these are, and how helpful Peter Ho is in enabling readers to engage with them!

John Goldingay, DD
Senior Professor of Old Testament,
Fuller Theological Seminary, California, USA

Peter Ho displays pastoral insight, literary sensitivity, and theological nuance in this commentary on Habakkuk and Zephaniah. Dr. Ho deploys his careful scholarship appropriately, drawing insights from current research as well as contextual theology. Perspectives from the Majority World interact with those of the West, creating a robust theological reading of these books for today. I shall return to this commentary again and again.

Heath A. Thomas, PhD
President and Professor of Old Testament,
Oklahoma Baptist University, USA

In this age of visual and pictorial learning, Dr. Peter Ho not only provides contextual readings but also offers visual representations in this commentary on the books of Habakkuk and Zephaniah. His work includes helpful charts, timelines, images, and photos to aid comprehension and bring life to these two ancient texts. Along with highlighting the historical and literary features of the books, the author emphasizes their importance in the context of Book of the Twelve, making his work a necessary and valuable addition to any theological library. His pastoral and contextual expositions are informed by contemporary cultural and ecclesial references and grounded in multidisciplinary scholarship, making these relevant and beneficial for modern readers seeking to understand these books with ease.

Shirley S. Ho, PhD
Associate Professor of Old Testament,
China Evangelical Seminary/
China Evangelical Graduate School of Theology, Taiwan

Prophetic literature of the Old Testament is often intimidating to those who are unfamiliar with the cultural and geopolitical contours shaping the context in which the literature was born. Peter Ho's commentary does an excellent job, making the books of Habakkuk and Zephaniah accessible and deeply meaningful to the uninitiated. His treatment of this divinely inspired literature – which contributes to the symphonic voice of a canon of Scripture that ultimately reveals redemption from the guilt and power of sin through Jesus Christ – is not only accessible, clear, and properly ordered, but it is also backed by the most rigorous of research and is informed by contemporary academic debates surrounding the corpus. This is a great resource for anyone – ranging from Old Testament scholars to average Christians – who wishes to go deeper in their study of these prophetic books.

Matt Ayars, PhD
Former President
Wesley Biblical Seminary, Mississippi, USA

Many find it daunting to read and study the Minor Prophets. However, if we truly believe in the centrality of God's word as the supreme standard for life and conduct, then, in these challenging times, it is more crucial than ever to apply our minds to study God's word and anchor our lives upon his truth. In this commentary on Habakkuk and Zephaniah, Dr. Peter Ho has combined incisive biblical exegesis, robust theological reflection, and astute cultural observation. Preachers, Bible study leaders, and lay Christians will find in this Asia Bible Commentary Series a biblically faithful and culturally relevant guide through which they will hear the timeless word of God speak truth in their own time and for their own context.

Rev. Darryl Chan
Senior Minister,
Prinsep Street Presbyterian Church, Singapore

This exceptional work achieves a delicate balance between the historical and cultural contexts of the biblical texts and their relevance to readers in Asia – Singaporean-Chinese contexts. In addition, the interpretations of the two books consistently uphold the identity of the historical people of Yahweh in the Old Testament while acknowledging the new identity founded in the coming King, Jesus Christ.

Through the prophetic discourses of Habakkuk and Zephaniah, Dr. Ho skilfully presents God as the Divine Warrior who is the source of hope in a world marked by wars, suffering, persecution, and uncertainty. While Dr. Ho's scholarly approach ensures a solid academic foundation, he makes the material accessible to a broad range of readers, including scholars, pastors, teachers, students, and other Bible-reading Christians from various backgrounds.

In a nutshell, Dr. Ho's well-informed scholarship and deeply reflective spirituality create an enriching commentary that is faithful to the historical texts and relevant to the current situation.

Clement M. S. Chia, PhD
Principal and Associate Professor of Systematic and Contextual Theologies,
Singapore Bible College

The books of Habakkuk and Zephaniah speak to us today. They demonstrate our need both for faith in God and faithfulness in how we live. This commentary is based on careful scholarship and explains these books and their significance in a way that is accessible to contemporary readers. Peter Ho clearly summarizes important concepts and emphasizes the importance of both the sociohistorical and the literary or textual contexts. Illustrations of ancient artifacts illumine the texts. He diligently traces the coherence and unity of the text, opening our eyes to the ways in which repetitions, patterns, and structure hold the text together and create the flow of each book's message. Both books are understood in light of their place within the Minor Prophets. Contemporary stories that illustrate the text's truths, with a special emphasis on examples drawn from and applied to Asian culture, build bridges to our lives.

Kenneth H. Cuffey, PhD
Professor of Biblical Studies,
Urbana Theological Seminary, Illinois, USA

Here is a commentary that builds a festoon of bridges: bridges between the ancient world of the Bible and the oracles of the prophets; bridges between scholarship and ministry; and bridges between the everyday realities of ancient West Asia and Asia today. These are easy bridges to tread, built with engaging

Dr. Peter Ho has crafted a delightful blend of solid scholarship and devotional thought in an accessible form that specialists and ordinary Christian readers may imbibe for deeper appreciation of the literary artistry and theological insights of the ancient writers. The underlying Hebrew language and poetic structures come to the forefront through Dr. Ho's penetrating analysis and clear exposition, highlighting key features that show how themes and major thoughts are developed and brought forth movingly in such a way that modern readers may vicariously experience the prophets' emotions and concerns. Sprinkled throughout the exposition are excerpts that bridge the divide between historical circumstances and modern challenges, helping the reader to perceive the continuing relevance of Scripture. Another feature is the numerous illustrations, diagrams, and photos that enable visualization and thus aids better understanding of the concepts and practices of the period. The style of this commentary is elegant yet straightforward, scholarly yet readily accessible to all, crisp, flowing, and highly readable. This commentary offers an excellent introduction into a relatively unfamiliar portion of Scripture and also invites the reader to dig deep for buried treasure.

Gilbert Soo Hoo, PhD
Professor of New Testament,
Singapore Bible College

Peter Ho states that he hopes to "demystify" the books of Habakkuk and Zephaniah – which are certainly obscure for most Christians – and he succeeds admirably in this task. His scholarly credentials are undeniable, and he regularly accesses the insights of sources like "recent poetic and discourse analyses and linguistic studies," mostly in footnotes. But he never lets such jargon interfere with his primary mission to unpack the messages of these books for the churches in Asia – a task he does well. I know I will benefit from using this fine work in the years to come. I recommend it highly.

David M. Howard Jr., PhD
Professor of Old Testament,
Bethlehem College and Seminary, Minnesota, USA

The Old Testament prophetic books of Habakkuk and Zephaniah are not so familiar to most readers. To help us grasp how these two "Minor Prophets" are far from being minor in significance, Dr. Peter Ho has produced this helpful commentary on Habakkuk and Zephaniah, which combines exegetical rigor, literary sensitivity, pastoral insight, and contextual relevance. Through the accessible bridges that Dr. Ho builds for readers of these books, God's word from the ancient Near East comes alive in its relevance for the modern Far East!

Jerry Hwang, PhD
Affiliate Research Professor, Advanced Studies,
Singapore Bible College

Habakkuk and Zephaniah are two of the "Minor Prophets" of the Bible who are majorly overlooked by Christians! So I am thrilled that Peter Ho shines the light of his expertise on their significance by reading them within the broader context of the Minor Prophets. One of the many strengths of Ho's work is his detailed outlines of the structure of each book and chapter, making them more accessible and easier to understand. He adds sharp exegetical observations of the text, reading them within their historical and cultural contexts. Moreover, Ho's attention to the Asian context brings a unique perspective to his analysis. Drawing on his own experience and cultural insights, Ho presents applications that resonate with contemporary Asian issues. Whether you are a scholar, pastor, student, or interested lay person, I highly recommend reading this book if you seek to gain a deeper understanding of these often-neglected biblical books.

Peter Lau, PhD
Lecturer in Old Testament,
Seminari Theoloji Malaysia and Equip Gospel Ministries

As a pastor who must preach regularly, I believe that this commentary will greatly help preachers. Peter has worked hard to give us both the context of the times and the relevance for today. There are many Asian perspectives and illustrations to help us communicate insights in our sermons. I highly recommend this commentary which will be a valuable addition to our library.

Rev. Chua Seng Lee
Senior Pastor,
Bethesda Bedok Tampines Church, Singapore

During his sabbatical, the author dedicated his time to crafting this volume. Rather than feeling burdened by the project, he embraced it as a joyful journalistic endeavor, chronicling his delightful journey through these two books. This volume has several specific aims. First, it seeks to showcase a faithful God, who is ever-present even amid painful trials. Second, it endeavors to convey that mere faith without steadfastness is nothing more than an immature fantasy. Finally, it strives to effectively communicate with an audience who may lack technical training in Hebrew poetry. Upon reading this manuscript, I have concluded that Dr. Ho has achieved remarkable success in respect of all three objectives. Additionally, I greatly appreciate the introduction included in this volume. The introductory section not only offers valuable contextual information but also establishes a theological framework, making this book a comprehensive resource for studying Habakkuk and Zephaniah.

Rev. Peter Lin
President,
Serving Singapore, Blessing Asia

In this fine commentary on two vital prophetic books, Dr. Peter Ho has taken up the admirable challenge of bringing to life two vital prophetic books for a contemporary Asian context. The result is this fine commentary. With careful scholarship, he illuminates the texts in their historical settings, language, and forms. He also situates these books helpfully within the shape and flow of the Old Testament and relates them to the message of the New Testament.

At the same time, Dr. Ho brings out the powerful prophetic, pastoral, and theological character of these books. The Asian context is apparent in a wealth of allusions and attention to specifically Asian issues. Yet, this is never at the expense of the universality of the biblical and Christian mission.

The book is extremely well-written and is enhanced by a host of well-chosen graphic illustration of topics that occur in the texts. It is a truly Asian commentary that draws on the very best of international scholarship and theology. I commend it unreservedly.

Gordon McConville, PhD
Emeritus Professor of Old Testament Theology,
University of Gloucestershire, UK

Peter Ho's commentary skillfully blends the three Rs of a good commentary: readability, research, and relevance. Dr. Ho targets Christian ministers and seminary students by using nontechnical jargon that allows him to communicate his points effectively. Readability matters little if one has nothing of substance to communicate, but that is not a problem for this author. Virtually every page has multiple footnotes to point readers to academic works for those who wish to chase down the details of the author's comments. The lengthy bibliography at the end of the book covers an array of recent English-language scholarship cited in the volume. These references show that the author has mastered the history of research on these books, including the question of how these two books function within the Book of the Twelve. The author also keeps his audience in mind by continually mining his literary analysis for its theological payoff. He does not merely append a discussion of theological implications to the end of his literary work; rather, he weaves it into his exegetical observations.

James Nogalski, PhD
Professor of Old Testament,
Baylor University, Texas, USA

In this work, Dr. Ho does three things for the student of Habakkuk and Zephaniah. First, he shows how the literary structures of the books open up fruitful new ways of understanding their content. Second, he shows the coherency of their message and content. Third, he shows how that content intersects with contemporary life. In these ways, he makes a solid contribution to the study of this literature.

John N. Oswalt, PhD
Visiting Distinguished Professor of Old Testament,
Asbury Theological Seminary, Kentucky, USA

Dr. Peter Ho brings his expertise on the Psalms to this terrific commentary on the prophetic books of Habakkuk and Zephaniah. These books, which are often neglected by preachers today, have an important message in a world where "pain and injustice reign" and God's work often seems hidden. The key contributions of Dr. Ho's commentary include his analysis of the literary features of these books and how they serve to powerfully communicate God's message, his illustrations and explanations of the ancient Near Eastern context, his thoughts on how these books interact with the other books of the Twelve, and the way the themes of these books are drawn into the broader storyline of Scripture, which includes the life, death, resurrection, and return of Jesus Christ. Dr. Ho gives many illustrations and applications from his Asian context, and these will prove invaluable to all who desire to understand, to live out, and to teach these books.

Anthony R. Petterson, PhD
Lecturer in Old Testament and Biblical Hebrew,
Morling College and Australian College of Theology, Sydney

Readers of this volume will be greatly helped in their understanding of Habakkuk and Zephaniah. They will learn much about recent scholarship on these books, about their historical and literary contexts, about the details of the text (its structure and its interpretation), and about the fulfillment – in Jesus – of the prophecies in these books. There are many insightful and challenging applications for the contemporary Southeast Asian context. I recommend this book.

Philip Satterthwaite, PhD
Lecturer Emeritus,
Biblical Graduate School of Theology, Singapore

Proving that the messages of the Minor Prophets are far from obsolete, Dr. Peter Ho deftly guides us through the books of Habakkuk and Zephaniah, bringing their messages clearly into focus. Sensitive to both the original settings of the books and to our modern contexts, Dr. Ho ably applies the multifaceted messages of Habakkuk and Zephaniah to readers and their relation to issues as diverse as wealth and poverty, suffering, faith and doubt, and God's purposes in the world. Sprinkled with helpful maps and illustrations from the ancient Near East, this volume exemplifies holistic Christian interpretation of the biblical text's literary, historical, and theological facets.

Daniel C. Timmer, PhD
Director and Professor of Biblical Studies, Doctoral Program,
Puritan Reformed Theological Seminary, Michigan, USA
Professeur d'Ancien Testament, Faculté de théologie évangélique, Canada

Some readers may be familiar with the typical way in which precious diamonds are professionally classified – that is, according to their clarity, color, cut, and carat weight. I would characterize Dr. Peter Ho's consummate commentary on Habakkuk and Zephaniah in analogous terms as *clarity* – a lucid, highly readable composition that is most appropriate for the designated readership of "pastors, Christian leaders, cross-cultural workers, and seminary or Bible school students in Asia" (and, I might add, Bible translators as well); *color* – a text that literally comes alive with an abundance of helpful diagrams, pictorial illustrations, and life-related applications from Asia and elsewhere in the world; *correctness* – superlative accuracy exhibited by the author in expositing and explaining the biblical Hebrew texts of these two little-known prophets with reference to their style, structure, and intended sense; *conciseness* – the various topics treated have been carefully selected in terms of their contextual importance, relevance, and suitability with reference to the prescribed length of a medium-sized commentary; and, finally, *consequence* – with regard to the immense informative value and personal spiritual benefit that all readers (not only those living in Asia!) will derive from this insightful, deeply engaging, Scripture-saturated study. In God's gracious provision, I have an intensive workshop on Habakkuk scheduled later this year so I will be able to put this impressive commentary to immediate use!

Ernst R. Wendland, PhD
Professor Extraordinary in the Department of Ancient Studies,
Stellenbosch University, South Africa

Asia Bible Commentary Series

HABAKKUK AND ZEPHANIAH

GLOBAL LIBRARY

Asia Bible Commentary Series

HABAKKUK AND ZEPHANIAH

Peter C. W. Ho

General Editor
Andrew B. Spurgeon

Old Testament Consulting Editors
**Yohanna Katanacho, Joseph Shao,
Havilah Dharamraj, Koowon Kim**

New Testament Consulting Editors
Steve Chang, Finny Philip, Samson Uytanlet

© 2024 Peter C. W. Ho

Published 2024 by Langham Global Library
An imprint of Langham Publishing
www.langhampublishing.org

Langham Publishing and its imprints are a ministry of Langham Partnership

Langham Partnership
PO Box 296, Carlisle, Cumbria, CA3 9WZ, UK
www.langham.org

Published in partnership with Asia Theological Association

ATA
QCC PO Box 1454–1154, Manila, Philippines
www.ataasia.com

ISBNs:
978-1-83973-976-7 Print
978-1-83973-977-4 ePub
978-1-83973-978-1 PDF

Peter C. W. Ho has asserted his right under the Copyright, Designs and Patents Act, 1988 to be identified as the Author of this work.

All rights reserved. No part of this publication may be reproduced, stored in a retrieval system or transmitted, in any form or by any means, electronic, mechanical, photocopying, recording or otherwise, without the prior written permission of the publisher or the Copyright Licensing Agency.

Requests to reuse content from Langham Publishing are processed through PLSclear. Please visit www.plsclear.com to complete your request.

Unless otherwise stated, Scripture quotations are from the New International Version, copyright © 2011. Used by permission. All rights reserved.

British Library Cataloguing-in-Publication Data
A catalogue record for this book is available from the British Library

ISBN: 978-1-83973-976-7

Cover & Book Design: projectluz.com

Langham Partnership actively supports theological dialogue and an author's right to publish but does not necessarily endorse the views and opinions set forth here or in works referenced within this publication, nor can we guarantee technical and grammatical correctness. Langham Partnership does not accept any responsibility or liability to persons or property as a consequence of the reading, use or interpretation of its published content.

To Wendy, for your steadfast love and faithfulness

———

"And without faith it is impossible to please him,
for whoever would draw near to God must believe that he exists
and that he rewards those who seek him."
Hebrews 11:6 (ESV)

CONTENTS

Commentary

Series Preface xix
Author's Preface xxi
List of Abbreviations xxiii
Introduction 1
Commentary on Habakkuk 21
Commentary on Zephaniah 101
Selected Bibliography 173

Topics

Are There Prophets of Yahweh Today? 6
Trapped in Unending Violence and Injustice 34
Knowing God's Will and Living Faithfully 60
Where Does Our Security Come From? 65
Jesus, the Divine Warrior 86
Who Will God Condemn on That Day? 125
We Are Called to Seek Yahweh, His Righteousness, and
    Humble Ourselves 139
God's Determination to Love and Transform His People
    Steeped in Their Decadence 156

SERIES PREFACE

What's unique about the Asia Bible Commentary Series? It is a commentary series written especially for Asian Christians, which incorporates and addresses Asian concerns, cultures, and practices. As Asian scholars – either by nationality, passion, or calling – the authors identify with the biblical text, understand it culturally, and apply its principles in Asian contexts to strengthen the churches in Asia. Missiologists tell us that Christianity has shifted from being a Western majority religion to a South, Southeastern, and Eastern majority religion and that the church is growing at an unprecedented rate in these regions. This series meets the need for evangelical commentaries written specifically for an Asian audience.

This is not to say that Asian churches and Asian Christians do not want to partner with Western Christians and churches or that they spurn Western influences. A house divided cannot stand. The books in this series complement the existing Western commentaries by taking into consideration the cultural nuances familiar to the Eastern world so that the Eastern readership is not inundated with Western clichés and illustrations that they are unable to relate to and which may not be applicable to them.

The mission of this series is "to produce resources that are biblical, pastoral, contextual, missional, and prophetic for pastors, Christian leaders, cross-cultural workers, and students in Asia." While using approved exegetical principles, the writers strive to be culturally relevant, offer practical applications, and provide clear explanations of the texts so that readers can grow in understanding and maturity in Christ, and so that Christian leaders can guide their congregations into maturity. May we be found faithful to this endeavor and may God be glorified!

Andrew B. Spurgeon
General Editor

AUTHOR'S PREFACE

Writing this volume has taught me that God's steadfast love and power will carry us through the fires and pains of life even though we may have long given up in despair. God remains faithful even when we are buried in our trespasses. The books of Habakkuk and Zephaniah are God's word to Israel, his people, set at the lowest point in their history – the time of the Babylonian captivity. In the horizon of these books, the looming national disaster is not simply contrasted with the prophetic hope of deliverance; rather, the brightest light that shines in these books is the display of God's unchanging faithfulness, power, and holiness, which were the foundations for divine actions for the well-being of the remnant of Judah. These books show us the faith of the righteous among the rebels and the ruins. They demonstrate that *faith without faithfulness is infantile fantasy*. I hope that this volume will speak to all God's people who continue to desire God in life's dark places and dark times.

While I have tried to write in accessible language, keeping in mind the audience of the Asia Bible Commentary Series, I also want to guide readers into the world of Hebrew poetry in these texts. I do this in hope that the Scripture itself will reveal its beauty and power as we persist in seeking to understand its intricacies. I trust that the many pictures and illustrations included will help readers make sense of what is being said despite the technical terms that are sometimes used.

This project was only possible because of the opportunity offered by the editors of the Asia Bible Commentary Series as well as the sabbatical afforded to me by the Singapore Bible College (SBC) from July to December 2022. I wish to thank Samuel Law, Andrew B. Spurgeon, Jerry Hwang, Jason Chen, Chen Chieh Ning, and also my colleagues at SBC's Centre for Teaching and Learning, who stood in the gap of my absence and supported the project in prayers and other generous ways. I am deeply appreciative to specialists in this field – Thomas Renz, Anthony R. Petterson, and others – who offered helpful critiques of this volume when I reached out to them. A special word of appreciation to Janis Lim, a student of mine at the Singapore Bible College, for her willingness to painstakingly proofread this work and offer numerous suggestions to make it better. My daughter, Priscilla, read a version of the manuscript and offered numerous corrections. She is more skillful with words than I realized! Bubbles, and other editors at ATA/Langham were amazing! All remaining errors are mine.

As I write this preface, in December 2022, I have been asked by various people how my sabbatical was going. My tongue-in-cheek response was that it had barely started! But on reflecting further, I realized that I have *indeed* rested in the word of God. Studying, waiting, and writing have kept me from squandering my time on less fruitful pursuits. Writing can be burdensome. Yet, at times, I feel like a journalist, happily recording the wondrous things I have seen (Ps 119:18). It is my prayer that just as God shows me what he wants me to see, he will also show you what he wants you to see so that, by his grace, we may all find rest and joy in faithful obedience of his word.

Peter C. W. Ho
Singapore, December 2022

LIST OF ABBREVIATIONS

BOOKS OF THE BIBLE

Old Testament

Gen, Exod, Lev, Num, Deut, Josh, Judg, Ruth, 1–2 Sam, 1–2 Kgs, 1–2 Chr, Ezra, Neh, Esth, Job, Ps/Pss, Prov, Eccl, Song, Isa, Jer, Lam, Ezek, Dan, Hos, Joel, Amos, Obad, Jonah, Mic, Nah, Hab, Zeph, Hag, Zech, Mal

New Testament

Matt, Mark, Luke, John, Acts, Rom, 1–2 Cor, Gal, Eph, Phil, Col, 1–2 Thess, 1–2 Tim, Titus, Phlm, Heb, Jas, 1–2 Pet, 1–2–3 John, Jude, Rev

BIBLE TEXTS AND VERSIONS

Divisions of the canon

NT	New Testament
OT	Old Testament

Ancient texts and versions

LXX	Septuagint
MT	Masoretic Text

Modern versions

ESV	English Standard Version
KJV	King James Version
NIV	New International Version
NASB	New American Standard Bible
NASB 1995	New American Standard Bible 1995
NRSV	New Revised Standard Version

Journals, reference works, and series

AcT	*Acta Theologica*
ANEM	Ancient Near East Monographs
ANET	*Ancient Near Eastern Texts Relating to the Old Testament*

Ant.	*Jewish Antiquities*
ArOr	*Archív orientální*
AS	Assyriological Studies
Bib	*Biblica*
BLS	Bible and Literature Series
BZAW	*Beihefte zur Zeitschrift für die alttestamentliche Wissenschaft*
CBQ	*Catholic Biblical Quarterly*
CM	Cuneiform Monographs
CTM	*Concordia Theological Monthly*
DCH	*Dictionary of Classical Hebrew*
HBM	Hebrew Bible Monograph Series
IEJ	*Israel Exploration Journal*
JBL	*Journal of Biblical Literature*
JETS	*Journal of the Evangelical Theological Society*
JSOTSup	Journal for the Study of the Old Testament Supplement Series
NAC	New American Commentary
NICOT	New International Commentary on the Old Testament
NIDOTTE	*New International Dictionary of Old Testament Theology and Exegesis*
OBO	*Orbis Biblicus et Orientalis*
OTE	*Old Testament Essays*
SSN	*Studia Semitica Neerlandica*
StBibLit	Studies in Biblical Literature
TDOT	*Theological Dictionary of the Old Testament*
TNTC	Tyndale New Testament Commentaries
TOTC	Tyndale Old Testament Commentaries
Transeu	*Transeuphratène*
TS	*Theological Studies*
VT	*Vetus Testamentum*
VTSup	*Vetus Testamentum* Supplements
WBC	Word Biblical Commentary

INTRODUCTION

In cosmopolitan Singapore, meritocracy – which has been a fundamental governing principle since the nation's independence – is a nonnegotiable, sacrosanct term that Singaporeans live by. Meritocracy means that one's standing and advancement in society are governed by merit and ability rather than status, wealth, or connections. As a lived reality, the person on the street understands meritocracy as a system where achieving success is achieved by being "good." For schoolchildren, *good* means achieving academic excellence. For grown-ups, *good* means credentials, pedigree, and an excellent résumé. So, meritocracy is construed as a system of fair rewards for those with merits. But meritocracy can also be understood negatively – if you do not have merits, you are not "successful." After more than half a century, it is fair to say that meritocracy has become the Singaporean *modus vivendi* (a way of life). In recent years, this ideology has been increasingly critiqued. One reporter notes that "the system of meritocracy perpetuates a national narrative that is too simplistic to capture the complexity of our lives, and the dominance of this narrative forces citizens to conform to it in a harmful manner."[1]

You may wonder what this meritocratic ideology has to do with the prophetic books of Habakkuk and Zephaniah. Theologically speaking, the meritocratic concept can be seen as a version of the retribution principle typically found in Deuteronomic and Wisdom literature. The retribution principle works like a meritocracy – if you do well by keeping the Torah, you will be rewarded (Zeph 3:5). Similarly, if you fail to comply with the rules, you will suffer the consequences. One's ability to perform (in every sense of the word) brings weal, and one's falling short will result in suffering woes. Nevertheless, there are instances when this retributive principle does not work.[2]

Perhaps you may find a similar principle at work in your own context, with people failing to do what they ought to do and indulging in what they ought not to do. Justice flounders, while the wicked flourish. Meanwhile, you cry out to God because you want his justice to go forth immediately and

---

1. Yip Brandon Zhen Yuan, "Understanding the Four Critiques of Singapore's Meritocracy," TODAY, April 29, 2019, https://www.todayonline.com/commentary/understanding-four-critiques-singapores-meritocracy.
2. The retribution principle enshrined in Deuteronomy 28:15–68 is undermined in Deuteronomy 9:4–10:11. J. Gordon McConville, "Retribution in Deuteronomy: Theology and Ethics," *Interpretation: A Journal of Bible & Theology* 69.3 (2015): 288–298, [294].

not tarry. How do pastors, missionaries, and servants of Jesus Christ who have made themselves poor continue in a world that systematically favors the meritorious, those who have it all? What should we do when our cherished ideologies no longer make sense?

In the books of Habakkuk and Zephaniah, we catch a glimpse of the prophets' inner struggles and their cries for God to act according to his decree. Although God eventually does act, he does so in a way that is beyond our notion of justice or timeliness. At the end of all the theological haggling, we must learn – as these OT prophets and their audiences did – how to endure in hope and patience. Perhaps God does not deliver us when we want him to precisely because he is making us more like him. The righteous shall live by faith because God is faithful.

The prophecies of Habakkuk and Zephaniah were received at a critical historical juncture in the story of God's people. These books have an important message, transcending time, geography, and culture, that we must hear afresh today. Unfortunately, these prophetic books have not always been interpreted and are often neglected in the pulpit. Why is this? First, they are hard to understand and seem far removed from our time. Readers today struggle to appreciate the sociohistorical contexts that cradled the text. Second, the textual content and its literary expressions may seem somewhat strange. What does "God came from Teman" (Hab 3:3) mean? Why do prophets speak in mysterious lyrical utterances? We fail to understand *what* is said because we do not understand *how* it is said. Third, we lack the ability to connect the theological dots because we read texts atomistically. We can only catch sight of the larger concerted and coherent message when we read texts within their larger contexts, such as an entire book or the entire collection of the Book of the Twelve (XII).[3]

Therefore, the following approach will be adopted in this volume. First, I hope to demystify Habakkuk and Zephaniah by explaining their literary and historical character. Second, I illustrate a way of reading these texts holistically by showing how Habakkuk and Zephaniah, as individual books, relate to the collection of the XII. Third, I mine the theological message, exploring its connections to the rest of the Bible – both Old Testament and New Tes-

---

3. The twelve books, from Hosea to Malachi in the current order, is often known as the Minor Prophets in the modern English Bible. In the Hebrew Masoretic tradition (MT), these twelve books are counted as one, hence the Book of the Twelve. The Greek tradition has the same books but with a slightly different order.

tament – and asking how this message is still relevant to us in our time and contexts. The assumption here is that God continues to speak to readers of the Bible today. And that knowing what God says involves living out what God says (Ezra 7:10).

According to an article in the *South China Morning Post*, Asia is now the "new hotbed" of Christian persecution.[4] Christians in this region will increasingly find themselves in situations similar to those depicted in Habakkuk and Zephaniah and will long desperately for the breaking forth of God's justice. Like Habakkuk, we cry, "How long, Lord?" (Hab 1:2). How must the just live by faith when justice is perverted, and God is silent (1:4; 2:4)? Like the prophet Habakkuk, we continue to wait. If you are reading this and find yourself in a similar pit of despondency, I pray that God will cause your strength to rise as we journey with God through these pages.

THE PROPHETIC OFFICE AND THE PROPHET'S CALL

In ancient Israel, the prophet was God's spokesperson. To be a prophet of Yahweh was to be Yahweh's mouth (Jer 15:19).[5] While prophets of God spoke for God at appointed times and places to God's people, their words were sometimes directed to Israel's enemies and the nations at large (see Hab 2:6–19; Zeph 2:4–15). Note that the phenomenon of prophets was not unique to ancient Israel. For instance, 1 Kings 18:19 reminds us of the 450 Canaanite prophets of Baal and 400 prophets of Asherah. The prophets in the ancient Near East often spoke oracles for kings and princes. Similarly, Israel's prophets were often connected to the royal court.[6] However, the prophetic literature of the Bible is unique.[7]

OT prophets can be classified into several groups based on time periods and functions. The earliest *premonarchic* prophets – such as Moses and Deborah – spoke primarily for God and functioned as leaders of the nation. Samuel was a transitional prophet. Next, the *preclassical* prophets – such as

---

4. Charles McDermid, "Christians in Asia: Persecuted, Oppressed . . . but Keeping the Faith," *South China Morning Post*, January 18, 2019, https://www.scmp.com/week-asia/politics/article/2182800/christians-asia-persecuted-oppressed-keeping-faith.
5. Aaron, for instance, is called the *mouth* of Moses (Exod 4:15–16; 7:1).
6. James Pritchard, ed., *Ancient Near Eastern Texts Relating to the Old Testament: Third Edition with Supplements* (Princeton: Princeton University Press, 1969), 450, http://archive.org/details/Pritchard1950ANET_20160815.
7. The term "Israel" is polyvalent. In this volume, unless distinctions are made in context (e.g., northern and southern kingdoms), "Israel" will refer to the people of God who came out of Egypt and their posterity up until their return from exile.

Nathan, Elijah, Elisha, and Micaiah – spoke for God and confronted kings or peoples for their religious and ethical failings. Finally, the *classical* prophets, such as Isaiah and Hosea, are the literary prophets who have given us many prophetic books.

The OT prophets seem to have undertaken three roles. First, they predicted the future and spoke about the new covenantal age (foretelling).[8] This type of text occurs in less than five percent of all prophetic texts.[9] Second, and with some overlap with the previous role, the prophets spoke specifically of messianic expectations and hope. Again, this occurs infrequently, in less than two percent of the body of prophetic writings. Third, and most frequently, OT prophets dealt with the immediate situation of God's people, speaking words of condemnation to both people and kings, seeking to turn them from their wicked ways. This occurs in more than ninety percent of the prophetic texts. In this way, the prophetic writings are overwhelmingly characterized by *forthtelling* rather than *foretelling*. This implies that the social, religious, and historical contexts in which the prophets spoke are highly significant. Hence, to understand the prophetic speeches, it is necessary to understand the socio-historical and theological backgrounds.

There are roughly fifty-five named prophets in the OT, compared to at least four hundred unnamed ones (1 Kgs 22:6). Out of these fifty or so prophets, a small percentage are literary or writing prophets, who gave us the prophetic books in the OT. The most common term for a prophet is *nabi* (prophet), but *roeh* (seer), *hozeh* (seer), or *ish-elohim* (the man of God) are used as well. A parenthetical remark in 1 Samuel 9:9 – "Formerly in Israel, if someone went to inquire of God, they would say, 'Come, let us go to the *seer*,' because the *prophet of today* used to be called a *seer*" (emphasis added) – suggests that by the time 1 Samuel was composed, these distinctions were no longer apparent (compare Amos 7:12–14). In 2 Kings, we see many unnamed prophets going out in large numbers to meet and interact with Elisha at places such as Bethel, Jericho, and Gilgal (2:3–5; 4:38). This has led to scholarly debates on whether there were training schools for professional prophets (literally, "sons of the prophets") in ancient Israel.

---

8. Peter J. Gentry, *How to Read and Understand the Biblical Prophets* (Wheaton: Crossway, 2017).

9. Aaron Chalmers, *Interpreting the Prophets: Reading, Understanding and Preaching from the Worlds of the Prophets* (Downers Grove: IVP Academic, 2015), 6.

Introduction

From the limited information available in the Bible, we know that prophets of God were called from all walks of life and served in different capacities. Nathan and Gad were probably court prophets (1 Sam 22:5; 2 Sam 24:11; 1 Kgs 1:22–23). Amos was a herdsman and sycamore farmer (Amos 7:14). Zephaniah could have been of royal stock by connection to Hezekiah.[10] In the OT, prophets were, sometimes, simultaneously priests (Ezekiel and Jeremiah) or judges (Samuel).[11] Yet, what is common among all prophets of Yahweh is that they all received divine messages or visions to proclaim. A prophet – as in the case of Micaiah – might have been privy to the divine council (1 Kgs 22:19–23; Jer 23:18; compare Job 1:6; 2:1; Pss 29:1; 82:1, 6; 89:7) or be sent to carry out Yahweh's purposes (Isa 6:8). Nonetheless, there were also many false prophets, who were recognized by the inaccuracy of their prophecies (Deut 13:1–5; Jer 14:14; Lam 2:14; Ezek 13:9).

Unlike in the case of false prophets, all the words of genuine prophets of Yahweh came true. The bona fide prophet was called by God and displays most, if not all, the following characteristics: a) God's call and interruption of the prophet's life in a significant way; b) God's personal appearance to the prophet; c) God's commissioning; and d) the prophet's response to the commission (compare Exodus 3; Isaiah 6; Jeremiah 1; Ezek 3:15). Sometimes, the prophet functioned as an intercessor (Amos 7:1–6) or watchman (Ezek 33:7).

Interestingly, the writing prophets of God rarely referred to themselves as prophets. Although the prophetic books bear their names, some even denied being prophets (Amos 7:14–15). In the XII, biographical information about the prophets is meager (perhaps found only in Hosea 1:2–3:5, Amos 7:14–15, and in the book of Jonah). According to Nogalski, this is not because later redactors removed the prophets' biographical details but because such details were "never selected for inclusion. The individual writings are not interested in the prophet's life because the prophet's message – the word from Yahweh comprising the writing – is the key to the structure, rhetoric, and collection of material."[12] While Jewish tradition may venerate these prophets, Scripture generally does not give many details about their personal life. They served

---

10. See our discussion of Zephaniah 1:1 below. Scholars debate this because some manuscript variants have "Hilkiah" instead of "Hezekiah."
11. Marti J. Steussy, *Samuel and His God* (Columbia: University of South Carolina Press, 2010), 29.
12. James D. Nogalski, "Where Are the Prophets in the Book of the Twelve?," in *The Book of Twelve & The New Form Criticism*, eds. Mark J. Boda, Michael H. Floyd, and Colin M. Toffelmire, ANEM 10 (Atlanta: SBL Press, 2015), 163–182, [169].

their generation by speaking for God and then faded silently into the background. Where more information is available, as in the case of Jeremiah, it is often unglamorous. The prophet's life was usually fraught with suffering by oppression, as described in the NT (Matt 23:30; Rev 16:6).

In brief, the dominant characteristics of a prophetic message include a) an *accusation* of wrongdoing, b) a *pronouncement* of judgment, and c) a *proclamation* of future deliverance and restoration.

ARE THERE PROPHETS OF YAHWEH TODAY?

Does the office of Yahweh's prophet still exist today? Do preachers and pastors operate as prophets of God? In many ways, there are clear parallels. God interrupts a person's life with a call. Then the person is commissioned and sent to preach and teach the word of God. It would be fair to say that preachers and pastors carry out prophetic functions. Cessationists believe that the gift of prophecy and the prophetic office have ceased today. Continuationists believe that prophecies continue, although such prophecies do not rise to the same status as Scripture. While the former argue from the vantage point of authority, inerrancy, and impeccability of genuine prophetic utterances, the latter argue that Paul requires his readers to pursue the gift of prophecy (1 Cor 13:8–14:1), pointing out that just as God has spoken through prophets in the past with words that were not always recorded, God can also speak through prophets today with words not recorded in the Bible.

It must be noted that both sides include proponents with a high view of the Scripture, who believe that the canon of the Bible is closed. While we cannot resolve all the issues here, in this brief article, two points can be made. First, we can understand the gift of prophecy described in 1 Corinthians 14:24–25 as a kind of message that, when spoken, causes unbelievers to hear and be convicted of sin, as the secrets of their hearts are disclosed. We recall the words of Hebrews 1:1–2: "In the past God spoke to our ancestors through the prophets at many times and in various ways, but in these last days he has spoken to us by his Son." While we affirm that the canon is closed and that the Bible is sufficient for all things pertaining to life and salvation, it is quite a different matter to say that God cannot speak through his chosen spokespeople today in unique ways through the work of the Spirit. Jon

Introduction

Bloom cites a fascinating story from Charles Spurgeon's autobiography, one that bears a remarkable resemblance to what is described in 1 Corinthians 14:24–25.

> [Spurgeon] suddenly broke off from his [sermon] subject, and pointing in a certain direction, said, "Young man, those gloves you are wearing have not been paid for: you have stolen them from your employer." At the close of the service, a young man, looking very pale and greatly agitated, came to the room which was used as a vestry, and begged for a private interview with Spurgeon. On being admitted, he placed a pair of gloves upon the table, and tearfully said, "It's the first time I have robbed my master, and I will never do it again. You won't expose me, sir, will you? It would kill my mother if she heard that I had become a thief."[1]

Spurgeon, a cessationist, used the term "impressions of the Holy Spirit" rather than the word "prophesying." If we allow that such experiences are possible, then the issue might merely be one of semantics. In other words, the prophetic ministry in 1 Corinthians 14:24–25 continues, though not in the same way as with the prophets of old.

Second, it is important to note that although the prophets and apostles are included in lists of God-appointed offices (1 Cor 12:28; Eph 4:11), this does not negate the fact that these offices are linked, as well as clearly distinct from other offices and gifts (Eph 2:20; 3:5; 2 Pet 3:2). While the prophets of the OT prophesied about Christ, the apostles in the NT explained how Jesus is the Christ. Together, they form the basis and foundation on which the church is built. There is no new gospel beyond what has been revealed. Pastors, preachers, evangelists, and teachers alike speak the word of God prophetically into the lives and situations of their audience, and God may use their words at specific moments, beyond their own consciousness, to speak to people prophetically in their specific situations.

As in the OT, there were also false prophets in NT times. Likewise, there are false prophetic ministries today. We are not to despise prophecies but must test everything (1 Thess 5:19–22). We are to test every spirit (1 John 4:1–3), and watch out for false prophets, recognizing them by their fruits (Matt 7:15–21).

---

1. Jon Bloom, "Should You Earnestly Desire to Prophesy?" Desiring God, 21 Sep 2018, https://www.desiringgod.org/articles/should-you-earnestly-desire-to-prophesy.

THE WORLD OF HABAKKUK AND ZEPHANIAH

Habakkuk and Zephaniah prophesied during a critical period in Israel's history. These two prophets were probably contemporaries, ministering in Jerusalem within two to three decades of each other at a time of impending doom for the nation. Their message was urgent and threatening. As with many other books of the Bible, we cannot be sure about the dating of these books. The political situation in the Near East in the seventh century BCE was fast changing. Judah's sister kingdom, Israel, had fallen to Assyria about a century earlier (722 BCE). The superpowers Assyria and Egypt were gradually losing their military power to a new superpower, Babylon, whose domination over the region of Syro-Palestine was firmly established by 605 BCE with the battle at Carchemish that eventually crushed the Assyrian-Egyptian alliance. In this topsy-turvy geopolitical situation, Judah found herself in the crosshairs of Nebuchadnezzar's expanding conquest.

Habakkuk and Zephaniah were probably written before the Babylonian captivity. Habakkuk was probably composed around the time of the events described in the book (Hab 1:5–7). Perhaps Habakkuk had seen the violence and aggression of the Babylonians when Nineveh fell to them in 612 BCE. In Habakkuk 1:6–11, the prophet might have been looking ahead to the Babylonian military expansion – specifically, the battle at Carchemish in 605 BCE, the siege of Jerusalem in 597 BCE, or the destruction of Jerusalem in 587 BCE.[13]

Moreover, the wickedness mentioned in Habakkuk (1:2–4, 12–17) in the contexts of the "paralyzed Torah" and "perverted justice" could well be describing the deplorable situation in Judah under the reign of King Jehoiakim from 609 to 605 BCE (Jer 22:13–23). Jehoiakim and his family were deported when Babylon attacked Jerusalem in 597 BCE. Zedekiah (Mattaniah), who succeeded Jehoiakim, revolted against the Babylonians. But Babylon, by this time, was weary of such revolts. They soon returned with their armies and lay the entire city to waste, thereby bringing to an end the southern kingdom, Judah.

---

13. For a vivid description of the battle in the "Babylonian Chronicles," see D. Winton Thomas, trans., *Documents from Old Testament Times* (London: Thomas Nelson and Sons, 1958), 76–79, http://archive.org/details/documentsfromold0000unse_d7h3.

Introduction

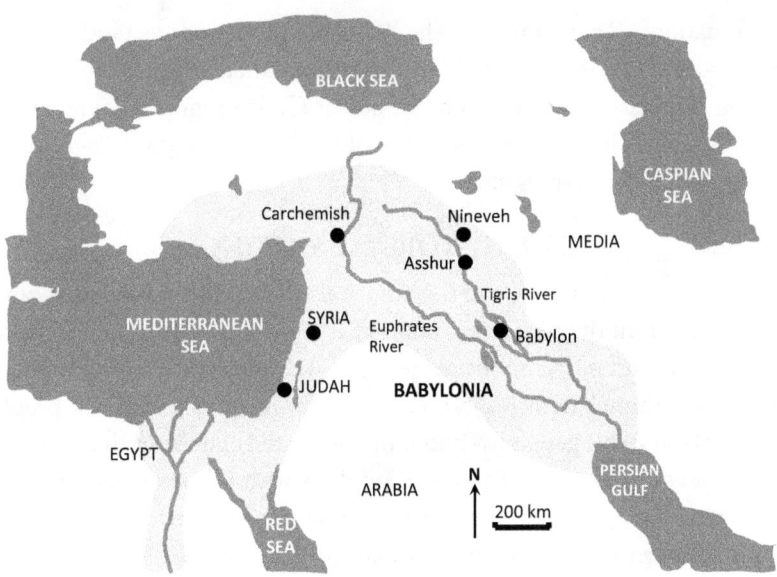

Figure 1: Babylonian Empire (ca. 600 BCE)

Zephaniah's message can be dated to the Judean king Josiah (Zeph 1:1), who died at the battle of Megiddo (640–609 BCE). Because of Zephaniah's oracle on the destruction of Assyria – which took place in 612 BCE – scholars think that the book was composed before this date. Moreover, the idolatrous situation mentioned in Zephaniah 1:4–9 suggests the book might have been written when the book of the law was found, before Josiah's reforms in 622 BCE (2 Kgs 23:1–27).[14] In this way, Zephaniah's message provided the support for Josiah to carry out his reforms.

Chronologically, Zephaniah comes before Habakkuk. However, Zephaniah follows Habakkuk within the XII because the content of Zephaniah – which speaks of the judgment of Judah – fits well after Habakkuk, when Judah was on the cusp of a national crisis by the end of the seventh century BCE. Significantly, these books spoke to a generation who witnessed the crumbling of the inviolable Zion city. These words emerged in the context of persistent wickedness and aggravating despair. Habakkuk tells of a time when the righteous, severely tested in their faith, cried out to a silent God (Hab 1:2). Zephaniah speaks of the coming day of Yahweh that would be unleashed on Jerusalem and

---

14. O. Palmer Robertson, *The Books of Nahum, Habakkuk, and Zephaniah*, NICOT (Grand Rapids: Eerdmans, 1990), 15.

foreign nations. Read consecutively, Zephaniah functions as God's response to the issues raised in Habakkuk. The original audience had heard about the looming disaster – which they understood as God's judgment – presented in these books. Yet, both books also speak of the hope of God's deliverance and salvation beyond that judgment.

THE HISTORICAL SETTING

Why should we pay attention to the historical setting? The written texts cannot be separated from their historical and social moorings. God speaks in history to real people and relates to his people within the framework of a covenantal relationship. This relationship and framework were assumed when the prophets spoke for God to his people. Without plumbing the context of the situation,[15] we cannot appreciate how and why God dealt with his people in the way he did; nor can we appreciate the larger metanarrative of how God has worked out his purposes for his people, of whom we ourselves are a part.

In the *larger metanarrative* – the grand scheme of things – the significance of these events, specifically the impending fall of Judah, is not merely historical but theological. God used the national catastrophe of Israel as part of his salvation plan for his people of all time. Childs's view of prophecy in the context of Israel's history is helpful: "Election [for Israel/Judah] was not a privilege to be enjoyed, but a calling to be pursued. The whole thrust of the prophetic witness is directed against those abusing this sacred trust."[16] As we shall see in Habakkuk and Zephaniah, the vision of the destruction of the human Davidic kingship and the Jerusalem temple is part of the salvation history of God's people. Abraham might have departed from Ur of Babylon, but Habakkuk and Zephaniah envisaged Judah's journey back to Babylon. In the trajectory of the XII, by the time we arrive at Haggai, we observe that God has brought his people out of Babylon and back into Canaan again. Five centuries later, the Romans destroyed the Second Temple (70 CE), and God's people were sacked from Jerusalem yet again! Only when the modern Jewish state of Israel was established in 1948 did many Jews gradually return to the

---

15. Colin M. Toffelmire, "Sitz Im What? Context and the Prophetic Book of Obadiah," in *The Book of Twelve & The New Form Criticism*, eds. Mark J. Boda, Michael H. Floyd, and Colin M. Toffelmire, ANEM 10 (Atlanta: SBL Press, 2015), 221–244, [228].
16. Brevard S. Childs, *Biblical Theology of the Old and New Testaments: Theological Reflection on the Christian Bible* (Minneapolis: Fortress, 1992), 445.

land.¹⁷ So, God's relationship with his people continues, and, from a theological vantage point, the story of his people continues. All this is to say that history and God's purposes are intertwined. And when we, in and through Christ, read ourselves into the storyline of God's people in the NT, we weave ourselves into the historical fabric of God's people.

When the people of God see a cloud rising in the west, they know that the rain is coming. Yet, the ability to "interpret the appearance of the earth and the sky" does not mean that one can "interpret this present time" (Luke 12:56). What is the interpretation of God's larger purposes for his people, especially today in Asia? Where do we stand today – historically and theologically? Is judgment coming? As Robertson rightly points out, "Central to this entire cosmic drama is faith; and it is the prophets of Israel who interpret and apply the demands of faith to their generation. The ministries of Nahum, Habakkuk, and Zephaniah fit within this scheme of God's redemptive purposes."¹⁸

Therefore, the demand for faith and God's supply of strength are timely and crucial and stand out as the key messages of these books. In relation to his rebellious people, Yahweh waits and longs to be gracious to them. But all who wait for Yahweh are blessed (Isa 30:18). Hosea – right at the beginning of the XII – calls, "Wait for your God always" (Hos 12:6). Similarly, on the brink of captivity, God calls to his people to "wait" (Zeph 3:8). During our earthly exile, awaiting our return to God's eternal home, we are to heed Habakkuk's words: "The righteous person will live by his faithfulness" and "the Sovereign LORD is my strength!" (Hab 2:4; 3:19).

HABAKKUK AND ZEPHANIAH IN THE BOOK OF THE TWELVE (XII)

In the earlier part of the twentieth century, scholars were interested in the oral tradition of the prophets and the relationships between the prophet, cultus, law, and covenant. From the 1980s, interest turned to the redaction and canonical formation of the XII.¹⁹ Currently, in their study of the prophetic

---

17. Discussions on whether post-biblical Israel is viewed as a continuity/discontinuity from biblical Israel is an important topic though it is beyond the scope of this volume. For a discussion of the people of God between the OT and the NT, see Childs, *Biblical Theology of the Old and New Testaments*, 441–451; Norbert Lohfink, *The Covenant Never Revoked: Biblical Reflections on Christian-Jewish Dialogue*, trans. John J. Scullion (New York: Paulist, 1991).
18. O'Palmer Robertson, *The Books of Nahum, Habakkuk, and Zephaniah*, NICOT (Grand Rapids: Eerdmans, 1990), 9.
19. James Nogalski, *Literary Precursors to the Book of the Twelve*, BZAW 217 (Berlin: Gruyter, 1993); *Redactional Processes in the Book of the Twelve*, BZAW 218 (Berlin: De Gruyter, 1993);

corpus, many scholars see the XII as a structural unit by design and not simply an anthology (amalgamated collection) of prophetic books.[20] In this way, the books of Habakkuk and Zephaniah are set within a larger literary context, and their messages are intended to be heard within the theological movement across the XII. For instance,

> Zephaniah was likely positioned last in the sequence [prior to the postexilic books of the XII] because of all the Minor Prophets it brings us closest to a reflection on the big historical turning point which is the destruction of Jerusalem before its conclusion looks forward to the restoration which is beginning to be implemented in the final three compositions of the Twelve.[21]

In this volume, we will adopt this approach, viewing the XII as a unified and coherent whole.

This paradigm of integrated reading is sometimes called the "new" form criticism.[22] In the "old," scholars were on a quest for the most "original" and historical utterances – *ipsissima verba* (the very words) – of the prophet by delimiting speech units, assigning genre (*Gattungen*), and postulating the specific life settings of those texts. This sort of reading fragments and layers the text. To some extent, it assumes a worldview based on a historically reconstructed Israelite religion for interpretive work. In the new form criticism, analyses of the text begin on the basis that the final form is received as a literary whole. According to Brevard Childs, this approach

> focuses its attention on the final form of the text itself. It seeks neither to use the text merely as a source for other information obtained by means of an oblique reading, nor to reconstruct a history of religious development. Rather it treats the literature

---

James Watts and Paul House, eds., *Forming Prophetic Literature: Essays on Isaiah and the Twelve in Honor of John D. W. Watts*, JSOTSup 235 (Sheffield: Sheffield Academic, 1996).
20. G. Michael O'Neal, *Interpreting Habakkuk as Scripture: An Application of the Canonical Approach of Brevard S. Childs*, StBibLit 9 (New York: Peter Lang, 2006); Jason T. LeCureux, *The Thematic Unity of the Book of the Twelve*, HBM 41 (Sheffield: Sheffield Phoenix, 2012).
21. Renz, "Habakkuk and Its Co-Texts," 23.
22. See Michael H. Floyd, "Introduction," in *The Book of Twelve & The New Form Criticism*, eds. Mark J. Boda, Michael H. Floyd, and Colin M. Toffelmire, ANEM 10 (Atlanta: SBL, 2015), 1–15, [11]; Floyd, "New Form Criticism and Beyond: The Historicity of Prophetic Literature Revisited," in *The Book of Twelve & The New Form Criticism*, 17–36; "Basic Trends in the Form-Critical Study of Prophetic Texts," in *The Changing Face of Form Criticism for the Twenty-First Century*, ed. Marvin A. Sweeney and Ehud Ben Zvi (Grand Rapids: Eerdmans, 2003), 298–311.

INTRODUCTION

in its own integrity. Its concern is not to establish a history of Hebrew literature in general, but to study the features of this peculiar set of religious texts in relation to their usage within the historical community of ancient Israel.[23]

There is also a hermeneutical move away from studying the prophet's utterances for his original audience to the *final composer's* written words for a later audience, presumably shaped with some overarching agenda for the entire book.[24] By moving away from the *ipsissima verba* to the voice of the whole book, historical concerns are somewhat conflated and generalized, though not invalidated. Prophetic speeches are now "written representations of prophecies uttered by living prophets that were produced not long after their proclamation."[25]

One aspect of the new form criticism is to see the prophetic books as cohesive and coherent,[26] with some logic undergirding its overarching design. This search for a unifying logic has been extended beyond the single book to the entire XII. According to Sweeney, this "new paradigm introduces an important dimension into the study of the Twelve Prophets in that it considers the presentation of the Twelve Prophets as a single prophetic book – one of the major forms in which the Twelve is encountered by its audience – to be a constitutive element in interpretation."[27] The study of the XII as a single unit is still debated, and not everyone is convinced of this perspective.[28] But as Lyons notes, "we should at least consider the possibility that our initial impressions of incoherence may be based on incomplete information; the things that we

---

23. Brevard Childs, *Introduction to the Old Testament as Scripture* (Philadelphia: Fortress, 1979), 73.
24. Some scholars look for underlying sociological, political, or liturgical factors that brought about the final composition of the prophetic book. See especially Erhard S. Gerstenberger, "Twelve (and More) Anonyms: A Biblical Book without Authors," in *The Book of Twelve & The New Form Criticism*, eds. Mark J. Boda, Michael H. Floyd, and Colin M. Toffelmire, ANEM 10 (Atlanta: SBL Press, 2015), 119–136.
25. Ehud Ben Zvi, "The Concept of Prophetic Books and Its Historical Setting," in *The Production of Prophecy: Constructing Prophecy and Prophets in Yehud*, eds. Diana Vikander Edelman and Ehud Ben Zvi (London: Routledge, 2014), 1–14.
26. Lyons notes, "cohesion refers to formal connections at the surface structure of a text, and coherence refers to connections in one's mental model formed during the reading process." Michael A. Lyons, "Standards of Cohesion and Coherence: Evidence from Early Readers," *Hebrew Bible and Ancient Israel* 9, no. 2 (2020): 183–208, [184].
27. Marvin A. Sweeney, "Sequence and Interpretation in the Book of the Twelve," in *Reading and Hearing the Book of the Twelve*, eds. James D. Nogalski and Marvin A. Sweeney, SBL Symposium 15 (Atlanta: Society of Biblical Literature, 2000), 50.
28. Thomas Renz, "Habakkuk and Its Co-Texts," *The Book of the Twelve: An Anthology of Prophetic Books or The Result of Complex Redactional Processes?*, edited by Heiko Wenzel (Göttingen: V&R Unipress, 2017), 13–36, [33].

perceive as incohesive or incoherent on a local level may actually play an important role on a global level."[29] Hence, the term, "The Book of the Twelve" (XII), as opposed to "the twelve prophetic books," has already clued us in on the fundamental perspective that the twelve discrete books of the Minor Prophets are to be seen as a unity.[30]

The moniker "Twelve," referred to as a single book, has been attested in Hebrew, Greek, Jewish, and Latin manuscripts.[31] In terms of length, the XII is comparable to the Major Prophets (Isaiah, Jeremiah, and Ezekiel). The books of the XII in modern versions of the English Bible (for example, ESV, NIV, NASB, RSV) follow the Masoretic order, but the Septuagint and Qumran traditions reflect a different order.[32] According to Sweeney, the Masoretic version on which our English version is based is close to the second-century (proto-)Masoretic consonantal manuscript uncovered at Wadi Murabba'at. This gives us confidence in the antiquity of the version we hold in our hands.[33]

THREE STAGES OF OLD TESTAMENT HISTORY

In the prophetic literature, the history of Israel as a nation is generally described in three stages. We shall adopt this same framework in discussing the XII. In the first stage, we have the early books – Hosea, Amos, and Micah – which are set in the eighth century BCE, up until the northern kingdom of Israel was destroyed by Assyria in 722 BCE. Next, at the center of the XII, are the books of Nahum, Habakkuk, and Zephaniah, set between the destruction of the northern kingdom in 722 BCE and the exile of Jerusalem in 587 BCE. Concerns about invading enemies and the judgment of God are understandably foregrounded

---

29. Lyons, "Standards," 207.
30. Ehud Ben Zvi and James D. Nogalski, *Two Sides of a Coin: Juxtaposing Views on Interpreting the Book of the Twelve/the Twelve Prophetic Books*, Analecta Gorgiana 201 (Piscataway: Gorgias, 2009).
31. For a detailed treatment of the textual traditions of Habakkuk and Zephaniah, see Thomas Renz, *The Books of Nahum, Habakkuk, and Zephaniah*, NICOT (Grand Rapids: Eerdmans, 2021), 206. Marvin A. Sweeney, *Zephaniah: A Commentary*, ed. Paul D. Hanson, Hermeneia (Minneapolis: Fortress, 2003), 1–45.
32. The LXX sequence: Hosea, Amos, Micah, Joel, Obadiah, Jonah, Nahum, Habakkuk, Zephaniah, Haggai, Zechariah, and Malachi. See Craig Petrovich's fascinating analysis on the Septuagint's order of the XII, "Toward the Originally Authored Book of the Twelve: Testing the Coherence of the Variant Shapings of the Twelve Prophets" (MA Thesis, Talbot School of Theology, Biola University, 2015). See also Marvin A. Sweeney, "Form and Eschatology in the Book of the Twelve Prophets," in *The Book of Twelve & The New Form Criticism*, eds. Mark J. Boda, Michael H. Floyd, and Colin M. Toffelmire, ANEM 10 (Atlanta: SBL Press, 2015), 137–163, [139]; Sweeney, *Zephaniah*, 12.
33. Sweeney, *Zephaniah*, 11.

Introduction

in these books. Finally, we have the books of Haggai, Zechariah, and Malachi forming the third stage. These books, which are considered postexilic (586–450 BCE), are primarily concerned with the temple's restoration and life in the Persian period. Dating the remaining books – Joel, Jonah, and Obadiah – remains a challenge.

The figure below – reproduced from Nogalski's commentary – helps us locate the settings of Habakkuk and Zephaniah within the XII.

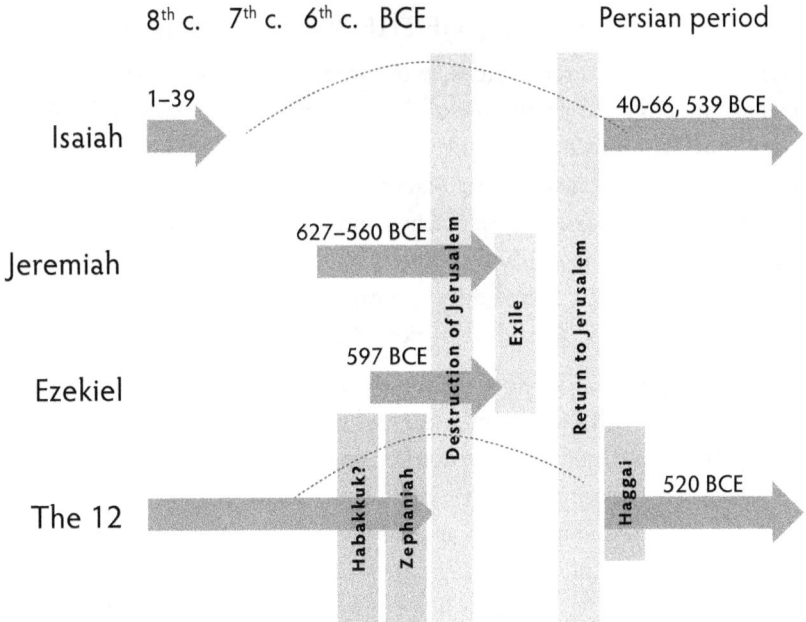

Figure 2: Habakkuk and Zephaniah within the Latter Prophets[34]

The shaded horizontal arrows identify the broad periods underlying the content of the specific body of prophetic writings. For instance, chapters 1–39 of the book Isaiah are situated in the eighth century BCE, while chapters 40–66 look back at the exile and are set in the Persian (postexilic) period. The books of Habakkuk and Zephaniah are located just before the exile. The books of Haggai, Zechariah, and Malachi, which are situated in the Persian period, view the exile in hindsight. This way, Isaiah and the XII are similar in their

---

34. Adapted from James D. Nogalski, *Hosea-Jonah* (Macon: Smyth & Helwys, 2011), 10.

historical contexts. Both these books "skipped" the period of the captivity. In contrast, Jeremiah and Ezekiel are associated with the exile, and their messages address the people of Jerusalem just before the city fell and the people went into Babylonian captivity.

Seen with this historic-literary macro image, these four prophetic corpora (collection of books) form a symmetric structure, with the exile at the center. The books of Habakkuk and Zephaniah, located at the onset of Jerusalem's fall, are central to the larger message of the XII.

LOGIC AND THEMES OF THE BOOK OF THE TWELVE

Over the last two to three decades, many attempts have been made to identify the logic underlying the structure of the XII.[35] From a literary standpoint, one reason the XII is considered a unity is because of some interesting surface features of the texts. For instance, scholars frequently find catchwords connecting the end of one book to the next – "the LORD will roar from Zion" (Joel 3:16) and "the LORD roars from Zion" (Amos 1:2). We are not able to detail the list of catchwords here, but what does it mean that a book has structural unity? Edgar Roberts gives a helpful definition of book structure:

> Structure describes how the writer arranges and places material in accord with the general ideas and purpose of the work. While plot is concerned with the conflict or conflicts, structure defines layout – the way the story, play, or narrative poem is shaped. Structure is about matters such as placement, balance, recurring themes, true and misleading conclusions, suspense, and the imitation of models of forms like reports, letters, conversations, or confessions . . . . To study structure is to study these arrangements and the purpose for which they are made.[36]

---

35. Heiko Wenzel and Georg Fischer, eds., *The Book of the Twelve: An Anthology of Prophetic Books or the Result of Complex Redactional Processes?*, Osnabrücker Studien Zur Jüdischen Und Christlichen Bibel 4 (Göttingen: V&R Unipress, 2018); James D. Nogalski and Marvin A. Sweeney, eds., *Reading and Hearing the Book of the Twelve*, SBL Symposium 15, ed. Christopher Matthews (Atlanta: Society of Biblical Literature, 2000); Lecureux, *The Thematic Unity of the Book of the Twelve*; Paul R. House, *The Unity of the Twelve*, BLS 27 (Sheffield: Sheffield Academic, 1990); Paul L. Redditt and Aaron Schart, eds., *Thematic Threads in the Book of the Twelve*, BZAW 325 (Berlin: De Gruyter, 2003).

36. Edgar V. Roberts, *Writing about Literature*, 8th ed. (Englewood Cliffs: Prentice Hall, 1995), 54, http://archive.org/details/writingaboutlite00robe.

Introduction

Paul House argues that "the Twelve are structured in a way that demonstrates the sin of Israel and the nations, the punishment of the sin, and the restoration of both from that sin."[37] He identifies a model (see below) that traces a Sin-Punishment-Restoration theological plot to explain the order of the XII.[38]

Sin: Covenant and Cosmic	Punishment: Covenant and Cosmic	Restoration: Covenant and Cosmic
Hosea: Spiritual infidelity of covenant people	Nahum: Punishment of Nineveh as sign for all nations	Haggai: New temple as symbol of restored worship
Joel: Adds sins of all peoples	Habakkuk: Chastisement of Jerusalem	Zechariah: Restoration of Jerusalem and covenant people as holy to Yahweh
Amos: Names nations and details outward sins	Zephaniah: Israel and neighbors suffer Day of Yahweh but may call on Yahweh's name	Malachi: Covenant people must do something to bring about a new order brought by Messiah
Obadiah: Sin of nations and denouncing heartless neighbors		
Jonah: Inward-outward sin of nationalistic spiritual prejudice		
Micah: Summarizes sin and adds keys to repentance and faith		

Figure 3: Paul R. House's Sin-Punishment-Restoration Model of the Twelve[39]

Beginning with Hosea and Joel, this framework shows Israel's spiritual infidelity, which resulted in various social problems and brokenness. The downward trend of the nation's moral decay continues from Amos to Micah

---

37. House, *The Unity of the Twelve*, 68.
38. This U-shaped plot is sometimes called a "comedy." Northrop Frye, *Anatomy of Criticism: Four Essays* (Princeton: Princeton University Press, 1973), 163–171.
39. Table adapted and redrawn from Barker and Bailey, *Micah, Nahum, Habakkuk, Zephaniah*, NAC 20 (Nashville: Broadman & Holman, 1998), 262.

and reaches its lowest point with Habakkuk, where national judgment and destruction are at hand. But the picture turns positive toward the end of the book of Zephaniah, where hope will be kindled after a display of God's day of wrath[40] and we are told that nations will call upon the name of Yahweh and the prophetic hope for deliverance. While Haggai and Zechariah show restoration as having begun, Israel's ultimate deliverance and restoration remain in the future, as envisioned in the last prophetic book of Malachi. House's work shows a theological metanarrative across the XII.

In this introduction, we have looked briefly at the prophetic office, the world of Habakkuk and Zephaniah, and the larger historical and literary contexts of the OT that cradled these books. We have also discussed how these two books fit logically within the theological structure of the XII.

---

40. It does not mean that individual books are chronologically arranged according to the historical information in the superscriptions at the beginning of the books. If that's the case, Zephaniah, set in the days of Josiah (Zeph 1:1), should come before Nahum-Habakkuk, which are set toward the end of the Assyrian empire (fall of Nineveh, 612 BCE), and near to the Babylonian ascendency (605 BCE onwards) respectively. See Renz, "Habakkuk and Its Co-Texts," 17.

HABAKKUK

OUTLINE

1:1	The Superscription of Pronouncement
1:2–4	Habakkuk's Complaint: God Is Deaf to Wrong
1:5–11	God's Speech about the Warring Chaldeans
1:12–17	Habakkuk's Remarks about God
2:1	Habakkuk's Self-Centered Outlook
2:2–5	God's Speech: The Vision and the Proud Man
2:6–19	Five Woe Oracles
	2:6–8 Those Who Heap Stolen Goods
	2:9–11 Those Who Profit from Unjust Gains
	2:12–14 Those Who Build through Bloodshed
	2:15–17 Those Who Incite Others to Get Drunk
	2:18–19 Those Who Practice Idolatry
2:20	Habakkuk's God-Centered Outlook
3:1	The Superscription of Prayer
3:2	Habakkuk's Remarks about God
3:3–15	God as Warrior
	3:3–7 From Teman to Midian
	3:8–15 Over the Rivers and the Sea
3:16–19c	Habakkuk's Transformation: I Hear You, God!
3:19d	Postscript

HABAKKUK IN A NUTSHELL

Since Habakkuk has two separate superscriptions (1:1; 3:1),[1] some see the book as having two main parts: 1:1–2:20 and 3:1–19.[2] A literary connection between the first two chapters is also evident, especially in Habakkuk 1:2–2:5, which encapsulates the two cycles of Habakkuk's complaint and God's corresponding speeches. While this commentary maintains the distinction of three main units in the three chapters as shown in the outline above, I will also argue that the entire book is a unity, as made clear below.

Chapter 1 begins with a superscription (1:1), followed by three units (1:2–4; 1:5–11; 1:12–17) that address three different topics. The first unit presents Habakkuk's first complaint against God and the prophet's evaluation of the circumstances in Judah (1:2–4). This is followed by God's first speech, which describes the warring Chaldeans (1:5–11). The third unit records Habakkuk's second complaint and his assessment of the Chaldeans' wickedness against the nations (1:12–17).

Chapter 2 has four text units. The first unit shows Habakkuk stationing himself on the ramparts (2:1). The second unit is God's speech (2:2–5). The third unit is a series of five woe oracles (2:6–19),[3] each beginning with the word "woe" and summarizing some of their sins (2:6–8, 9–11, 12–14, 15–18, and 19). The final unit is the final verse (2:20), where the subject is once more God. The first and last units function as bookends for the whole chapter (2:1, 20).

Chapter 3 is a prayer that vividly describes ways in which God manifests himself. Although some scholars question whether Habakkuk originally penned this chapter, suggesting that another priest or scribe added it, most scholars see this chapter as integral to the whole book.[4] This chapter is chiastic

---

1. In the commentary on Habakkuk and Zephaniah below, Bible references without book names indicate references from these two books accordingly.
2. Marvin Sweeney, "Structure, Genre, and Intent in the Book of Habakkuk," *VT* 41.1 (1991): 63–83.
3. The interjection, "woe" (*hoy*), is found at least fifty times in the OT. In the Latter Prophets, note their presence in Isaiah 5:5; Jeremiah 23:1; Ezekiel 13:18; Amos 6:1; Micah 2:1; Nahum 3:1; Zephaniah 2:5; 3:1. For more details on the prophetic speech and woe oracles, see Claus Westermann, *Basic Forms of Prophetic Speech* (Philadelphia: Westminster, 1967); Erhard Gerstenberger, "The Woe-Oracles of the Prophets," *JBL* 81.3 (1962): 249–263.
4. For a technical survey of the critical issues concerning Habakkuk 3, see G. T. M. Prinsloo, "Reading Habakkuk 3 in Its Literary Context: A Worthwhile Exercise or Futile Attempt?" *Journal for Semitics* 11, no.1 (2002): 83–111.

in shape, meaning that it has a symmetry in which one half of the text mirrors the other. To see this chiasmus clearly, look at both ends of the chapter. Notice that there is a superscript (3:1) and a postscript (3:19d) that form bookends, just like in chapter 2. As we move inward from the bookends, we see Habakkuk's first-person remarks about God (3:2) and Habakkuk's posture (3:16–19c). The center of chapter 3 has an extended depiction of the power and sovereignty of God (3:3–15). This depiction is called a *theophany* – the manifestation of God in power and glory.[5]

THE SHAPE AND MESSAGE OF HABAKKUK

The more we linger over the book of Habakkuk, the more we see how well-crafted it is. The composer uses changes of subject or speaker, shifts in grammatical or morphological forms, repetitions, parallelisms, strategic placements of formulaic phrases, and specific genres to shape the text. Consider some *parallelisms* and *repetitions* in Habakkuk. Chapter 1 begins and ends with Habakkuk's questions (1:2–3, 17), and questions also bind the last unit of the chapter (1:12–17). These strategically placed questions capture the audience's attention at the onset and solicit their response at the end of a unit. Also notice how the phrases "therefore" and "so" or "so that" – based on the same Hebrew phrase (*al-ken*) – are repeated at the end of Habakkuk's two complaints (1:4, 15d–16). These phrases are not found anywhere else in chapter 1.[6]

> Therefore [*al-ken*] the law is paralyzed, and justice never prevails. The wicked hem in the righteous, so that [*al-ken*] justice is perverted (1:4).

> And so [*al-ken*] he rejoices and is glad. Therefore [*al-ken*] he sacrifices to his net and burns incense to his dragnet, for by his net he lives in luxury and enjoys the choicest food (1:15d–16).

Note how the composer uses the imperative mood (volitional speech) each time God begins to speak to Habakkuk.[7] At the beginning of Habakkuk 1:5, the listeners are commanded by God to "look" and "watch" and be "utterly

---

5. For this chapter, I have arrived at a similar structure to Prinsloo's "Reading Habakkuk 3," 101–102.
6. Interestingly, these four occurrences of *al-ken* form a chiastic shape, with the first and last occurrences beginning a sentence and the two middle occurrences beginning the final clause of a line.
7. For a list of rhetorical and literary devices used in Habakkuk 3, see Michael L. Barré, "Newly Discovered Literary Devices in the Prayer of Habakkuk," *CBQ* 75, nos. 3 (2013): 446–462.

amazed"! These are the only verbs in imperative form in chapter 1. In God's response to the prophet in Habakkuk 2:2, the verbs "write down" and "make it plain" are also in the imperative form.

Another technique used to shape the text is the change of person. When Habakkuk cries out to God and God responds to him, we observe the use of *I-You* pronouns (1:2–3, 5–6, 12–14) and first- or second-person speeches. However, when Habakkuk begins to describe the decadent situation around him in relation to the Torah (1:3–4) and the brutal violence of the invading Chaldeans (1:15–17), the text shifts to the third-person. These shifts in person correspond well to changes in the semantic and sense units.[8] The movement of the semantic content across the book fits well with the literary structure we have proposed. If the composer of Habakkuk had indeed chosen to shape this book in this way, we should ask how this shape serves to carry its message.

The overarching message of Habakkuk highlights a theology-versus-reality conundrum and a metamorphosing power that turns one from despair to hope in God. At the center of the book, we see a vision and five woe oracles that highlight God's retributive justice – something Habakkuk had already known but needed to hear anew. However, two significant manifestations of power – a vision of the Chaldeans and the theophany of Yahweh – ultimately altered Habakkuk's outlook even though his circumstances remained unchanged. Habakkuk's vision of the Chaldeans might have been traumatizing, but his vision of Yahweh as a warrior was *transformational*, and enabled Habakkuk to tolerate the intolerable. In this way, the book of Habakkuk is helpful to all who struggle with a similar theology-versus-reality conundrum.

This message, I believe, is corroborated by the structural design of the book, echoing Wendland's argument: "The macrostructure of Habakkuk is one of the most clearly defined of all the prophetic books."[9] The short analysis below explains how I think the shape of the book works. On the one hand, we see a linear movement across the book – that is, we see a development of the concerns between the prophet and God. There is a forward sense of time, and, toward the end of the book, we see a development in Habakkuk's inner

---

8. Using insights from recent poetic discourse analyses and linguistic studies, we observe that shifts in the grammatical or morphological forms of verbs also correspond to the identified text units. For instance, the perfective verbs in Habakkuk 1:1 and 1:2, as well as 1:8 and 1:12, mark the major sectional seams in chapter 1. These features, however, are only visible in the Hebrew text.

9. Ernst Wendland, "'The Righteous Live by Their Faith' in a Holy God: Complementary Compositional Forces and Habakkuk's Dialogue with the Lord," *JETS* 42, no. 4 (1999): 591–628, [593].

disposition and attitude. This change begs the question of how. From a linear and progressive point of view, the shift in Habakkuk's attitude from one of sorrow and a deflated spirit to one of hope and assurance in God (3:16–19) can be seen as the climax of this trajectory.[10]

But linearity is not the only way this text is organized. While repetitions of words and motifs across discrete units of texts can appear random, this apparent randomness disappears once we realize *how* the composer has created repetitions (in a concentric way, as shown above in the structural proposals). Concentricity means that significant motifs in the book recur at locations that are symmetrical around the center. The concentricity of a book functions not only to highlight repeated motifs but also directs the reader's attention to the book's center. A concentric structure is also called a chiasmus or a palindrome.[11]

The book of Habakkuk is concentric. We can detect a shift in a particular motif of interest before and after 2:2–19, which is the pivotal center of the book. After 2:19, Habakkuk makes no further complaint. By 3:1, his complaints have turned into a prayer. By this point, Habakkuk's understanding of God has deepened, and his hope is resolute.

The outline of Habakkuk shown above is now illustrated concentrically below.

---

10. Hiramatsu sees a two-part structure with climaxes at 2:4 and 3:16–19. Kei Hiramatsu, "The Structure and Structural Relationships of the Book of Habakkuk," *Journal of Inductive Biblical Studies* 3.2 (2016): 106–129.
11. Other chiastic structures for the book of Habakkuk have been proposed. Wendland, "'The Righteous,'" 594; H. H. Walker and N. W. Lund, "The Literary Structure of the Book of Habakkuk," *JBL* 53, no. 4 (1934): 355–370; David A. Dorsey, *The Literary Structure of the Old Testament: A Commentary on Genesis-Malachi* (Grand Rapids: Baker Academic, 2004), 308.

Habakkuk in a Nutshell

A	The Superscription of Pronouncement	1:1a	Superscription
B	Habakkuk's Complaint: God Is Deaf to Wrong	1:2–4	Lament
C	God's Speech about the Warring Chaldeans	1:5–11	Chaldeans
D	Habakkuk's Remarks about God	1:12–17	Introducing God
E	Habakkuk's Self-Centered Outlook	2:1	Anticipating God
F	God's Speech on Vision and the Proud Man	2:2–5	Vision
F′	Five Woe Oracles	2:6–19	Woe Oracles
E′	Habakkuk's God-Centered Outlook	2:20	Anticipating God
A′	The Superscription of Prayer	3:1a–b	Superscription
D′	Habakkuk's Remarks about God	3:2	Introducing God
C′	God as Warrior	3:3–15	God as Warrior
B′	Habakkuk's Transformation: I Hear You, God!	3:16–19c	Praise
A″	Postscript	3:19d	Postscript

Figure 4: Structural Design of Habakkuk

HABAKKUK 1

The first chapter of Habakkuk is an exchange between Habakkuk and God, in which the prophet complains about the deplorable and unjust situation in Jerusalem. God's word to Habakkuk announces his intention to raise up the Chaldeans as his instrument of judgment (1:5–11). But the prophet struggles to accept how a holy God would use a people who were even more wicked to accomplish his purposes. Written with poetic finesse, using vivid metaphors and techniques of doubling, this chapter heightens the sense of fear about the impending invasion of the Chaldeans and shows that the perpetual hardening of God's people in their sins would hasten the inescapable punishment of God.

1:1 THE SUPERSCRIPTION OF PRONOUNCEMENT

The word "prophecy" in the superscription is translated from an enigmatic Hebrew term, *massa*, which likely means a kind of "prophetic utterance."[1] Scholars have made several suggestions about the possible meaning of *massa*.[2] First, in its basic or root meaning (etymology), *massa* means "burden" (or "load") or "responsibility." Second, *massa* might refer to a category of prophetic utterance in which the prophet, based on a vision already received, gave clear and usable insight to his hearers in order to elicit a response from them. The *massa* often expresses God's transcendental intentions or acts in the human arena concerning the immediate or near future. The prophecy might be aurally or visually communicated to the prophet before it was composed as text.[3] There is a visual quality underlying the word "received" (1:1), rendered from a Hebrew verb that means "to see."

---

1. The Hebrew lexeme, *massa*, occurs 67 times in the HB/OT but 28 of these function as an introduction to a prophecy. It is rendered "oracle" in the ESV, RSV, and "message" in the NET. Michael H. Floyd, "The אשָּׂמַ (Maśśā') as a Type of Prophetic Book," *JBL* 121, nos. 3 (2002): 401–422.
2. For an in-depth study of the term, *massa*, see Mark J. Boda, "Freeing the Burden of Prophecy," in *Exploring Zechariah, Volume 2: The Development and Role of Biblical Traditions in Zechariah* (Atlanta: SBL Press, 2017), 135–152. Available online: https://www.sbl-site.org/assets/pdfs/pubs/9780884142010_OA.pdf; "Freeing the Burden of Prophecy: Maśśā' and the Legitimacy of Prophecy in Zech 9-14," *Bib* 87, no. 3 (2006): 338–357.
3. Elsewhere, it is often verbal (e.g., Jer 23:38; Ezek 12:10) or written (Zech 9:1; 12:1; Mal 1:1). K. W. Weyde, "Once Again the Term Maśśā' in Zechariah 9:1; 12:1 and in Malachi 1:1: What Is Its Significance?" *AcT* (2018): 251–267.

The name "Habakkuk" (1:1; 3:1) does not appear anywhere else in the OT. Habakkuk, who is given the title "the prophet" (*hannabi*), was probably connected to the temple since his vision was received at the "ramparts" of the temple (2:1; and "temple" in 2:20).[4] In contrast, prophets like Gad and Isaiah were associated with the royal court (2 Sam 24:11; Isa 37:1–7).[5]

Habakkuk, who possessed the scribal skills necessary to record his visions (2:2), might have been a musician or skilled literary poet who wrote down his words. The Bible provides little background information on Habakkuk, but tradition has helped to fill the gap. Since "Habakkuk" resembles the verb *chabak* (meaning "to embrace"), Jewish traditions in the medieval period linked Habakkuk to the Shunammite's son based on the phrase, "you shall embrace (*chabak*) a son" (2 Kgs 4:16 ESV).[6] The deuterocanonical *Bel and the Dragon* (composed in Greek and added to the book of Daniel) gives us Habakkuk's pedigree – the son of Joshua, a Levite. This text also records that the prophet Habakkuk delivered stew to Daniel in the lion's den.

> [33] Now the prophet Habakkuk was in Judea; he had made a stew and had broken bread into a bowl and was going into the field to take it to the reapers. [34] But the angel of the Lord said to Habakkuk, "Take the food that you have to Babylon, to Daniel, in the lions' den." [35] Habakkuk said, "Sir, I have never seen Babylon, and I know nothing about the den." [36] Then the angel of the Lord took him by the crown of his head and carried him by his hair; with the speed of the wind, he set him down in Babylon, right over the den. [37] Then Habakkuk shouted, "Daniel, Daniel! Take the food that God has sent you." [38] Daniel said, "You have remembered me, O God, and have not forsaken those who love you." [39] So Daniel got up and ate. And the angel of God immediately returned Habakkuk to his own place. (Bel 1:33–39 NRSV)

---

4. Most likely, Habakkuk was standing on the ramparts of the temple – which divided the temple from the city outside – and seeing what was both outside and inside the temple. Similarly, God's speech, too, would take place both outside the temple area and inside the temple.
5. Sweeney cites 2 Chronicles 7:6; 8:14; 35:2, where the priests and Levites took their positions at the temple as they praised God. Sweeney, "Structure, Genre, and Intent," 70.
6. Richard Coggins and Jin H. Han, *Six Minor Prophets through the Centuries: Nahum, Habakkuk, Zephaniah, Haggai, Zechariah, and Malachi* (Chichester: Wiley-Blackwell, 2011), 50.

Figure 5: Habakkuk delivering stew to Daniel in the lion's den (fifteenth century)
Public Domain: https://commons.wikimedia.org/wiki/
File:Daniel_dans_la_fosse_aux_lions.jpg

These traditions are not necessarily true or historical. However, what we do know is that Habakkuk spoke for God since the expression "the prophet" is a bona fide epithet for God's spokesperson. The OT recognizes a few similar terms: "prophet" (*nabi*), "seer" (*roeh* or *hozeh*, 1 Sam 9:9; Amos 7:12–15), and "man of God" (*ish-elohim*).[7] Yahweh's prophet was expected to represent God before the recipients of God's message. Sometimes, that meant going directly to people of authority with rebukes and threats (1 Kgs 21:17–19). The prophet's life was not his own. Frequently, the suffering prophet himself *was* God's symbolic message, expressed through austere practices.[8]

As noted earlier, the prophetic message includes a) an *accusation* of wrongdoing, b) a *pronouncement* of judgment, and c) a *proclamation* of future deliverance or restoration. The Bible often lists three types of punishment as judgment: famine, plague, and sword. This trinary expression likely originated

---

7. From the Mari Letters or Ebla documents, we find the title of *nabiutum*, which is a close parallel to the term *nabi* in the OT. P. A. Verhoef, *NIDOTTE* 4:1068, 1072; Chalmers, *Interpreting the Prophets*, chapters 1–2.
8. Chalmers, *Interpreting the Prophets*, 18.

with the Torah (Deut 32:24), was used nationally with David's sin (2 Sam 24:13), and acquired formulaic status by the time of Jeremiah and Ezekiel.[9]

> "You have not obeyed me; you have not proclaimed freedom to your own people. So I now proclaim 'freedom' for you, declares the LORD – 'freedom' to fall by the sword, plague and famine. I will make you abhorrent to all the kingdoms of the earth." (Jer 34:17)

> This is what the LORD says: "Whoever stays in this city will die by the sword, famine or plague, but whoever goes over to the Babylonians will live. They will escape with their lives; they will live." (Jer 38:2)

> "For this is what the Sovereign LORD says: How much worse will it be when I send against Jerusalem my four dreadful judgments – sword and famine and wild beasts and plague – to kill its men and their animals!" (Ezek 14:21)

But judgment is not the last word on the lips of the prophets. They also declare hope for God's people, a future when God will manifest not only power and holiness but also his mercy and compassion. More specifically, in Habakkuk and Zephaniah, Yahweh promises to bring deliverance through a messianic warrior figure who will restore his intended blessings to his people. The essence of the prophetic utterance is thus a display of God's nature and his covenantal purposes for a people he calls his own.

1:2–4 HABAKKUK'S COMPLAINT: GOD IS DEAF TO WRONG

The book begins with the prophet's cries and gives us a glimpse of his inner turmoil. It is a profoundly personal discourse that displays both Habakkuk's struggle and his relationship with God and the world. The book reads like a diary, in which the prophet converses, negotiates, and wrestles with God.

Habakkuk laments and even accuses God. With four rapid-fire rhetorical questions, he complains that God is not responding to his perpetual call for help or to his cries for deliverance from violence. Then he accuses God of being indifferent to injustice and wrongdoing, attributing the cause of his misery to God. These accusations assume that God ought to respond based on what Habakkuk knew about him. For Habakkuk, God's tardiness in this situation

---

[9]. See Jeremiah 14:12; 21:7, 9; 24:10; 27:8, 13; 29:17, 18; 32:24, 36; 34:17; 42:17, 22; 44:13; Ezekiel 5:12, 17; 6:11, 12; 7:15; 12:16; 14:21. This format also occurs in Revelation 6:8.

did not make theological sense. Because God did not address the situation, the lawless wicked ran amok, doing as they deemed fit. At the heart of this lament is Habakkuk's deep yearning for a world under God's righteous law, where justice and peace would flourish. The expectation of how things ought to be conflicted with the way things actually were in Habakkuk's time. And this theology-versus-reality tension had reached a breaking point.

Habakkuk 1:2–3 consists of carefully composed parallel lines with *I-You* speeches. Both lines begin with interrogative markers – "How long?" and "Why?" In his first-person speech, Habakkuk says, "*I* call," and "*I* cry out," and each of these statements is met with a contrasting "but *you* do not."[10] Also, note the aural and visual aspects of these verses. Verse 2 contrasts Habakkuk's loud cries with God's deafness, and verse 3 focuses on what Habakkuk sees.[11] This dual seeing-hearing nature follows from our earlier discussion of the *massa* prophecy.

If we find the form of Habakkuk's questions familiar, that is because we have seen this elsewhere.[12] In Psalm 13:2, we find a similar lament against God by the Psalmist: "How long must I wrestle with my thoughts and day after day have sorrow in my heart? How long will my enemy triumph over me?" A similar cry against God is found in Jeremiah 47:6, where the prophet yearns for respite from the enemy's sword, which was the result of God's judgment. In these instances, God's people cried out to God, but God was silent.

Strikingly, this line of questioning was first adopted by God when speaking to his people – instead of the other way round – when they refused to hear and keep his commandment.

> Then the LORD said to Moses, "How long will you refuse to keep my commands and my instructions?" (Exod 16:28)

> The LORD said to Moses, "How long will these people treat me with contempt? How long will they refuse to believe in me, in spite of all the signs I have performed among them?" (Num 14:11)

The people's perpetual refusal to listen to and obey God eventually led to punishment and judgment, as we see in the books of Isaiah and Jeremiah.

---

10. Although, here, Habakkuk accuses God of doing nothing, in the following verse he accuses God of forcing Habakkuk to witness injustice and tolerate evildoers (1:3).
11. The NIV's translation, "Why do you tolerate wrongdoing?" is literally "Why do you make me look at wrongdoing?" The Hebrew verb uses the Hiphil with a causative thrust.
12. Compare Job 8:2; 18:2; 19:2; Ps 62:3.

> "I will destine you for the sword, and all of you will fall in the slaughter; for I called but you did not answer, I spoke but you did not listen. You did evil in my sight and chose what displeases me." (Isa 65:12)
>
> Therefore this is what the LORD says: "I will bring on them a disaster they cannot escape. Although they cry out to me, I will not listen to them . . . Do not pray for this people or offer any plea or petition for them, because I will not listen when they call to me in the time of their distress." (Jer 11:11, 14)

God's unwillingness to listen to petitions for his people was a mark of his determination to bring judgment. And Habakkuk's cry against God's unhearing ears was a reversal of the people's spurning of God and the fulfillment of God's indictment on his people. God had not denied himself or those who cried out to him. Rather, God was being true to his earlier warnings. The people's refusal to listen had earned them the same "unhearing." Now the chickens have come home to roost! The tables have turned. So, the opening cries of the book of Habakkuk signal what is to come – God's judgment is at hand.

Habakkuk found himself among those who were enduring God's judgment – a significant point in the book of Habakkuk, which concerns the faith of the righteous among the rebels and the ruins. And the rest of the book reveals how the righteous – as seen through the life of the prophet Habakkuk – ought to live.

Ten different words are used to heighten the comprehensiveness of the dire circumstances that Habakkuk describes. Of these, six are nouns – "violence," "injustice," "wrongdoing," "destruction," "strife," and "conflict" – and four are either verbs or adverbs – "paralyzed," "never prevails," "hem in" [the righteous], and [justice is] "perverted." Some of these words are characteristic of the Psalms and Wisdom literature. For instance, the word "conflict" is frequently rendered "strife" or "quarrelsome" in Proverbs. Similarly, "toil" – which is the repeated refrain in the book of Ecclesiastes – is rendered "wrongdoing" in Habakkuk. Habakkuk's choice of words conveys the same sense of exasperation that Qoheleth expresses in Ecclesiastes.

The link to Wisdom literature is also evident in verse 4 in the use of words like "justice," "prevail," and "perverted." In Hebrew, verses 4b and 4d form a parallel, using the same words "justice" (*mishpat*) and "go out" (*yetze*). When the law is suppressed, "justice does not go out" (NIV: "justice never prevails") and "justice goes out" with perversion – that is, in the hands of the wicked, justice is twisted (NIV: "justice is perverted"). Similarly, words such as "law" (Torah), "justice," "righteous," and "wicked" – which find currency in the Wisdom literature – are also prevalent in Habakkuk.

The decadence we see around us now is also a departure from the instructions of the Torah and, more generally, the Judeo-Christian value system. Although this value system was once seen as underpinning Western and European laws, unfortunately, this view is no longer in vogue and is now associated with fundamentalism and division.[13]

The call for the righteous to live faithfully (2:4) suggests that the righteous lived among the wicked who failed to keep covenantal faith in Judah. Historically, this moral decadence could have described Judah under King Jehoiakim from 609 to 605 BCE (Jer 22:13–23). But the deplorable imagery used in Habakkuk 1–2 may also refer to the Babylonians' rise to power in 605 BCE and portray their aggression as they ravaged the lands of Canaan. In any case, it is impossible to accurately identify the righteous and the wicked in this text. The generic nature of the text allows us to readapt it for different situations and different times.

What is clear, nonetheless, is Habakkuk's despondency and misery. The prophet's evaluation of the situation in 1:4 is poignant: God's laws were not kept. Interestingly, the words chosen to describe this situation occur in decreasing frequency in the Bible. It is as if Habakkuk had run out of words to describe this deplorable situation. The verbs "paralyzed" and "hem in" are used only a handful of times in the entire OT; and the final word in this verse – "perverted" – occurs just once in the Bible.

---

13. James Loeffler, "The Problem With the 'Judeo-Christian Tradition,'" *The Atlantic*, August 1, 2020, https://www.theatlantic.com/ideas/archive/2020/08/the-judeo-christian-tradition-is-over/614812/.

TRAPPED IN UNENDING VIOLENCE AND INJUSTICE

Habakkuk's situation reminds me of the Dalit people, who are often called the "untouchables." In Nepal, the Dalit people face unimaginable oppression.

> This distinction defines every conceivable aspect of a Dalit's existence; her citizenship, her access to land, her education, her livelihood, her choice of spouse, her place of worship, her security, her health, and her bodily integrity are all principally limited by caste. The grossest manifestation of this discrimination system is the practice of "untouchability" – the complete repudiation and segregation of Dalits from members of other castes, including a prohibition on touching non-Dalits and their possessions based on the belief that Dalits are "polluted." Caste discrimination and the practice of "untouchability" have ensured the complete subordination of Dalits . . . In addition, Dalit women and girls in Nepal endure the intersectional burden of both caste and gender discrimination.[1]

How should the Christian Dalit live? Dalits who have embraced the Christian faith have gradually built up their contextual theology, which is a form of liberation theology "aiming for the emancipation of the poorest of the poor, restoration of their lost rights, and the recovery of their human status."[2] But the theological propositions established over the years since Christianity penetrated the community are still resisted by the lived reality of the Dalits. Even within the church, Dalit Christians face discrimination from non-Dalit Christians. There remains a genuine "practical efficacy" problem[3] – a problem of incompatibility between theory and practice.

Although there are fundamental differences between Habakkuk's situation and that of the Dalits, it is correct to say that Habakkuk experienced the same existential and theological crisis: If the wicked are not punished and the righteous are not blessed, how can anyone reconcile this with the concepts of retribution and justice that are underscored in the Torah? At the core, the existential challenge of Habakkuk and Christian Dalits is the same – it is a struggle with God. While the godless will not face this problem since they deny God, the righteous must carry their crosses and deny themselves daily. When will one's faith break? When will the faithful "curse God and die" (Job 2:9)? The laments of

> Habakkuk, the Dalits, and Christians living under cruel oppression reflect this liminal state.
>
> ---
>
> 1. "Recasting Justice: Securing Dalit Rights in Nepal's New Constitution," Center for Human Rights and Global Justice (New York: NYU School of Law, 2008), 3; https://chrgj.org/wp-content/uploads/2016/09/recastingjustice.pdf.
> 2. Daniel Jeyaraj, "The Struggle of Dalit Christians in South India for Their Identity and Recognition," *Theology* 100, no. 796 (1997): 242–251, [249].
> 3. See Peniel Rajkumar, *Dalit Theology and Dalit Liberation: Problems, Paradigms, and Possibilities* (London: Routledge, 2016).

At the end of verse 4, Habakkuk seemed to have run out of words to describe the situation. He had no more strength to continue the struggle. The perfect storm of rampant wickedness and the apparent silence of God had pushed the prophet to the precipice of his faith. How long could Habakkuk hang on to a "theoretical" God before life slipped away from the prophet himself?

1:5–11 GOD'S SPEECH ABOUT THE WARRING CHALDEANS

We lament that our problems are big, and that God has hidden himself from us. To use modern slang, have we been *ghosted* by God? That is, we cannot get a response from God even after we have prayed repeatedly. But the surprising factor is that when God finally speaks, we find ourselves overwhelmed, "paralyzed," and unable to respond – much like Job (Job 42:1–6).

The silence at the end of verse 4 is broken by four successive imperative verbs in verse 5. God, in a first-person speech, commands Habakkuk and the people of Judah to "look," "watch," and be "utterly amazed"![14] God was saying, in effect, "All of you be stunned and be aghast at what I am going to do – the likes of which you [plural] would not believe!" Only in Isaiah 29:9–10 do we find a parallel form of astonishment (and Hebrew construction). There, the Israelites (not the nations) would be astonished by the state in which God had placed them – blind and drunk (not from wine but because of God's punishment).

---

14. The NIV's "utterly amazed" is an emphatic translation of two underlying plural verbs of the same root.

Habakkuk speaks of a similar kind of astonishment. Verse 5 draws the hearers' (or readers') attention to God's rousing act.[15] Verse 6 begins in a similar way, with a Hebrew interjection – "behold" (untranslated in the NIV) – that emphasizes God's act of raising up the "Babylonians" or "Chaldeans" (NASB, ESV).[16] The first-person present participles – "I am *going to do* something in your days" and "I am *raising* up the Babylonians" – highlight God's ongoing actions. The rest of the chapter simply expands on the description of the invading Babylonians.

The words "Babylonians" and "Chaldeans" are often interchangeably used in English translations, even though the Hebrew word is the same – *kasddim*. While Chaldeans referred to the people group, Babylonians referred to the place from where they came – that is, Babylon. Although the term "Chaldeans" is used as early as Genesis 11:28, in Habakkuk, "Chaldeans" refers to the Neo-Babylonians, who were a superpower from about 626–539 BCE. The Old Babylonian Empire can be traced back to the eighteenth-century BCE under the rule of Hammurabi.[17] Archaeological data trace the Chaldeans back to a group that emerged around 900 BCE in southeastern Mesopotamia, between the Tigris and Euphrates rivers.[18] From the ninth to the seventh centuries BCE, the Chaldeans gradually gained political and military power and vied with the Assyrians for control over the region. Under the leadership of Nabopolassar (626–605 BCE), the Neo-Babylonians eventually established themselves in the Near East when they defeated the Assyrians at Carchemish in 605 BCE.

Soon after this victory, King Nebuchadnezzar II – Nabopolassar's son – invaded Palestine and besieged many cities. Jerusalem fell to the Babylonians, and King Jehoiakim was captured and made a vassal. Daniel and his friends were also captured at that time (Dan 1:1–7). This was the first deportation. Jehoiakim soon died, and his son Jehoiachin took over. In 597 BCE, the Babylonians came against Judah again and captured the city. They deported Jehoiachin and his family to Babylon and made Zedekiah (Jehoiachin's uncle) a vassal king in Jerusalem. This was the second deportation. Finally, in 588

---

15. The LXX reads verse 5 differently, having "scoffers" instead of "nations" (MT), and "be destroyed!" instead of "astounded!" (MT).
16. The LXX adds an additional term, "warrior," to the Chaldeans.
17. Bill Arnold, "Babylonians," in *Peoples of the Old Testament World*, Alfred J. Hoerth et al., eds. (Cambridge: Baker Academic, 1998), 43–75.
18. Trent C. Butler, "Chaldea," *The Lexham Bible Dictionary* (Bellingham, WA: Lexham, 2016); W. G. Lambert, "The Babylonians and Chaldeans," in *Peoples of Old Testament Times*, ed. D. J. Wiseman (Oxford: Clarendon, 1973), 179–196.

BCE, Nebuchadnezzar besieged the city, destroyed Jerusalem, and deported the people a third time.

The term Chaldean can also function metaphorically. The Chaldeans' ruthless, impetuous, self-aggrandizing, and violent nature (1:6–9) recalls the Egyptian pharaohs who rose and challenged Yahweh. Scholars also compare the Chaldeans' ruthless killing of people to Sheol's insatiable appetite for the dead.[19]

Habakkuk 1:6–10 gives a vivid depiction of the Chaldeans, with no less than twenty different descriptions of their military prowess. Apart from the plural description of horses and horsemen (1:8), the Hebrew verbs and pronouns used to refer to the Chaldeans in this section, particularly in 1:9–11, are in the collective singular form (although translated "they" in the NIV). It is as if they would come as one massive, unstoppable horde. The Chaldeans were filled with unbridled pride and swollen with arrogance. They promoted their own honor and showed no respect for any laws but their own. They mocked kings, scoffed at rulers, and laughed at fortified cities. They gloried in violence and in their own strength. Like rampaging bulls, they crushed and trampled everything in their way. Such vivid descriptions in the text are not a neutral record of events. They capture the violence and bloodshed of the Chaldeans, who would not go unpunished.

Images of predatory animals and the desert wind are used to describe the Chaldeans, whose captives were as numerous as grains of sand (1:8–9). The swiftness of their battle horses is compared to the leopard, their aggression to the wolves, and their intense focus as they seek to devour their enemies is likened to an eagle swooping down on its prey. Their military advance is compared to the desert wind (compare "whirlwinds" in Isaiah 21:1) – perhaps the Mediterranean *sirocco*, the Persian *shamal*, or the *simoon* of the Arabian Peninsula. These suffocating winds sometimes reach the speed of a gale, last for hours, and often cause damage to infrastructure. Similarly, the prophet Joel compares the Babylonian invasion to a dense cloud of locusts, which obliterate everything in their path without care or compassion and leave nothing in their wake.

These descriptions, however, may be more poetic than historically exact. The *Babylonian Chronicle 5*, the OT, and Josephus's *Antiquities of the Jews* (X, chs 6–8) record that the exploits of Nebuchadnezzar II and the expansion of

---

19. B. T. Arnold, "Babylon," in *Dictionary of the Old Testament: Prophets: Prophets*, eds Mark J. Boda and J. Gordon McConville (Westmont: InterVarsity Press, 2012), 52–60, [59].

his empire took decades.[20] Although Habakkuk's references to the besieging warfare and the building of earth ramps describe how the Babylonians overcame fortified cities and captured numerous prisoners – Josephus notes the number of 10,832 prisoners at the sack of Jehoiachin[21] – according to the biblical account, the siege of Jerusalem actually took about two years (2 Kgs 25:1–4; Jer 39:1–2; 52:4–7). In reality, the conquests were not as swift and complete as depicted in Habakkuk. Nebuchadnezzar's siege of Tyre was also less than successful (Ezek 29:17–21), and Egypt was only completely subdued by Cambyses in 525 BCE.

Yet, the fall of Jerusalem was inevitable. From the vantage point of the prophet Habakkuk and the righteous (2:4), who were called to witness the vision, these things were still unfolding. Nevertheless, the mercury was rising rapidly. Not only was the situation exacerbated by an impending ruthless invasion, but there was also an escalating internal rebellion:

> [13] He [Zedekiah] became stiff-necked and hardened his heart and would not turn to the LORD, the God of Israel. [14] Furthermore, all the leaders of the priests and the people became more and more unfaithful, following all the detestable practices of the nations and defiling the temple of the LORD, which he had consecrated in Jerusalem . . . [16] they mocked God's messengers, despised his words and scoffed at his prophets until the wrath of the LORD was aroused against his people, and there was no remedy. (2 Chr 36:13–14, 16)

Eventually, Jerusalem's capitulation, the plundering of the temple, and the exile of her priests and people came to pass (2 Kgs 25:1–26; 2 Chr 36:15–23). For Habakkuk, the vision God gave him in response was too much to bear. God had not merely failed to answer his cry for help but had aggravated the situation!

God's wisdom and his ways are always higher than ours. He sees what we need beyond what we think we need. His actions may seem at odds with our desires because he sees the future and knows what is better for us in the longer term. I once took my toddler to a huge toy section in a departmental store. The toys were stacked in piles, forming several islands that towered over

---

20. Israel Eph'al, "Nebuchadnezzar the Warrior: Remarks on His Military Achievements," *IEJ* 53.2 (2003): 178–191.
21. Josephus, *Ant.* X, vii, i. An English translation is available online: https://www.gutenberg.org/files/2848/2848-h/2848-h.htm#link102HCH0006.

my toddler as he wandered through this giant maze in amazement. At one point, my son was "stuck" at a particular island of toys and refused to leave. But I was ahead of him and saw that beyond the island lay something more interesting. So, I said to him, "Come here, there are better toys here." Yet, he refused to budge. He was unable to see what I had seen. All he could see was the toy before him. When I picked him and moved him away from his "prize," he began to cry. To him, it seemed that I was doing a terrible thing; yet, that temporary departure was necessary for him to achieve greater joy, which came when I eventually put him down beside the "better" stack of toys. God allows us to go through pain because he knows that pain is necessary for greater joy. Only a sovereign God, who knows the future and who has the power to lead us there, can do that for us.

1:12–17 HABAKKUK'S REMARKS ABOUT GOD

This literary unit (1:12–17) parallels 1:2–4. Both these units begin with Habakkuk questioning God (1:2–3, 12–13) and end with an evaluation of the situation that are introduced by a pair of phrases – "therefore" and "so" or "so that" – translated from the Hebrew phrase *al-ken*. Both 1:2–4 and 1:12–17 open with first- and second-person speeches that capture an *I-You* exchange before transiting to third-person speeches in which Habakkuk offers an evaluation of the situation. Based on these linguistic and grammatical features, 1:12–17 can be further divided into two groups of three verses each (1:12–14 and 1:15–17).

Several compositional ingenuities help us to interpret this unit. The first three verses are often deemed to be Habakkuk's second complaint against God. This complaint focuses on God's character and the apparent incongruity of God using a wicked horde to accomplish his purposes.

Carefully consider the lines presented visually below. Verses 12 and 13 have similar syntactical constructions, each consisting of a *bicolon* (two short clauses that form a unit). The first bicolon in both verses is chiastic (1:12a–b, 1:13a–b; ABB´A´//DEE´D´), and the second bicolon consists of parallel lines (1:12c–d, 1:13c–d; CC´//FF´).

Habakkuk and Zephaniah

P	A	1:12a	Are <u>you</u> <u>not</u> from everlasting, Lord?[22]
	B		<u>my</u> God,
	B′		<u>my</u> Holy One,
	A′	1:12b	<u>you</u> will <u>never</u> die.
Q	C	1:12c[23]	Lord, you have appointed them to execute judgment;
	C′	1:12d	[My] Rock, you have ordained them to punish.
Q′	D	1:13a	<u>Your</u> eyes are too pure to look
	E		on <u>evil</u>;
	E′	1:13b	at <u>wrongdoing</u>,
	D′		<u>you</u> cannot tolerate.
P′	F	1:13c	Why then do you tolerate the treacherous?
	F′	1:13d[24]	[Why are] you silent while the wicked swallow up those more righteous than themselves?
R	G	1:14a	You have made people
	H		like the fish in the sea,
	H′	1:14b	like the sea creatures
	G′		that have no ruler.

The second-person reference to God in 1:12a (A) – "are you not from everlasting"[25] – is a parallel to 1:12b (A′) – "you will never die."[26] Written as negative statements, they form a frame around B and B′, where we have the

---

22. The underlying Hebrew is "Yahweh." But the LXX has κύριε ("Lord"). I have used the NIV translation but modified the lines to show the Hebrew syntax.
23. The Hebrew syntax for this verse, which has "Lord" and "Rock" fronted.
24. The words in bracket, [why are], are not in the underlying Hebrew (poetic ellipsis).
25. The attribute of God, "from everlasting" can also be translated "from the east" (Isa 2:6). Renz notes that this reference could prepare the reader for Yahweh, who comes from Teman, a place in the southeast (3:1). Renz, *Nahum, Habakkuk, and Zephaniah*, 256.
26. In other translations, A′ is read, "we will/shall not die" (NASB 1995, ESV). The Hebrew reading "we should not die" and supported by ancient manuscripts. But ancient scribes provide marginal notes to suggest the written text may not have been intended by the author. Other translations like NET and NLT have the second person "you."

first-person "my God" and "my Holy One." In this way, 12a–b is chiastic or concentric (see underlined words).

Similarly, in lines D and D′, we have second-person references to God – "your eyes are too pure" (D) and "you cannot tolerate" (D′) – framing the lines E and E′, which have "evil" and "wrongdoing," at the center (see underlined words). So, lines 12a–b (ABB′A′) and 13a–b (DEE′D′) parallel each other in their description of God's character.

Lines 12c–d (C-C′) and 13c–d (F-F′) are also parallels by virtue of their syntax and semantic content. Both lines begin with God as the subject, addressed in the second person, and characterize the binary nature of God's righteousness vis-à-vis humankind's wickedness.

It may take some effort to see these parallelisms, but it is worth making that effort. Take a step back and look at 1:12–13 as a whole; notice how the larger text units P-Q-Q′-P′ are also structured concentrically. The P and P′ units – which form this larger unit's bookends – are questions directed to God regarding his nature.

At issue is the incongruity of God's holiness vis-à-vis his apparent tolerance of the wicked. The way Habakkuk calls God out on his acquiescence is unique in the Bible. Nowhere else does the OT apply "tolerate" (1:13, literally, "you are not able") to God in such a manner. The adage "silence means consent" seems to apply here. The reference to God as being "silent" (*hrs*) suggests that God is giving assent to the actions of the treacherous or the wicked.[27]

In short, these few verses recapitulate the tension we have seen in 1:2–4, namely, the incongruity of the silence of the Holy One in the face of wickedness. The intensity is ratcheted up another notch by the notion of executing punishment on the wicked by using an even more wicked instrument – which was simply too much for Habakkuk to comprehend. Not only had God's silence become deafening, but his plans had also shaken Habakkuk!

Consider one last point about the structure of 1:12–14. Verse 14 is a hinge verse, linking the verses before to the next unit (1:15–17), and also concentric in shape. References to human beings – "people" and "ruler" (G, G′) – wrap around the analogies of "fish" (H) and "sea creatures" (H′).

---

[27]. Perhaps Habakkuk has Numbers 30 in mind, where an oath-taking law states that when a woman vows "and her father hears about her vow or pledge but says nothing [*hrs*] to her, then all her vows and every pledge by which she obligated herself will stand" (Num 30:4, compare 7, 14).

The last three verses of chapter 1 are connected by *result* clauses, introduced by the result marker "therefore" or "so" (*al-ken*). The only other appearance of this marker in this chapter is in 1:4, but it occurs in three successive instances here (v. 17 has "thus," *ken*, in the Hebrew, which is not translated in the NIV). Third-person speech also points to 1:15–17 being a unit. While second-person (reported) speeches with God as the subject are used up to verse 14 – which is the hinge verse – from verse 15 onward, there is a transition to third-person speech. It is not always clear who is speaking in the text. Was Habakkuk recording God's description of the Chaldeans? Or was he describing the Chaldeans himself? Scholars tend to favor the latter suggestion. Either way, the topic of concern is the collective horde of invading Chaldeans. In verse 15, the Hebrew text simply uses the third-person singular pronoun "he," so the renderings "the wicked foe" (NIV) or "Chaldeans" (NASB 1995) are interpretive decisions of Bible translators.

The third reason these three verses are viewed as a unit is the repetitive metaphoric references to successfully catching fish. There are six direct references to fishing instruments, using three separate terms. The first term is "net" (*herem*), which occurs three times, once in each verse. The word *herem* can refer either to a net cast into the sea or a river or to a snare used on land (see Mic 7:2). Interestingly, all nine occurrences of this word in the Bible are used metaphorically.[28] In the phrase "by his net he lives in luxury" (1:16), the word "net" is supplied by the NIV translators and is not in the original Hebrew. The second term – "dragnet" or "seine" (*mikemeret*) – is a rare word, occurring only three times in the OT, with two of its uses here in 1:15–16. Again, they are used metaphorically to refer to the powerful military instrument for invasion. The third term, "hooks" (*hakkah*), occurs in verse 15.[29] References to these fishing instruments decrease in frequency in these verses: three times in verse 15, twice in verse 16, and only once in verse 17. The literary effect of this is to suggest that successful fishing expeditions have resulted in fewer and fewer fish.

Although the use of fishing imagery to describe military conquests is often found in the ancient Near East, large-scale industrial fishing metaphors are better suited for nations other than Israel, which has only two primary freshwater sources – the River Jordan and the Sea of Galilee.[30]

---

28. Ecclesiastes 9:12; Isaiah 19:8; Ezekiel 26:5, 14; 32:3; 47:10; Micah 7:2; Habakkuk 1:15–17.
29. On these three fishing instruments, see Tyler R. Yoder, "Fishing for Fish and Fishing for Men: Fishing Imagery in the Hebrew Bible and the Ancient Near East" (PhD Diss., The Ohio State University, 2015), 50–51, 57–61.
30. Yoder, "Fishing for Fish," 1.

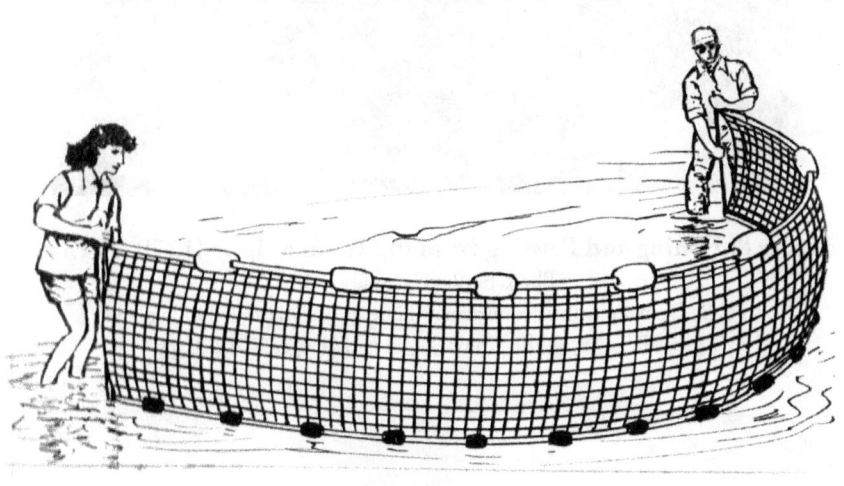

Figure 6: A basic dragnet or seine net
Illustration by Pearson Scott Foresman
Public Domain: https://commons.wikimedia.org/wiki/File:Seine_(PSF).png#filelinks

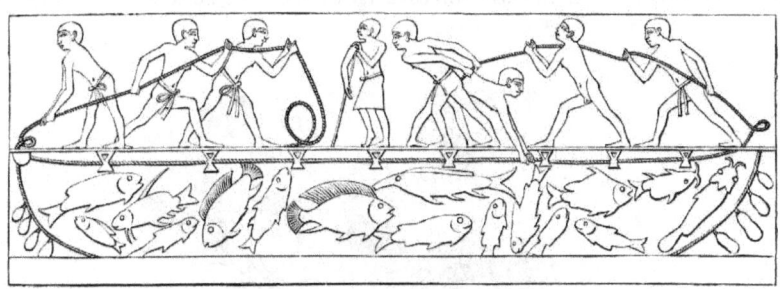

Figure 7: Ancient Fishing with Nets
Source: Georg Ebers, *EgDescriptive, Historical, and Picturesque*, volume 1
(New York, NY: Cassell & Company, 1878), 134.
Wikimedia Commons: https://commons.wikimedia.org/wiki/
File:Fishing_with_Net_(1878)_-_TIMEA.jpg

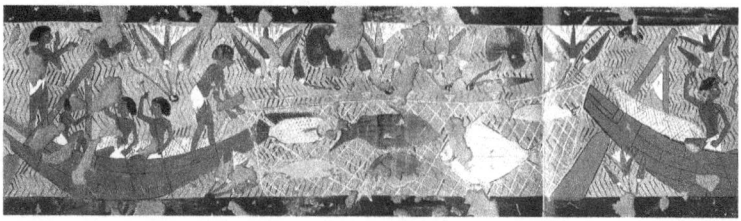

Figure 8: Fishing and Fowling from the Tomb of Ipuy (1279–1213 BCE)
Photo by Rogers Fund (1930)
Public Domain: https://commons.wikimedia.org/wiki/File:Fishing_and_
Fowling,_from_the_Tomb_of_Ipuy_MET_eg30.4.120.jpg

Figure 9: Ancient Egyptian Fishhook (1295–1070 BCE)
Source: https://www.metmuseum.org/art/collection/search/558135
Public Domain: https://commons.wikimedia.org/wiki/File:Fish_hook_MET_17.6.134.jpg

Figure 10: Edfu Temple relief showing a net filled with humans, fish, and birds
Photo by Karen Green
Wikimedia Commons: https://commons.wikimedia.org/wiki/File:Flickr_-_
schmuela_-_net_filled_with_fish,_birds,_and_enemies.jpg

Material evidence for the depiction of the fishing net as weaponry is found in the hexagonal clay prisms with Akkadian inscriptions of Esarhaddon I's military conquest. One such inscription states, "The one who fled into the sea to save his (own) life *did not escape my net* and did not save himself... Neither he who made the sea his fortress nor he who made the mountain his stronghold escaped me (or) succeeded in escaping."[31] Elsewhere, in another inscription, the fishing metaphor is even more vivid:

> Abdi-Milkūti, its king, in the face of my weapons, fled into the midst of the sea. By the command of the god Aššur, my lord, I caught him like a fish from the midst of the sea and cut off his head. I carried off his wife, his sons, his daughters, his palace retainers, silver, gold, goods and property, precious stones, garments with trimming and linen(s), everything of value from his palace in huge quantities, (and) took away (his) far-flung people (who were) beyond counting, oxen, sheep, and goats, (and) donkeys in huge numbers to Assyria. I gathered the kings of Ḫatti (Syria-Palestine) and the seacoast, all of them, and had (them) build a city in another place, and I named it Kār-Esarhaddon.[32]

Note that a large fish haul is equated to the fruitful plundering of the foe. Catching the fish with a net represents the loss of freedom and life. *Hauling* in the catch and *taking away* the fish from the sea to a place far away refer to the exile of the vassal nations and its people and the plunder of their valuables such as gold and silver.

Moreover, in ancient Mesopotamian texts, the *fisher* represents deities who wielded power and authority over the fish – who symbolize humans. Viewed in this way, the act of fishing symbolizes the divine subjugation (or punishment) of the human realm. The Mesopotamian Nanshe was a goddess of fishing; her husband, Nindara, was called the taxman of the sea.[33] Two Sumerian deities, Dumuzid and Papulegarra, were given the epithet "fishers" in the Sumerian King List.[34] Yoder notes that

---

31. Emphasis mine. Possibly composed in 673–72 BCE. Inscription on col. V lines 10–25. See Erle Leichty, *The Royal Inscriptions of Esarhaddon, King of Assyria (680-669 BC)*, vol. 4. Royal Inscriptions of the Neo-Assyrian Period (Winona Lake: Eisenbrauns, 2011), 22.
32. Leichty, *The Royal Inscriptions of Esarhaddon*, 4:48, compare 4:16, 28.
33. Niek Veldhuis, *Religion, Literature, and Scholarship: The Sumerian Composition of Nanése and the Birds, with a Catalogue of Sumerian Bird Names*, CM 22 (Leiden: Brill, 2004), 13–14.
34. The Sumerian King's List, col. three, line 14 reads, "dumu-zi ŠU-PEŠ," and suggestions are given to connect the deity Dumuzi to a fisherman. One scholar translates this passage: "The

the various representations of divine fishers emphasize their peerless authority over human life . . . . To a certain degree, the fisher is to the fish as the deity is to the human. There is an inherently authoritative, if not punitive, element to this manifestation of the divine-human relationship. Just as the human angler, charged with providing fish offerings for the local temple's patron deity, or simply the responsibility of providing for his or her family, held a position of authority, so does a deity wielding a cosmic net.[35]

Even if Habakkuk had been familiar with these references, how does the fishing metaphor work here? In metaphor theory, the *tenor* (the thing meant) represents what is signified. The *vehicle* (the thing said) is the metaphorical expression used to convey the idea about the tenor. The metaphor in Habakkuk 1:14–17 conveys the idea that *fishing is invasion*, and the following mapping of two domains – vehicle and tenor – helps us to understand the details of what is meant by what is said.

The use of metaphors aids receptivity. The function of a metaphor is to shock readers or hearers and to alter how they think about reality through a conceptual vehicle – in this case, fishing. For Yoder, "Their disparity [between the reality and vehicle] leads to the topic's reevaluation from an altogether new perspective."[36] This new perspective afforded by the metaphor would have forced the Judahite readers or hearers to consider themselves as *dead fish* because of the sweeping Babylonian military campaigns.

---

divine Dumuzi, the fisherman, whose city was Ku'ara, ruled for 100." See Thorkild Jacobsen, *The Sumerian King List*, AS 11 (Chicago: University of Chicago, 1939), 88–89, https://oi.uchicago.edu/research/publications/as/11-sumerian-king-list.
35. Yoder, "Fishing for Fish," 74–75.
36. Yoder, "Fishing for Fish," 12.

Vehicle (the thing said)	Tenor (the thing meant)	Text
Fish or sea creatures	Humans/Judah	1:14
Lack a ruler	Judah lacking real leadership (disobedient king); Babylonian gods as those to restore order	1:14
Fisher (Subject "he")	Nebuchadnezzar, or Chaldeans/Babylonians	1:15–17
Fisher as judge/punisher	Yahweh/Babylonian deities as restorer of justice and order	1:12
Fish caught unwittingly in the net	City of Judah suddenly besieged and the people finding themselves in a helpless situation	Ecclesiastes 9:12
Fish captured with hooks and nets	Judah captured, and its people killed and rounded up as prisoners and exiled. Items of value plundered and taken away	1:15
Hook, net, dragnet	Chaldeans' military weaponry, siege ramps, overwhelming force	1:15–17
Fisher rejoices and is glad	Celebration of victory	1:15
Fisher sacrifices to net/burns incense to his dragnet	Babylonian sacrificing to their deities for military success	1:16
Fisher lives in luxury and enjoys the choicest food	Plundering the wealth of Judah – the gold and bronze of the temple	1:16
Fisher empties his net and fishes again	Expansion of conquest, no escape for Judah	1:17

Figure 11: Vehicle and Tenor of the Fishing Metaphor

SUMMARY AND REFLECTION

The chapter begins with a cry of desperation: *Why is God allowing evil and suffering?* But God's response was not the answer that the prophet had hoped for. The righteous sufferers find themselves among the wicked, suffering the same judgment. Habakkuk's cry and God's corresponding response remind us of two things about God: His silence, which is not indifference but judgment and patience, and his judgment, which prefaces the salvation of all who would turn to God, including the wicked.

We may interpret God's silence as an abrogation of justice. But God says, through the psalmist, "When you did these things and I kept silent, you thought I was exactly like you. But I now arraign you and set my accusations before you" (Ps 50:21). Isaiah speaks along the same lines: "For a long time I have kept silent, I have been quiet and held myself back. But now, like a woman in childbirth, I cry out, I gasp and pant. I will lay waste the mountains and hills and dry up all their vegetation; I will turn rivers into islands and dry up the pools" (Isa 42:14–15).

In the NT, the parable of the weeds (Matt 13:24–30, 36–43) shows us the reasons for God's delay. Writing about this delay, Paul says, "What if God, although choosing to show his wrath and make his power known, bore with great patience the objects of his wrath – prepared for destruction?" (Rom 9:22). Similarly, Peter writes, "Bear in mind that our Lord's patience means salvation" (2 Pet 3:15).

Perhaps one of the most striking parallels in the NT is the parable of the net (Matt 13:47–51). As with Habakkuk 1:14–17, the parable uses a fishing metaphor to speak about God's coming judgment. Like fish caught in the net, there will be a great heavenly haul in the future. Humans, represented by the many kinds of (dead) fish, will be dragged to the shore and separated by the angels into two groups – the good and the bad. The good fish will be collected in baskets, while the bad – representing the wicked – will be thrown into God's blazing furnace.

Although Habakkuk 1 is set in the late seventh century BCE – with rampant wickedness in Judah and the invading Chaldeans on the horizon – we can easily relate to his situation in our own times. Do we not also wonder why God remains silent amid rampant wickedness in our own contexts? Where is the justice we so desperately need? We mentioned the Dalits earlier. On September 9, 2022, the UN News reported more than fourteen thousand civilian casualties in Ukraine, with "5,767 killed and 8,292 injured."[37] Most of these civilians were killed by wide area explosive weapons. Like dead fish hauled onto the boat, human lives are ended, suddenly and prematurely. The global COVID-19 pandemic has also destroyed many lives over the last three years. The poor, needy, and helpless suffered the most because they had the

---

37. "Ukraine: More than 14,000 Casualties to Date but 'actual Numbers Are Likely Considerably Higher'," UN News, September 9, 2022, https://news.un.org/en/story/2022/09/1126391.

least access to healthcare services and vaccines.[38] Habakkuk speaks about oppression, warfare, and plague to show that although all these things should not hurt God's people, they were piling up to a moment when God would unleash his righteous anger to punish and judge. If you parent young children, do you occasionally experience the same kind of pent-up frustration over their perpetual disobedience and end up unleashing that frustration on them at some point? Of course, God's anger is holy, while ours is often not (Jas 1:20). In the following chapter of Habakkuk, we will continue to explore the theological tension in Habakkuk's mind: What will become of God's people?

---

38. Mogomotsi Magome, "South Africa's Response to Pandemic Hit by Corrupt Contracts," *AP NEWS*, January 25, 2022, https://apnews.com/article/coronavirus-pandemic-health-pandemics-africa-covid-19-pandemic-9a0afd37e14d2a707f7785822b21eba7.

HABAKKUK 2

Chapter 1 concluded with a cliffhanger, leaving us wondering how Habakkuk would respond. Would he balk at God using wicked people to accomplish his work? How was that even theologically "kosher"? With some sense of déjà vu (where an event seems to repeat itself), chapter 2 – like chapter 1 – begins with a challenge. But this time, the author is challenging himself rather than challenging God. The chapter is bookended by two single verses that anticipate God's actions (2:1, 20); these verses frame a short introduction to the vision (NIV uses "revelation," 2:2–3) and then the vision itself at the center (2:4–19). Following the introduction, the vision is recorded in two parts. The first (2:4–5) distinguishes between the righteous and the proud or treacherous; the second part (2:6–19) consists of five woe oracles. These woe oracles pronounce trouble for those committing violence, injustice, and idolatry. Their indictment is spelled out – they would receive retributive judgment. The poetic reversals seen in these woes highlight God's holy justice and compassion for his people, which was the response Habakkuk was seeking. Chapter 2 is the centerpiece in the book of Habakkuk.

2:1 HABAKKUK'S SELF-CENTERED OUTLOOK

At the beginning of this chapter, we see Habakkuk speaking to himself in the first person with volitional verbs that show his intent and desire. The prophet seems to be responding to God's earlier speech. Habakkuk portrays himself as a watchman on the ramparts ("fortified city") of Jerusalem's walls. Four successive words or phrases – "stand," "my watch," "station myself," and "look" – and the infinitive (verbal noun) "to see" are closely connected to the work of manning the city's fortifications. Habakkuk's actions were prompted by the impending invasion of the Chaldeans, which was described in chapter 1. In such times, watchmen were on high alert, ready to give notice the moment the enemy was sighted (2 Kgs 9:17–20).

Habakkuk portrays himself as a watchman in a prophetic sense, not just in relation to impending invasion of Babylon but also in connection with deliverance from Babylon (see Isa 21:6–9; Ezek 33:7). He needed to be attuned to God and careful to relay what he would see or hear from God to the people. Spiritual watchmen must grapple with the tension and confluence of two realities – one that God has willed through his revelation and the other, that which he sees before him at the moment. The conflict between these two realities can weigh heavily on the prophet-watchmen. After being the first to bear the burden of the vision, Habakkuk also bore the extraordinary burden of communicating that vision to his audience, regardless of their readiness to receive it. Jeremiah could not hold back the word of God because it was like fire in his bones. Micaiah, son of Imlah, cynically went along with his stubborn hearers in a bid to spite them (1 Kgs 22:15). The prophet's inner world was a mixture of trepidation, sorrow, weariness, and danger (1 Kgs 22:15–16; Jer 20:9). While simultaneously witnessing the impending doom of the people and being rejected by them, the prophets could only weep and intercede continually on behalf of the people. Perhaps knowing this will help us better appreciate Habakkuk's inner turmoil.

The first verse can be divided into two halves and linked to the motif of the city watchman. The Hebrew syntax of the first half of the verse is symmetrically shaped with the nouns "watch" and "ramparts" on both ends of the line and the first-person verbs – "I will stand . . . station myself" – at the center. The second half of the verse opens with a purpose statement – "I will look to see" – and the rest of the line identifies what Habakkuk is anticipating.

**Figure 12: Jerusalem City Wall (Ottoman)
Fortifications (photo by author)**

Figure 13: Modern Reconstruction of a Field Watchtower (photo by author)

Interestingly, although Habakkuk stood on the ramparts, the text does not say that he was looking out for the Chaldeans. Instead, he was waiting *to see* what he would hear from God. The noun "complaint" (*tokahat*) – the last word in verse 1 – is a key word in the book of Proverbs, where it is often translated "rebuke" or "correction" (see Prov 1:23, 25; 5:12). In its twenty-four occurrences in the OT, this is the only instance where the NIV translates this word as "complaint." Perhaps the translators sought to connect 2:1 with the prophet's complaint in chapter 1. But the point in Habakkuk 2:1 is that while the prophet knew that the invasion was inevitable, he had not accepted its theological coherency or logic. Hence, on the ramparts, Habakkuk was ready for a debate with God – like a lawyer waiting to give his rejoinder. At this point, we see a Job-like Habakkuk.

While scholars generally view 2:1–5 as God's second response to Habakkuk's second complaint (1:12–17), the focus on Habakkuk's action in 2:1 suggests that 2:1–5 cannot simply be seen as a single textual unit containing God's response or as evidence of an ongoing dialogue. Moreover, we have seen that 1:12–17 parallels 1:2–4, which is the first cycle of God's response to Habakkuk's complaint with God's description of the Chaldeans.[1]

Therefore, I have set 2:1 apart from 2:2–5 and propose that this first verse and the last verse – "The Lord is in his holy temple; let all the earth be silent before him" (2:20) – be viewed as this chapter's bookends. In both 2:1 and 2:20, there is a deep yearning for God's response. In both cases, volitional verbs are used in expectation of God's answer and we see a geographical connection to either the city or the temple – the only two direct references to the city of Jerusalem and the Jerusalem temple in the book of Habakkuk.

This framing brings the reader to the geographical heart of Judah – the Jerusalem temple – where God begins to address the book's key theological issue. The problem was no longer just social or moral decadence but a national existential crisis. Why did God allow things to get to this point?

2:2-5 GOD'S SPEECH: THE VISION AND THE PROUD MAN

Verse 2 begins with a speech marker, with Habakkuk quoting what Yahweh had said. The first part of the speech (2:2–3) is directed at Habakkuk, instructing him on what he must do and the effects of doing so. The second part of the speech (2:4–5) focuses on the impending invasion of the Chaldeans. Habakkuk highlights the rampant social wickedness and the impact of this on those who want to live righteously.

Habakkuk was commanded to write down and make plain God's "revelation" or vision (*hazon*). This word occurs twice in Habakkuk (2:2–3) and is frequently used in superscriptions and introductions to divine revelation (Isa 1:1; Dan 8:1; Obad 1:1; Nah 1:1). The *hazon* is a revelatory event through which God speaks to a prophet. The prophet could be "encouraged, chosen, shocked, pardoned, etc."[2]

---

[1]. Sweeney also notes, "The reporting language of Hab. ii 1-4 (5) indicates that this text cannot be identified as the divine response to the complaint in Hab. i 12-27, but as the prophet's report of God's response. Because the prophet speaks in this section, Hab. i 2-ii 4 cannot be viewed generically as a dialogue between Habakkuk and God." Sweeney, "Structure, Genre, and Intent," 64.
[2]. Jakie A. Naudé, "הזח," *NIDOTTE* 2:56–61.

The second command to "make it plain" is a rare verb that occurs only two other times in the OT (Deut 1:5; 27:8). In Habakkuk, it simply means to write down the vision clearly. The plural form, "tablets," suggests a vision of some length – perhaps the entirety of 2:2–19. These "tablets" were flat surfaces, possibly stone, clay, or even wood coated with wax (Ezek 4:1; Luke 1:63); such tablets might have been used to record the Ten Commandments and covenantal laws (Exod 24:12; Deut 9:9).

This written vision was to be transmitted via a courier or messenger who runs to deliver the message.[3] Evidence from Mari – an ancient city located in modern-day Syria – suggests that such runners could cover more than one hundred kilometers in a single day.[4] These runners might have been a class of trained, selected, and trustworthy persons who could also read and write, and were familiar with the logistical and geographical demands of the journey. As sources of intelligence, they were often targeted and captured. Such couriers were likely to have been both courageous and highly skilled. The need to transmit the vision to others indicates that God intended the community to receive the vision and act on it.

Verse 3 highlights the nature of this revelation. Four phrases emphasize that the vision's fulfillment, though perhaps delayed, was never in doubt. First, the text uses a double negative – "will *not* prove *false*." Second, Habakkuk (along with the recipients of the revelation) was commanded to "wait" despite the fact that the fulfillment of the revelation would "linger." Third, this fulfillment would "*certainly* come."[5] The fourth expression is another negative statement – "it will *not* delay" – that stands in direct contrast to the earlier phrase "though it linger."

The line, "For the revelation awaits an appointed time; it speaks of the end," is difficult to understand.[6] With Habakkuk stationed on the ramparts in expectation of the Chaldeans' invasion, it is natural to link the revelation of 2:2 to the Chaldeans' impending arrival. One interpretation is to see the revelation, which includes the entirety of the woe oracles in chapter 2, as the indictment of the Chaldeans for their wicked aggression. If this approach is

---

3. On different ways of relaying messages in the ancient world, see Alan D. Crown, "Tidings and Instructions: How News Travelled in the Ancient Near East," *Journal of the Economic and Social History of the Orient* 17.3 (1974): 244–271, [251].
4. Crown, "Tidings and Instructions," 265.
5. The pairing of a Hebrew infinitive construct "to come" with the imperfective verb, "it will come" functions as an emphatic.
6. ESV has "*hasten* to the end." The LXX translates it as "culminates [ἀνατελεῖ] to the end."

adopted, the fulfillment of the revelation would only take place further along the time horizon when the Chaldeans were punished. But if the woe oracles were an internal indictment against the wicked people of Judah, it leaves the problem of the wicked Chaldeans unresolved.

The "revelation" that encompasses 2:2–19 does not require an explicit connection to the Chaldeans. While the Chaldeans would fit the descriptions in the woe oracles (2:6–19), especially the descriptions in verse 5, much of the woe sayings are generic and could apply equally to the proud and wicked among the people of Judah, as well to other foreign invaders further down the road. Without being historically unmoored, the woe oracles do have a universal and generic aspect. Note that although the NIV refers to "the enemy" (2: 4), which is suggestive of the Chaldeans, the word "enemy" is not in the Hebrew text.

If God's speech here (2:2–19) parallels his first speech (1:5–11), then the "revelation" in chapter 2 is, again, not a one-to-one response to Habakkuk's second complaint. This is because God's word that follows Habakkuk's speech lies beyond the prophet's immediate concerns – a non sequitur, so to speak. When Habakkuk first sought God's action in response to the problematic situation in Judah, God's speech in 1:5–11 escalated a social problem into a national crisis. In response to Habakkuk's complaint against the Chaldeans, God's speech is a universal indictment of the proud, greedy, and wicked (which includes the Chaldeans). So, as we read chapter 2 along the grain of chapter 1, the revelation that tarries and "speaks of the end" can be viewed more generically. The problem does not lie in giving it a historical interpretation but, rather, in trying to unequivocally pin it to a particular historical event.

The pairing of the words "appointed time" and "end" adds to the difficulty of tying the fulfillment to just one specific time in history. These words only occur together within single verses in Daniel's prophecy (Dan 8:19; 11:27, 35). Daniel wrote of the judgment of God beyond the days of Persian rule, extending to the period of the Greeks and the Romans. The NT also speaks of a delayed end time when judgment will come upon proud, greedy, and idolatrous people.

The phrase "appointed time" is also applied to Jesus's work on the cross (Matt 26:18) and to his second coming (1 Cor 4:5). As Renz notes, "In Habakkuk, the end is first of all the end of Babylonian injustice and oppression; in Hebrews [Heb 10:38], the end of all injustice and oppression will come with the second coming of Christ."[7] If we understand the revelation that "waits for an appointed time" in such a way, then the invasion of the Chaldeans as God's instrument of judgment on the wickedness of Judah (1:12) is a type or foreshadowing of God's judgment on evil and injustice when Christ comes with his angels.

Verse 4 is famous for its use in Romans, Galatians, and Hebrews.

> For in the gospel the righteousness of God is revealed – a righteousness that is by faith from first to last, just as it is written: "The righteous will live by faith." (Rom 1:17)

> Clearly no one who relies on the law is justified before God, because "the righteous will live by faith." (Gal 3:11)

> And, "But my righteous one will live by faith. And I take no pleasure in the one who shrinks back." (Heb 10:38)

I have grouped verses 4 and 5 together because of the use of the grammatical singular subject. Both verses begin with interjections – "see" and "indeed."[8] Habakkuk 2:5 also functions as a hinge verse that prepares the reader for the woe oracles (2:6–19).

The call to "see" (or "behold") at the beginning of verse 4 creates a link with Habakkuk's desire to "look to see" in verse 1. Here, the object in view – which is described using a singular pronoun – is a puffed up and greedy man, whose desires are crooked and insatiable. This unnamed man is contrasted with another anonymous person who is described as "righteous" (2:4; see also 1:4 and 1:13). The sum of all these references expresses a bifurcation or division between the righteous and the wicked, with the latter characterized as being wrongdoers, puffed up, drunkards, greedy, and arrogant.

This contrast between the righteous and the wicked goes further. The righteous shall "live," but the arrogant man is greedy, and this greed is likened to "death." This distinction between the righteous and the wicked is seen as early as Genesis 18:23–25, where Abraham pleaded with God to not sweep away the righteous with the wicked. This bifurcation is not only central to the Pentateuch but also introduces the book of Psalms and is a key motif in the Wisdom literature and prophetic books (Pss 1:5–6; 37:12–21; Prov 10:3–32; Eccl 3:17; Ezek 33:12; Mal 3:18).

---

7. Renz, *Nahum, Habakkuk, and Zephaniah*, 283.
8. Note that a series of perfective verbs frame verses 4 and 5. Also, perfective verbs mark the beginning of verse 2.

In Habakkuk, what sets the righteous man apart is his "faithfulness" or steadfastness (*emunah*). This attribute is introduced with the preposition "by." In the NIV and ESV, we have the instrumental "by his faithfulness," but the NET sees a causal relationship with its translation "*because* of his faithfulness." In the ESV, the noun is rendered "faith" rather than "faithfulness" (also NASB 1995). Note that most translations of the NT quotations cited earlier – from Romans 1:17, Galatians 3:11, and Hebrews 10:38 – have "faith" rather than "faithfulness."[9]

The nuances between these translations are not trivial. Whereas *faith* is putting trust in an object – in Romans and Galatians, that object is Jesus Christ – *faithfulness* may be understood as *covenantal faithfulness*, which is a persistent and faithful keeping of God's laws.[10] The NT understands righteousness – or justification – by faith as being the result of believing in Jesus as the Christ. In contrast, justification *because* of covenantal faithfulness seems to suggest that the justification is based on a person's ability to remain in right standing within the framework of the OT covenant. The NET's use of "faithfulness," coupled with the causal use of the preposition "because," evokes to some extent the familiar OT idea of covenantal faithfulness – that is, the righteous shall live because of their covenantal fidelity. A third reading can be seen in the Greek translation: "from *my* faithfulness."[11] In this case, since Habakkuk reports the words of God, "faith" or "faithfulness" does not belong to the righteous person but to Yahweh. So, the righteous will live because of God's faithfulness to his promises.[12]

Nonetheless, translating *emunah* as "faithfulness" is not without merit. In the context of Habakkuk, the whole struggle is because the concept of covenantal faithfulness is in crisis. Habakkuk laments that violence, wickedness, and the perversion of the law (1:2–4) were flourishing. If the righteous, who kept the law, suffered, while the wicked thrived, why continue to remain right-

---

9. The Septuagint renders the Hebrew *emunah* in Habakkuk 2:4 as *pisteos* (faith), from the noun *pistis*. The Greek of all three NT texts, Romans 1:17, Galatians 3:11, and Hebrews 10:38, are rendered from the same noun, *pistis* (faith).
10. Janzen reads *emunah* as "reliability" (his translation: "but the righteous through its reliability shall live"). J. Gerald Janzen, "Eschatological Symbol and Existence in Habakkuk," in *When Prayer Takes Place*, eds. Brent A. Strawn and Patrick D. Miller (Cambridge: The Lutterworth, 2012), 218–238, [227].
11. The last clause of Septuagint Habakkuk 2:4 reads, "but the righteous, from *my faithfulness*, shall live."
12. Baker notes another LXX reading with "my righteous one," whose identity is understood as Christ, "the Coming One," in his delayed return. David W. Baker, *Nahum, Habakkuk, Zephaniah*, TOTC 27 (Leicester: Inter-Varsity Press, 1988), 60–61.

eous? The covenantal framework that Habakkuk knew was crumbling before his eyes. The wicked and unjust continued to flourish, while God seemed to maintain a ridiculous silence. God's announcement that he would use the violent Chaldeans as his instrument of punishment exacerbated this situation. Faced with such a predicament, *faithfulness* or fidelity to all that God stands for is impossible without *faith*. Put differently, *faith without faithfulness is fantasy*. When our faithfulness or fidelity is challenged to the core by circumstances, genuine faith is the only thing that keeps our faithfulness going. As James says, "You see that his faith and his actions were working together, and his faith was made complete by what he did" (Jas 2:22). Clendenen is right to argue that the translation should be rendered "faith."[13] At the same time, this faith is demonstrated by faithfulness.[14] So, the adoption of "faithfulness" in our translation need not and cannot exclude the prophet's faith in God and in the Lord's promise to judge the wicked, despite delays in the fulfilment of that promise. As F. F. Bruce points out, in his study of how Paul used Habakkuk, "The righteous would endure to the end, directing their lives by a loyalty to God inspired by faith in his promise."[15]

Moving on to verse 5, the greedy drunk[16] – who is compared to the insatiable grave and the invading horde – may represent the Babylonians mentioned in the previous chapter (1:5–11, 15–17). The word "arrogant" (*yahir*) is rare and is used elsewhere only in Proverbs 21:24. The NIV's rendering of "greedy" is based on an underlying word that means "opening wide." In this case, it describes the infinite capacity of the grave or Sheol (the realm of the dead) to keep swallowing humans (see Num 26:10). This insatiable nature of the grave is also seen in Wisdom literature and the prophetic books (Prov 27:20; 30:16; Isa 5:14). The grave is the abyss into which a person goes down and never returns (Job 7:9; Pss 28:1; 30:3; 88:4); death has the power to keep captive everyone who enters through its doors.

In Egyptian mythology, this insatiable ability to keep devouring the dead is represented by a hybrid creature called Ammit, the "Devourer of the Dead"

---

13. Ray Clendenen, "Salvation by Faith or by Faithfulness in the Book of Habakkuk?" *Bulletin for Biblical Research* 24.4 (2014): 505–513.
14. Renz, *Nahum, Habakkuk, and Zephaniah*, 289–290.
15. Frederick F. Bruce, *The Epistle of Paul to the Romans: An Introduction and Commentary*, TNTC 6 (London: Inter-Varsity Press, 1974), 80.
16. The Habakkuk pesher has "wealth" instead of "wine" in 2:5. But scholars believe "wine" is likely the original. G. T. M. Prinsloo, "Habakkuk 2:5a: Denouncing 'Wine' or 'Wealth'? Contextual Readings of the Masoretic Text and 1QpHab," *HTS Theological Studies* 72, no. 4 (2016): 1–12.

or the "Eater of Hearts." The ancient Egyptians believed that a dead person's heart was weighed against a feather of truth before Anubis, the god of death. If a dead person had lived an evil life, the scale would reveal it, and the person's heart would be eaten by Ammit, who functioned as the devourer of the wicked. In the OT, both the evil and the righteous descend into "the realm of the dead" (or "grave," Ps 89:48), but Yahweh can redeem a person from the dead (Pss 16:10; 30:3; 49:15; Hos 13:14). The powers of death and destruction are superintended by Yahweh (Prov 15:11).

Figure 14: Ammit, the Devourer of the Dead, a hybrid creature made up of a crocodile, lion, and hippopotamus
Public Domain: https://commons.wikimedia.org/wiki/File:Ammit_BD.jpg

KNOWING GOD'S WILL AND LIVING FAITHFULLY

An essential part of living faithfully is knowing the will of God. Habakkuk knew *what* God would do but not *when* he would do it. Faith is moving forward despite the immediate reality. Consider the story of George Müller and how he ran orphanages by the currency of faith and faithfulness.

One evening, Müller's wife came to him and told him they had run out of milk and were low on food for the following day. By this time, the orphanage had over a hundred children. Müller was determined to depend on God alone for all their provisions and had resolved not to solicit or borrow funds. The Müllers simply prayed to God about the needs of the orphanage, and they did so again that day. Soon after, someone visited them and handed over some money – it was more than enough to cover their next meal. Envelopes of funds, whether delivered by hand or through the mail, kept coming whenever they had a need.

Figure 15: George Müller, his faith and faithfulness
Public Domain: https://commons.wikimedia.org/
wiki/File:George_Muller_Bristol.jpg

Yet, again and again, Müller said that he did not have the gift of faith. He simply believed that "Jesus Christ is the same yesterday and today and forever" (Heb 13:8). Müller's ministry demonstrates that God still delivers and that people should turn to the same God of Israel. Müller wrote:

> His glory was my chief aim, i.e., that it might be seen that it is not a vain thing to trust in the living God – and that my second aim was the spiritual welfare of the orphan-children – and the third their bodily welfare; and still continuing in prayer, I was at last brought to this state, that I could say from my heart.[1]

> But we ask: How does faith work in practical terms? How did Müller do it? Müller's own words give us a glimpse of the inner workings of his faith. May these words help us in our own journey of faith.
>
>> I seek at the beginning to get my heart into such a state that it has no will of its own in regard to a given matter. Nine-tenths of the trouble with people is just here. Nine-tenths of the difficulties are overcome when our hearts are ready to do the Lord's will, whatever it may be. When one is truly in this state, it is usually but a little way to the knowledge of what His will is. 2. Having done this, I do not leave the result to feeling of simple impression. If I do so, I make myself liable to great delusions. 3. I seek the will of the Spirit of God through, or in connection with, the Word of God. The Spirit and the Word must be combined. If I look to the Spirit alone without the Word I lay myself open to great delusions also. If the Holy Ghost guides us at all, He will do it according to the Scriptures and never contrary to them. 4. Next I take into account providential circumstances. These often plainly indicate God's will in connection with His Word and Spirit. 5. I ask God in prayer to reveal His will to me aright. 6. THUS, THROUGH PRAYER to God, the study of the Word, and reflection, I come to deliberate judgment according to the best of my ability and knowledge, and if my mind is thus at peace, and continues so after two or three more petitions, I proceed accordingly. In trivial matters, and in transactions involving most important issues, I have found this method always effective.[2]
>
> ---
>
> 1. George Müller, *Answers to Prayer: From George Müller's Narratives. Compiled by A. E. C. Brooks* (Chicago: Moody), 9, https://www.georgemuller.org/uploads/4/8/6/5/48652749/answers_to_prayer_g_muller.pdf.
> 2. Müller, *Answers to Prayer*, 5.

2:6–19 FIVE WOE ORACLES

The woe oracle is a genre of literature that is found primarily, but not exclusively, in the prophetic books. Such oracles are often clustered together as a unit. In Habakkuk 2:6–19, the five woe oracles follow a similar general shape, usually beginning with the *interjection* "Woe!" (*hoy*). Next, using participles – for example, "who piles up" (2:6) – a particular group of people is identified as the object of the woes. While this identification is mainly in the third person, the second person is also used in a few places (2:7, 10, 16). These referents are not defined by their nationalities but presented as a single collective group who are defined by their actions. Third, the text records the *indictments* on this group of people because of their wickedness and idolatry. Fourth, there is a *pronouncement* of judgment or condemnation of these people presented as retributive justice. Finally, the woe oracle ends with a short *evaluation* of the situation, usually introduced by the dependent clause marker "for."[17]

Figure 16: Pattern of Woe Oracles in Habakkuk

Interestingly, the first and last of the five woe sayings do not begin a new verse and have additional rhetorical questions added *before* the woe interjection (2:6, 18). The other woe sayings do not have these additions, and the verse starts with the woe interjection (2:9, 12, 15).[18] The five woe oracles identify five different referents: a) those who pile up stolen goods and grow wealthy by extortion, b) those who profit from unjust gain, c) those who build a city with bloodshed, d) those who make others drunk in order to take advantage of them, and e) those who worship idols.

While these indictments could apply to the Chaldeans (in particular, 2:8), they could also apply to a smaller class of wealthy and arrogant Judeans during the rule of Jehoiakim. Precise identification eludes us, but what is significant in the woe oracles is that they connect well with Habakkuk's first complaint, which raised the issue of God's righteousness and justice in a society devoid of these qualities.

2:6–8 Woe to Those Who Heap Stolen Goods

This unit (2:6–8) is the first of the five woe sayings. In verse 6, there is an additional line before the woe interjection. It is unclear who is being referred to by the pronouns "them" and "him." While "them" could refer to the "nations" and "peoples" in the preceding verse (2:5), the context is open-ended enough to elude precise identification. The use of the words "taunt," "ridicule," and

---

17. See 2:8, 14, 18. In 2:11 "for" is not translated in the NIV ("[for] The stones").
18. For those familiar with Hebrew, consider the other grammatical characteristics that set the woe oracles apart such as the use of verbless clauses, infinitive construct forms, and *weyyiqtols*.

"scorn" carry a lasting disparaging tone, as if the indictment would become a perpetual shame. The woe saying is directed at those who had accumulated stolen wealth by extortion (2:6), and verse 8 suggests that the Chaldeans might have been in view. The word "extortion" is found only once in the OT – and probably means unjustly taking over ownership of a security item for a loan or unfairly charging interest.[19] This indictment might have been based on contraventions of OT laws which forbid creditors to profit unjustly by lending to the needy (Exod 22:25; Lev 25:36–37; Deut 23:19). In the context of Habakkuk, the Babylonians were guilty of the crime of extortion of the Judeans.

In the pronouncement of judgment, notice the reversal whereby the creditor would become the debtor and the plunderer would be plundered. Retributive justice is at work here. This sharp and sudden reversal contrasts with the seemingly unending period of oppression. Finally, note how the evaluative comment, introduced by the word "for" (2:8), explains that the punishment was due to the oppressors acts of physical violence and human bloodshed.

2:9–11 Woe to Those Who Profit from Unjust Gains

This woe is similar in focus to the first woe and also emphasizes the futility of self-preservation. The connecting motif in these three verses is the security of one's dwelling – represented by the word "house," which occurs twice, and related words such as "nest." The need for security is also seen in the repeated phrases of purpose: "*setting* his nest," "to *escape* the clutches," and "plotted the *ruin* of many peoples."[20] Setting a house on high carries connotations of pride and self-sufficiency (Jer 49:16). Elsewhere, this is linked to Babylon – that is, the Chaldeans – who "fortifies her lofty stronghold" (Jer 51:53).

The use of the phrase "on high" can be found in three semantic groups of texts, which is helpful for our interpretation. First, this phrase is associated with Yahweh or God (Isa 33:5). Second, it is used to describe the place of protection God gives to his people (Jer 31:12). Third, it is associated with the insolent (2 Kgs 19:23; Isa 37:24). The use in Habakkuk fits well with the last group and characterizes a combination of self-centeredness and sense of insecurity. In short, we have a grabber, who grabs from others to guarantee his own security but, ultimately, finds this guarantee nothing more than a fool's gamble. The pronouncement of judgment reverses this self-security. Eventually, the grabber would be shamed and lose the life he had sought hard to preserve. Verse 11

---

19. David Clines, "טִיבְעַ," *DCH* 6:232.
20. In the Hebrew, these words are infinitives.

provides the evaluation for their downfall. The very stones and beams of the house – built through unjust means that resulted in ruining many lives – seem to "cry out" for justice.

The stones and the beams of the house, built with the ruins and blood of its victims, cried out. This verse echoes Genesis 4:10, where the blood of Abel cried out from the ground and sought for God's justice that would bring evil back on the head of the oppressor.

WHERE DOES OUR SECURITY COME FROM?

It is human to desire security. And the fact that human beings search for security presumes both the value and the risks of life. Much of our waking life is spent providing security for ourselves and our families, and most of us do this by acquiring wealth and provisions. Gradually, our *need* for money may become a *love* of money, and our love of money then becomes *covetousness* and *trust* in money. When family and livelihood are at stake, it is difficult to separate whom we serve: God? Or mammon?

Security in wealth is a gamble, but "blessed is the one who trusts in the LORD" (Jer 17:7). Jesus made this clear in one of his parables:

[18]"Then [the rich man] said, 'This is what I'll do. I will tear down my barns and build bigger ones, and there I will store my surplus grain. [19]And I'll say to myself, "You have plenty of grain laid up for many years. Take life easy; eat, drink and be merry."' [20]But God said to him, 'You fool! This very night your life will be demanded from you. Then who will get what you have prepared for yourself?' [21]This is how it will be with whoever stores up things for themselves but is not rich toward God." (Luke 12:18–21)

Likewise, Paul instructed Timothy about what to say to the rich among the believers:

[17]Command those who are rich in this present world not to be arrogant nor to put their hope in wealth, which is so uncertain, but to put their hope in God, who richly provides us with everything for our enjoyment. [18]Command them to do good, to be rich in good deeds, and to be generous and willing to share. [19]In this way they will lay up treasure for themselves as a firm foundation for the coming age, so that they may take hold of the life that is truly life. (1 Tim 6:17–19)

> Of the 70 or so references to "being rich" or "riches" (root: πλοῦτος) in the NT, practically all references to a person's earthly wealth have negative connotations.[1] Where the word is not used negatively, it is either used metaphorically (see Rom 2:4; 9:23; 10:12; 11:12; 1 Cor 1:5) or applies to someone else (see Luke 12:16; 2 Cor 6:10). The NT does not allow us to justify our pursuit for earthly wealth as a form of security!
>
> Philip Wijaya, writing about the believer's security in the Lord, identifies four main areas in which God provides security: a) our material needs, b) protection from evil and calamity, c) our relationship with God, and d) the assurance of our eternal salvation.[2] Money sometimes gives us a false sense of security because it can satisfy many of our physical needs.
>
> But ultimately, our love of money may lead to a futile trust in money and to covetousness, which is idolatry (Eph 5:5, ESV).
>
> ---
>
> 1. Matthew 13:22; 19:23, 24; 27:57; Mark 4:19; 10:25; 12:41; Luke 1:53; 6:24; 8:14; 12:16, 21; 14:12; 16:1, 19, 21, 22; 18:23, 25; 19:2; 21:1; Romans 2:4; 9:23; 10:12; 11:12, 33; 1 Corinthians 1:5; 4:8; 2 Corinthians 6:10; 8:2, 9; 9:11; Ephesians 1:7, 18; 2:4, 7; 3:8, 16; Philippians 4:19; Colossians 1:27; 2:2; 3:16; 1 Timothy 6:9, 17, 18; Titus 3:6; Hebrews 11:26; James 1:10, 11; 2:5, 6; 5:1, 2; 2 Peter 1:11; Revelations 2:9; 3:17, 18; 5:12; 6:15; 13:16; 18:3, 15, 17, 19.
> 2. Philip Wijaya, "What Does It Mean That Our Security Is in the Lord?," Christianity.com, https://www.christianity.com/wiki/salvation/what-does-it-mean-that-our-security-is-in-the-lord.html.

2:12–14 Woe to Those Who Build through Bloodshed

In the third woe oracle, the search for security takes the form of building an entire community that is founded on injustice and oppression. The indictment in this third woe has "worsened." It is no longer about building an individual's house but about building a whole city. Note that references to injustice and bloodshed are common across the first four woes (compare 2:8, 11, 12, 17). Verse 12 consists of two syntactical parallel clauses where the actions of building and establishing are paired with the instruments of "bloodshed" and "injustice."

| builds | a city | with bloodshed |
| establishes | a town | by injustice! |

In the OT, the term "the Lord Almighty" (literally, "Yahweh of Hosts/Armies") is significant. It conveys the idea of Yahweh as a warrior leading a victorious battle against divine or human enemies. This terminology is used about 285 times, employing different word combinations, and is found primarily in prophetic books like Isaiah, Jeremiah, Zechariah, and Malachi.[21] In Habakkuk, this term occurs only in 2:13, where it anticipates the warrior God of chapter 3.

The pronouncement in verse 13 begins forcefully. First, it starts with a verbless rhetorical question: "Has not the Lord Almighty determined . . . ?"). Second, the interjection "behold" (left untranslated in the NIV) directs readers to what is immediate on the literary horizon and connects with words like "look" and "revelation" seen earlier (2:1–2, 4). Third, two corresponding parallel lines subsequently depict the futility of the oppressor's actions: "the people's labor is only fuel for the fire," and "the nations exhaust themselves for nothing." Although these two lines use plural pronouns, they refer to the single oppressor identified in the woe (2:12). Again, the pronouncement denies the oppressor the security that he had sought. The act of building a city or town is futile, ending with destruction by fire. Once again, we see retributive justice at work.

The final line of this woe contains the evaluative comment. The reference to the earth being filled by something, which is found in at least two dozen places in the OT, can be grouped in three contexts. In the first group, the earth is filled by God's creation.[22] In the second group, the earth is filled with violence, blood, injustice, or human tears,[23] as in Ezekiel 9:9:

> The sin of the people of Israel and Judah is exceedingly great; the land is full of bloodshed and the city is full of injustice. They say, "The Lord has forsaken the land; the Lord does not see." (Ezek 9:9)

In the third group, the earth is filled with the knowledge of God, glory, steadfast love, and praise.[24] By considering these three domains together, we gain a deeper understanding of what being "filled" means. While the first category

---

21. Dempsey Rosales Acosta, "Lord of Hosts," *The Lexham Bible Dictionary* (Bellingham: Lexham, 2016); Zobel, "Tseva'oth," *TDOT* 12:215–232, [218].
22. Genesis 1:22, 28; 9:1; Exodus 1:7; Psalms 80:9; 104:24.
23. Genesis 6:11, 13; Leviticus 19:29; Ezra 9:11; Psalm 74:20; Jeremiah 23:10; 46:12; Ezekiel 7:23; 8:17; 9:9; 30:11.
24. Numbers 14:21; Psalms 33:5; 48:10; 72:19; 119:64; Isaiah 6:3; 11:9; Jeremiah 23:24; Habakkuk 2:14; 3:3.

is positive and orderly, the second is a distortion of all that is good. The third semantic domain offers hope that there will be a reorientation of God's purposes and that his glory will fill all the earth. Habakkuk 2:14 combines "knowledge" with God's "glory" and the filling of the earth. This verse, together with Habakkuk 3:3, may allude to several OT references (Num 14:21; Isa 6:3; 11:9; Ps 72:19), in which we see God rising to act against the oppression of his people to bring about a new era of restoration. Thus Habakkuk 2:14, in its context, fits well with the third domain. If the choice of words was deliberate, then this shows that the prophet was conversant with OT Scripture and was looking forward to God's restoration.

2:15–17 Woe to Those Who incite Others to get Drunk

The fourth woe is directed at those who incite their friends (or neighbors) to get drunk so that they may gaze on their "naked bodies" (literally, "genitalia").[25] The act of "pouring it [the drink] from the wineskin" is difficult to translate (literally, "joining with your wrath"[26]) and has been rendered differently across Bible versions – for example, "pour out your wrath" (ESV). To look upon drunk, naked bodies recalls Ham, who saw his father Noah's genitalia when Noah was in a state of intoxication. On account of Ham's sin, his offspring, Canaan, was cursed.

The pronouncement in verse 16 – which has a symmetrical construction with several phonetical parallels – shows the reversal by which the perpetrator will experience judgment:

> You will be filled with shame (*qalon*) instead of glory (*mikkabod*).
> Now it is your turn! . . . be exposed!
> The cup . . . is coming around to you,
> and disgrace[27] (*qiqalon*) will cover your glory (*al-kebodeka*).

The perpetrator is now commanded to drink and expose himself. To drink from God's cup is an expression that refers to experiencing God's judgment (compare Isa 51:17; Jer 51:7). Babylon was like the cup in God's hand, making the whole earth, especially Judah, drunk with her wine.[28] In the NT, the sinless Christ drank from the cup of God's wrath on behalf of God's people.

---

25. The underlying Hebrew word, "nakedness" (*maor*) in verse 15, occurs only once in the OT and sounds like the word "nakedness" (*arel*) in verse 16, though the latter is of a different root.
26. The Greek translation *anatrope tholera* is as obscure as both words are *hapax legomenon*.
27. This word occurs only once in the OT.
28. On references to God's cup of wrath, see Job 21:20; Isaiah 51:22; Jeremiah 25:15.

But unrepentant idolaters (Rev 14:10) and the metaphorical Babylon, who drank the blood of humans will one day drink from the cup of God's wrath (Rev 16:19).

The word "for" (2:17), gives the reason for this woe. The violence done to Lebanon alludes to the destruction of forests by the Babylonians – "you cut down the forests" (Isa 14:8 NLT). But here, the tables are turned. Violence would "overwhelm" (literally, "cover") the one who had committed violence. The object of the verb "to terrify" is in the third-person plural (i.e., "them," e.g. ESV, NASB 1995; NIV has "you"), perhaps referring to the animals terrified by the destruction. Besides the destruction of trees, animals, and humans, collateral damage included devastation of the land and other human establishments.[29]

2:18–19 Woe to Those Who Practice Idolatry

Like the first woe oracle, this last woe begins with rhetorical questions. The woe interjection appears only after these questions, which is probably intentional. Semantically, the final woe differs from the previous four in that it says nothing about violence or bloodshed. Instead, this woe oracle is directed at the idolater. At least ten nouns and verbs in these two verses are connected to idolatry – for instance, calling for guidance to lifeless and breathless wood and stones, rather than to the living God.[30] We see the same kind of reversal as in the previous woes. Those who sought guidance from idols and trusted in these images fashioned by their own hands would only receive lies or silence. All that the idolaters would hear were their own voices.

Archaeological findings that reveal the assimilation of Yahwism and the Asherah and Baal cultures demonstrate that Israel was an idolatrous nation.[31] Asherah was the fertility goddess, often depicted as a pillar or a woman with large breasts. The Motza cultic site, where multiple deities were worshiped and which was probably in use from the tenth to sixth centuries BCE, was

---

29. S. D. Snyman, *Nahum, Habakkuk and Zephaniah: An Introduction and Commentary*, TOTC 27 (Downers Grove: IVP Academic, 2020), 85.
30. The archive of Esarhaddon records a "mouth opening" ritual in Babylon that turns a newly carved idol into a physical embodiment of deity. John Hilber et al., *The Minor Prophets, Job, Psalms, Proverbs, Ecclesiastes, Song of Songs*, ed. John H. Walton, Zondervan Illustrated Bible Backgrounds Commentary 5 (Grand Rapids: Zondervan Academic, 2009), 172.
31. Philippe Bohstrom, "Israelites in Biblical Dan Worshipped Idols – and Yahweh Too, Archaeologists Discover," *Haaretz*, October 31, 2018, https://www.haaretz.com/archaeology/2018-10-31/ty-article-magazine/.premium/israelites-in-biblical-dan-worshipped-idols-and-yahweh-too/0000017f-db76-db5a-a57f-db7ebdd20000.

just a few miles away from Solomon's temple.³² Rabbi David Wolpe laments, "It seems every time they dig in Jerusalem there are idols. Especially fertility idols."³³ Archaeological finds increasingly confirm the Bible's description of God's people as being steeped in idolatry.

> ²²Judah did evil in the eyes of the LORD. By the sins they committed they stirred up his jealous anger more than those who were before them had done. ²³They also set up for themselves high places, sacred stones and Asherah poles on every high hill and under every spreading tree. ²⁴There were even male shrine prostitutes in the land; the people engaged in all the detestable practices of the nations the LORD had driven out before the Israelites. (1 Kgs 14:22–24)

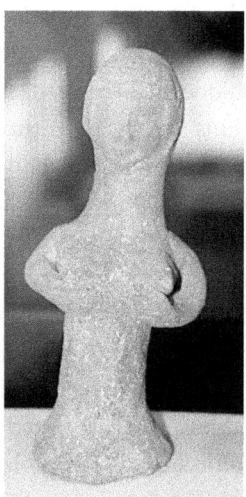

Figure 17: Pillar Figurine of the Fertility Goddess, Asherah (8th–6th century BCE)
Public Domain: https://commons.wikimedia.org/wiki/File:Ashera._Eretz_Israel_Mus.jpg

---

32. Brian R. Rickett, "Temple of Idol Worship Found Near Jerusalem," *Patterns of Evidence* (blog), February 20, 2020, https://patternsofevidence.com/2020/02/20/temple-of-idol-worship-found-near-jerusalem/.
33. Bari Weiss, "The Story Behind a 2,600-Year-Old Seal," *The New York Times*, March 30, 2019, Sunday Review, https://www.nytimes.com/2019/03/30/opinion/sunday/bible-josiah-david-seal.html.

This final woe is poignant because Habakkuk, who did not hear from God initially, eventually heard definitively from Yahweh. In contrast, the idolaters, who turned for guidance to wood and stones, were met with perpetual silence. Yet, history has shown that despite several national reforms, idolatry persisted in Jerusalem. If the book of Habakkuk was written after Josiah's reforms in 623 BCE and before the fall of Jerusalem in 587 BCE, then Josiah's reforms had failed by the time this book was composed.

2:20 HABAKKUK'S GOD-CENTERED OUTLOOK

Habakkuk 2:1 and 2:20 frame the chapter. These verses are connected either to the Jerusalem city or the Jerusalem temple, and both anticipate God's response. In 2:1, Habakkuk waited expectantly for God to speak. Now, in 2:20, God seemed to have taken his seat on his throne, while all the earth waited in anticipation for his word or judgment (compare Ps 29:1–11). It is also possible that God's verdict had been given by this time and that all the world fell silent because they were guilty before him.

If the interjection "silent" (*has*)[34] follows its usual function in the context of the Minor Prophets (see below), then its meaning in 2:20 would be that God was rousing himself from his dwelling place and pronouncing judgment. This fits nicely in the context of Habakkuk 2 and corroborates with our position here. Note how each reference below is connected to God's judgment and his seat in the temple:

> "In that day," declares the Sovereign LORD, "the songs in the temple will turn to wailing. Many, many bodies – flung everywhere! Silence [*has*]!" (Amos 8:3)

> Be silent [*has*] before the Sovereign LORD, for the day of the LORD is near. The LORD has prepared a sacrifice; he has consecrated those he has invited. (Zeph 1:7)

> "Be still [*has*] before the LORD, all mankind, because he has roused himself from his holy dwelling." (Zech 2:13)

SUMMARY AND REFLECTION

The heart of the book of Habakkuk is chapter 2, where we hear God's pronouncement of judgment on evil – which is precisely what the prophet

---

34. The occurrences of *has* in these references, including Habakkuk 2:20, are all in the Piel imperative form.

Habakkuk had wanted and needed to hear from the beginning. Recall how the book begins with a description of the rampant wickedness in society and the futility of the law to rein in injustice. God's speech about raising up the Chaldeans added fuel to an already burning oppressive situation. As one commentator said, "The remedy is worse than the disease [*Aegrecit medendo*]."[35] In this chapter, 2:1 and 2:20 bookend the vision contained within 2:2–19. After a short introduction (2:2–3), the vision is recorded in two parts. The first part (2:4–5) distinguishes the righteous from the proud or treacherous. The second (2:6–19) consists of five woe oracles. Each of these oracles pronounces trouble on a group of people who are characterized by bloodlust, injustice, and idolatry. These people are characterized by deep insecurity and the desire for self-preservation. Their indictment is spelled out, and their judgment is retributive in nature – the evil they had committed would return upon their own heads. This poetic reversal in the woe oracles highlights God's holy justice and compassion for his people and stands as the theological rationale of the entire book.

This vision in chapter 2 is important because it reveals that despite the perpetual evil in this world, a good and loving God exists. Furthermore, this God will set apart the righteous from the wicked and bring to justice the perpetrators of wickedness and violence. These five woe oracles call to mind the violence we have seen in the various wars around the globe in 2022-23 – the flying munitions, explosions, and the destruction of trees, cities, structures, and human lives. The fighting is motivated by fear, insecurity, and the need for self-preservation. These woe oracles are spot-on. Yet, the chapter also shows us that the righteous – who often become embroiled in these conflicts – are called to faith and faithfulness. The vision in this chapter is the foundation on which the faith and faithfulness of the righteous rests as they wait for God to act.

---

35. Eric J. Tully, *Reading the Prophets as Christian Scripture: A Literary, Canonical, and Theological Introduction* (Grand Rapids: Baker Academic, 2022), 331.

HABAKKUK 3

The final chapter of the book of Habakkuk is a prayer of Habakkuk that captures a spectacular theophany of Yahweh as the divine warrior who defeats the primordial chaos. Apart from the superscript (3:1) and postscript (3:19d), this chapter has three main units. First, we have Habakkuk's introductory remarks about the theophany (3:2). Then, the unit 3:3–15 contains a two-part depiction of the divine warrior, Yahweh, in battle (3:3–7, 8–15). This divine warfare in chapter 3 forms a symmetrical parallel to description of the Chaldeans' invasion in chapter 1. The final section (3:16–19c) depicts the prophet's wholly transformed attitude. Thus, Habakkuk 3, with its trajectory of lament to praise, is the critical denouement that unites the whole book.

3:1 THE SUPERSCRIPTION OF PRAYER

Apart from five occurrences in the book of Psalms (see Psalms 17, 86, 90, 102, and 142), a superscription of prayer is only found in Habakkuk 3:1. And apart from David and Moses, Habakkuk is the only other name mentioned in such superscriptions. In addition, the term *shigionoth* – possibly a literary or musical designation – is found elsewhere only in Psalms.[1] Like the bookends in chapter 2, Habakkuk 3:1 forms a bookend with the postscript in 3:19d. The phrase "for the director of music" occurs nowhere else except in the Psalter. Moreover, Habakkuk 3:19 is the only place such a colophon is found at the end of a poem. We also see the enigmatic term *Selah*, left untranslated in the NIV, in verses 3, 9, and 13. Again, this term occurs elsewhere only in Psalms. Therefore, as a prayer and psalm, Habakkuk 3 has been called "an old psalm depicting Yahweh as the Divine Warrior, expanded into a prayer for help."[2]

As in 1:1, the superscript assigns to Habakkuk the epithet "the prophet" (3:1). As a prayer, the superscription sets chapter 3 apart from the first two chapters. Bound by a superscript and a postscript, this chapter has often been

---

[1]. The term could be connected to the word, *saga* ("to go astray"), making a connection to a kind of lament with uneven meter. John Hilber et al., *The Minor Prophets*, 172.
[2]. Steven S. Tuell, "The Psalm in Habakkuk 3," in *Partners with God*, eds. Shelley L. Birdsong and Serge Frolov, vol. 2. Claremont Studies in Hebrew Bible and Septuagint (Claremont: Claremont Press, 2017), 263–274, [263].

considered an addition to the book.³ The Pesher Habakkuk (1QpHab) – a Jewish commentary on Habakkuk found at Qumran Cave 1 – does not include Habakkuk 3, lending weight to this suggestion. Nonetheless, there are many reasons to see this chapter as cohering with the rest of the book.

Figure 18: Pesher Habakkuk (1QpHab), first-century BCE
Source: The Israel Museum's "Dead Sea Scrolls Digital Project"
Public Domain: https://commons.wikimedia.org/wiki/File:Habakkuk_Pesher.png

3:2 HABAKKUK'S REMARKS ABOUT GOD

Verse 2 introduces the topic with five *cola* (the singular term *colon* refers to the shortest meaningful unit of a poetic line) consisting of impressive syntactical and phonetic parallels. Since this may not be obvious in English, I have rearranged the verse below according to its underlying Hebrew syntax.

---

3. In most English translations today, such superscriptions are relegated to secondary colophonic materials and not accorded the same value as the content. In my view, the superscript and postscript are part of the original text and should not be seen secondary to the text.

Habakkuk 3

Lord, I [Habakkuk] have heard of	your fame;
I [Habakkuk] stand, Lord, in awe of	your deeds;
In our day,	[Yahweh] repeat them;
In our time	[Yahweh] make them known;
In wrath	[Yahweh] remember mercy.

The first two cola begin with the same Hebrew letter (*yod*), and the following three lines all start with another letter (*bet*). Habakkuk is the subject of the first two cola and uses first-person speech. Yahweh is the subject of the following three cola. Notice that the first two cola end with a mention of God's fame and deeds in times past; and then in the next two cola, Habakkuk calls on God to repeat these deeds in Habakkuk's own time. The last colon speaks of wrath, which suggests a state of destruction leading to the prophet's cries for mercy (compare Job 3:17, 26; Isa 14:3).

The thrust of this verse echoes the sentiments of the prophet's calls to God at the beginning of the first two chapters (1:2–4; 2:1). Habakkuk's continual yearning for Yahweh's mighty deliverance, a display of his righteousness, and the manifestation of his power to save is the common thread that runs through all three chapters.

3:3–15 GOD AS WARRIOR

3:3–7 From Teman to Midian

This unit, which deals with Yahweh as the divine warrior (3:3–15), can be divided into two main sections (3:3–7 and 3:8–15). Earlier, we noted that 3:2–7 parallels 1:12–17 since both have a shared focus on God's power over nature and that the reference to the "Holy One" (*qadosh*) is found nowhere else in Habakkuk except in these two places (1:12; 3:3).[4] It is also striking that the book of Habakkuk has the highest usage of *qadosh* per thousand words in the entire OT.[5] The references to God's power and holiness are significant because God is the only source of hope in a world overwhelmed by evil and injustice. The unit 3:3–6 is composed of an impressive poetic doubling of seven three-word cola that depict the warrior God. I have delineated the lines below to illustrate this. Each of the seven cola has three synonymous bicolons

---

4. John N. Oswalt, *The Holy One of Israel: Studies in the Book of Isaiah* (Eugene: Cascade Books, 2014).
5. The books of Isaiah, Leviticus, and Psalms have the highest absolute occurrences of *qadosh*.

(two cola that form a unit of thought) followed by a transitional verbless line. This will be made clear below. The bicolons express various parallels such as semantic, syntactic, prepositional, and verbal (or nominal) forms. The last verse (3:7) shifts the subject from the third person (Yahweh) to the first person (Habakkuk) and has a different word length.

1	³God [*eloha*] came from Teman,	[three-word]	
2	the Holy One from Mount Paran. [*Selah*]	[three-word + *Selah*; mark the beginning]	
3	His glory covered the heavens	[three-word]	
4	and his praise filled the earth.	[three-word]	
5	⁴His splendor was like the sunrise;	[three-word]	} example of a bicolon
6	rays flashed from his hand,	[three-word]	
7	*where his power was hidden.*	[three-word transition colon, verbless line]	
1	⁵Plague went before him;	[three-word]	
2	pestilences followed his steps.	[three-word]	
3	⁶He stood, and shook the earth;	[three-word]	
4	he looked, and made the nations tremble.⁶	[three-word]	
5	The ancient mountains crumbled	[three-word]	
6	and the age-old hills collapsed –	[three-word]	
7	*but he marches on forever.*	[three-word transition colon, verbless line]	
End	⁷I saw the tents of Cushan in distress, the dwellings of Midian in anguish.	[nine-word concluding bicolon]	

---

6. It is also striking how God *stood* and *shook*; and *looked* and *trembled* the nations (3:6), drawing a parallel to Habakkuk's stance seen earlier in 2:1.

Notice how these five verses are framed by a pair of named locations. God (*eloha*) came from "Teman" and "Mount Paran" (3:3), and the tents of "Cushan" and "Midian" were in a state of distress (3:7). Teman was a city of Edom (Jer 49:7; Ezek 25:13); Mount Paran was located on the eastern side of the Sinai Peninsula (Num 13:3). Both were situated to the south of Jerusalem. The motif of God traveling could have been drawn from an earlier theophanic tradition of the blessing of the Israelites by Moses (Deut 33:2; compare Ps 68:7) or the Song of Deborah (Judg 5:4–5), where Yahweh came with his myriads from the south (Sinai, Seir [Edom], and Paran).

Identifying the region of Cushan is difficult because this name does not occur elsewhere in the OT. Although the Septuagint associates it with Ethiopia, this seems too far south to be correct. Perhaps Cushan was in Northern Syria, connected to the River Gihon (Gen 2:13), or is an alternate reference to a region of Midian,[7] which lay southeast of Jerusalem and east of the Gulf Aqaba.

The desert, like the sea, is to be seen metaphorically as the primordial chaos: "Immeasurable stretched-out spaces like the ocean and the desert, to their mind's eye, had no boundaries and were therefore orderless and feared as powers of chaos."[8] The use of these geographical locations shows how God had led the people of Israel as they journeyed from Egypt through the desert to Canaan. This journey through the realms of the power of chaos also depicts the *Chaoskampf* (German for "struggle against chaos"), an ancient motif where a divine warrior, representing order, defeats a serpent, perhaps the Leviathan or Rahab (Pss 74:14; 89:10; Isa 27:1; 51:9), representing chaos. In the context of Habakkuk, God is portrayed as the divine warrior who fought at the dawn of the chaotic sixth century BCE to bring about order as in days past.[9]

Verse 4 speaks of rays (literally, "horns") radiating from the divine warrior. This portrayal is common in the ancient Near East. The figure below shows a bas-relief of a Mesopotamian god with lightning bolts in his hands, battling a hybrid creature.[10] The iconography has been interpreted as Marduk fighting

---

7. David W. Baker, "Cushan (Place)." The Anchor Yale Bible Dictionary (New York: Doubleday, 1992).
8. Frances Klopper, "Aspects of Creation: The Water in the Wilderness Motif in the Psalms and the Prophets," *OTE* 18, no. 2 (2005): 253–264, [255].
9. Hermann Gunkel, *Creation and Chaos in the Primeval Era and the Eschaton: A Religio-Historical Study of Genesis 1 and Revelation 12*, trans. K. William Whitney, Biblical Resource Series (Grand Rapids: Eerdmans, 2006).
10. Such hybrid creatures are often depicted as terrifying monsters or deities in folklores or mythologies. The Assyrian Shedu or Lamassu are creatures with a human head, a body of a bull (or lion), and having wings. In Greek mythology, the Chimera is a monster with the head of a

Tiamat (primordial chaos) in the *Enuma Elish* story.[11] Canaanite mythology also had its version of *Chaoskampf*, where Baal fights Yaam (*yam* means "sea" – the sea monster).[12]

Figure 19: Mesopotamian god with lightning bolts battling Gryphon (half lion and half eagle)
Public Domain: https://commons.wikimedia.org/wiki/
File:Chaos_Monster_and_Sun_God.png

---

lion, body of a goat, and tail of a dragon. Deities who wield the lightning bolt are widespread. They include Zeus (Greek), Thor (Nordic), Indra (Hindu), Perun (Slavic), and Taranis (Celtic).
11. Several ancient Near East iconic objects depict deities holding axes, swords, mace, bows and arrows or spears. For illustrations of these, see especially Martin Klingbeil, *Yahweh Fighting from Heaven: God as Warrior and as God of Heaven in the Hebrew Psalter and Ancient Near Eastern Iconography*, OBO 169 (Göttingen: Vandenhoeck & Ruprecht, 1999), especially 168–195.
12. John Day, *Yahweh and the Gods and Goddesses of Canaan*, eds. David J. A. Clines and Philip R. Davies, JSOTSup 265 (London: Sheffield Academic, 2002), 94–95.

Figure 20: Neo-Hittite storm god, Tarhunzas, holding a thunderbolt and axe (Aleppo Museum)
Picture by Verity Cridland
Wikimedia Commons: https://commons.wikimedia.org/wiki/File:Hetite_God_in_Aleppo.jpg

In Habakkuk 3:5, God is presented as being preceded by plague and followed by pestilence, with death and destruction shown as marks of his coming. God's theophany was also accompanied by a trembling mountain (Exod 19:18; Nah 1:5) commonly seen in apocalyptic scenes (Isa 64:1–3; Ezek 38:20; 39:4).

One of the most striking scriptural parallels to our text is the divine warrior motif of Psalm 18. I quote at length here:

> ⁶In my distress I called to the LORD;
> I cried to my God for help.
> From his temple he heard my voice;
> my cry came before him, into his ears.
> ⁷The earth trembled and quaked,
> and the foundations of the mountains shook;
> they trembled because he was angry.

⁸Smoke rose from his nostrils;
   consuming fire came from his mouth,
   burning coals blazed out of it.
⁹He parted the heavens and came down;
   dark clouds were under his feet.
¹⁰He mounted the cherubim and flew;
   he soared on the wings of the wind.
¹¹He made darkness his covering, his canopy around him –
   the dark rain clouds of the sky.
¹²Out of the brightness of his presence clouds advanced,
   with hailstones and bolts of lightning.
¹³The Lord thundered from heaven;
   the voice of the Most High resounded.
¹⁴He shot his arrows and scattered the enemy,
   with great bolts of lightning he routed them.
¹⁵The valleys of the sea were exposed
   and the foundations of the earth laid bare at your
       rebuke, Lord,
   at the blast of breath from your nostrils.
¹⁶He reached down from on high and took hold of me;
   he drew me out of deep waters.
¹⁷He rescued me from my powerful enemy,
   from my foes, who were too strong for me.
¹⁸They confronted me in the day of my disaster,
   but the Lord was my support.
¹⁹He brought me out into a spacious place;
   he rescued me because he delighted in me.
²⁰The Lord has dealt with me according
 to my righteousness;
   according to the cleanness of my hands
 he has rewarded me.
²¹For I have kept the ways of the Lord;
   I am not guilty of turning from my God.
²²All his laws are before me;
   I have not turned away from his decrees.
²³I have been blameless before him
   and have kept myself from sin.

^{24}"The LORD has rewarded me according to my righteousness,
   according to the cleanness of my hands in his sight.
^{25}To the faithful you show yourself faithful,
   to the blameless you show yourself blameless,
^{26}to the pure you show yourself pure,
   but to the devious you show yourself shrewd. (Ps 18:6–26)

The parallels between Psalm 18 and Habakkuk 3 are clear. If Habakkuk had drawn from Psalm 18, then, in comparing himself with the psalmist, the prophet saw God not only as his deliverer but also as the rewarder of his righteousness. The last few verses above (Ps 18:23–26) show that God repays everyone according to their ways. A similar retribution principle underlies the text of Habakkuk.

3:8–15 Over the Rivers and the Sea

In this unit, we see a further expression of the *Chaoskampf* motif embedded within grammatical alternation of second-person speech to express Yahweh's actions as a warrior and a third-person speech to describe the effects of those actions. The reader can easily spot the list of references to water motifs in this passage: "rivers" (3:8, 9), "streams" (3:8), "sea" (3:8, 15), "torrents of water" (3:10), "deep" (3:10), "great waters" (3:15), and "waves" (3:10) – literally "its hands." The effect of the chaotic images of water is enhanced by the use of terms such as "roared and lifted," "stormed," "scatter," "trampled," and "churning" (3:10, 14, 15). The point of these repetitions is to portray the chaotic and destructive forces at work and describe the power wielded by the dragon or serpent of the sea (primordial chaos).[13] In the context of Habakkuk, these chaotic forces represented the invading Chaldeans.

In contrast to the chaotic waters, God is portrayed as a man of war. Yahweh represents the power of order and plays the antagonist (or protagonist) who is angry at the chaotic waters (3:8). This narrative of a hero slaying a serpent is an ancient one,[14] and this hero has an abode where he is enthroned and from which he rules. From Zion, Yahweh rose to deliver his people from the

---

13. Consider the references that Ramantswana cites of dragon: "Job 7:12; Ps 44:20; Ezek 29:3–6a; 32:2–7; Jer 51:34, 46, 42; Pss 2:28b–34"; and of the primordial sea, "Ps 104:5–9; Job 38:8–11; Prov 8:22–31; Jer 5:22b; Jer 31:35; Ps 33:6–8; Ps 65:7–8." Hulisani Ramantswana, "Conflicts at Creation: Genesis 1–3 in Dialogue with the Psalter," *OTE* 27, no. 2 (2014): 553–578, [556].
14. I am indebted to my colleague, Jerry Hwang, who has brought my attention to Miller's work. Robert D. Miller II, "Tracking the Dragon across the Ancient Near East," *ArOr* 82 (2014): 225–245, [226].

serpent (primordial chaos). As Miller notes, "This is precisely what the Esagil [Marduk's temple] does in Enuma Elish, as does Baal's Mount Zaphon and [Yahweh's] Zion in the Psalms; they are the axis Mundi [cosmic axis] both vertically and horizontally."[15]

Just as we have an impressive description of the primordial chaos, we find an equally impressive description of the divine warrior. At least five types of warfaring weaponry are listed for this warrior: "horses" (3:8, 15), "chariots" (3:8), "bow" (3:9), "arrows" (3:9, 11), and "spear" (3:11, 14).

Figure 21: Relief of the Battle of Kadesh with Egyptian horses and chariots in 1274 BCE
Picture by Roland Unger
Wikimedia Commons: https://commons.wikimedia.org/wiki/File:RamesseumPM10.jpg

---

15. Robert D. Miller II, "Dragon Myths and Biblical Theology," *TS* 80.1 (2019): 37–56, [46].

Figure 22: Pitched Warfare in the Battle of Magnesia in 190 BCE
Source: Alexander Conze, *Altertümer von Pergamon: Stadt und Landschaft* (Berlin: Reimer, 1913), 250-1.
Public Domain: https://commons.wikimedia.org/wiki/File:Battle_of_Magnesia.jpg

Surprisingly, the text portrays a pitched battle rather than a siege. This is significant as it suggests that Yahweh's battle with the serpent was fought on a plain, which carries eschatological connotations (like Zech 12:11, which refers to "the plain of Megiddo"). We first see the divine warrior riding forward on his horses and chariots (Yahweh also rides on the clouds and the wind, Isa 19:1; Ps 104:3). Riding in strength, the divine warrior led his army toward the battle lines.[16] As he neared the battlefield, he uncovered his bow and arrow in preparation for battle (3:8–9). Then there was a dramatic pause. As God's army arrayed itself the mountains writhed, torrents of water swept by, the deep roared and lifted its waves, and the sun and moon stood still (3:10–11). Time stopped, the chaos roared, and the world braced for the horrors of the battle. This recalls the mighty conquest of Canaan at the Valley of Aijalon [a plain], where time stopped for Yahweh's slaughter:

> [12]On the day the LORD gave the Amorites over to Israel, Joshua said to the LORD in the presence of Israel:
> "Sun, stand still over Gibeon,
>   and you, moon, over the Valley of Aijalon."
> [13]So the sun stood still,
>   and the moon stopped,
>   till the nation avenged itself on its enemies,

---

16. In the Ugaritic Baal Cycle, the deity Baal is also portrayed as a divine rider with the title "Cloudrider" in his victorious theophany. Mark Smith and Wayne Pitard, *The Ugaritic Baal Cycle: Volume II. Introduction with Text, Translation and Commentary of KTU/CAT 1.3–1.4*, vol. II of VTSup 114 (Leiden: Brill, 2009), 677.

> as it is written in the Book of Jashar.
> The sun stopped in the middle of the sky
> and delayed going down about a full day. (Josh 10:12–13)

In the battle depicted in Habakkuk, as the opposing sides approached each other, arrows were shot and spears unleashed, flying like lightning across to the other side (3:11). From verse 12, the text reads as if the enemy's battle lines had been breached, as God raced his army to a decisive victory, completely routing the enemy's forces. The crushing of the enemy's leader, the reference to dead soldiers being "stripped . . . from head to foot" (3:13),[17] and a spear being used to pierce the head may allude to the crushing of the head of the serpent (Gen 3:15), Jael crushing Sisera's head with a tent peg (Judg 5:26), and God crushing the heads of Leviathan (Ps 74:14).

Habakkuk's choice of words in verse 13 – "anointed," "crushed" (*mhts*), "to deliver," "to save" – carry messianic overtones, which might have been based on the following texts:

> "I see him, but not now;
>   I behold him, but not near.
> A star will come out of Jacob;
>   a scepter will rise out of Israel.
> He will crush [*mhts*] the foreheads of Moab,
>   the skulls of all the people of Sheth." (Num 24:17)

> ⁵The Lord is at your right hand; he will crush [*mhts*] kings on the day of his wrath. ⁶He will judge the nations, heaping up the dead and crushing [*mhts*] the rulers of the whole earth. (Ps 110:5–6)

The text unit Habakkuk 3:8–15 is framed by repeated descriptions of the watery chaos and the divine warrior riding a horse (3:8, 15). The final line (3:15) expresses, in poetic form, the subduing of the chaotic forces of the sea. Nature and human powers are now under the feet of God's trampling horses. This imagery of trampling the foe is also seen on the footstools of ancient victor kings, where pictures of vassal kings and subjects were drawn. Similar references of trampling over one's enemies are found in the Bible (1 Kgs 5:3; Pss 47:3; 110:1; Zech 10:5). Habakkuk 3:15 portrays Yahweh as victorious, and this victory is the highlight of the last segment of Habakkuk.

---

17. The Hebrew reads: "from base [thigh] to neck" (ESV, NASB 1995). The Complete Jewish Bible renders, "uncovering its foundation all the way to the neck."

**Figure 23: Tiglath-pileser III Stepping on the
Head of a Vassal (8th century BCE)**
Picture by Osama Shukir Muhammed Amin FRCP (Glasg)
Wikimedia Commons: https://commons.wikimedia.org/wiki/File:Tiglath-pileser_III_and_
submission_of_an_enemy,_8th_century_BC,_from_Nimrud,_Iraq._The_British_Museum.jpg

**Figure 24: King Tutankhamon's Throne and Footstool
with Images of Vassal Kings on the Footstool**
Source: E-Pics Bildarchiv online
Wikimedia Commons: https://commons.wikimedia.org/wiki/File:ETH-BIB-Tut-
Ank-Amons_Treasures,_the_Kings_coalesiastical_throne-Dia_247-11149.tif

JESUS, THE DIVINE WARRIOR

The NT clearly portrays Jesus Christ as the divine warrior – an understanding that follows on from a long line of divine warriors in the OT. Longman and Reid suggest that the biblical theology of the divine warrior has been developed across the Bible over five phases.[1]

In the first phase, God fights against Israel's "flesh-and-blood enemies." God, the warrior, was with Abraham as he fought to deliver Lot (Gen 14). Yahweh fought for his people as he led them out of Egypt (Exod 14:14) and again, when Israel fought the Amalekites in the wilderness (Exod 17:8–13). Speaking to another generation of Israelites, Scripture says: "The LORD your God, who is going before you, will fight for you, as he did for you in Egypt, before your very eyes" (Deut 1:30; compare 3:22; 20:4). We see this again as Yahweh led the people into battle in Canaan (Josh 5:13–15) and also after they had settled in the promised land (Josh 23:10). As noted earlier, David sang of God as the divine warrior who fought for his people (Ps 18; 74; Isa 27, 51 compare Ps 144).

In the second phase, God fights against Israel! The tables have turned. Here we see Israel's perpetual spurning of God and their sinning against him. Yahweh is now Israel's enemy. In this phase, God uses the Assyrians and Chaldeans as his instruments of judgment (Jer 21:3–7; Lam 2:3–5; Hab 1:6–11). This stage also sees the end of Israel as a nation, with the people of God being scattered among the nations.

In the third phase, the divine warrior is presented as a future savior who will deliver God's people (Zech 9:14–15; 14:3–5). This is especially prominent in Daniel's vision, in which we see God battling four beasts that came up from the sea, and we see the triumphant Son of Man who would come as a cloud rider (Dan 7; compare Ps 104:3–4; Isa 59:17–20; Nah 1:3). Messianic expectations of a deliverer continued to develop through the Second Temple period. Consider the messianic expression in 1 Enoch 46:3–5 (300–100 BCE):

> [3]This is the Son of Man, to whom belongs righteousness, and with whom righteousness dwells. And he will open all the hidden storerooms; for the Lord of the Spirits has chosen him, and he is destined to be victorious before the Lord of the Spirits in eternal uprightness. [4]This Son of Man whom you have seen is the One who would remove the kings and the mighty ones from their comfortable seats and the strong ones from their thrones. He shall loosen the reins of the strong and crush the teeth of the sinners. [5]He shall depose the kings from their thrones and

kingdoms. For they do not extol and glorify him, and neither do they obey him, the source of their kingship.[2]

The anticipation of the Messiah in this third phase finds fulfillment in Jesus's first coming. The period from Jesus's birth, ministry, death, resurrection, and ascension to his second coming is deemed phase four. In this phase, Jesus fights, primarily, against the spiritual forces of evil and darkness (Matt 12:28; Mark 3:11; 4:35–41).

The final stage of the divine warrior motif begins when Jesus, the cloud rider, will return to judge and destroy all human and spiritual enemies of God (Mark 14:62; 2 Thess 2:8; Rev 22:12–15). I have reproduced Longman and Reid's graphical representation below.

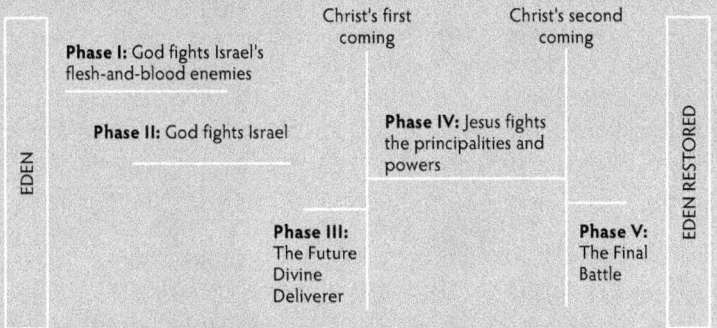

Figure 25: God's Cosmological Battle (Longman and Reid)
Source: Longman III and Reid, *God Is a Warrior*, 17

By acknowledging God as a divine warrior, we are recognizing that there is an ongoing battle. This battle, which began the moment Adam and Eve chose to submit to the serpent, continues to this day. At the Fall, came God's judgment – with his pronouncement of enmity between the serpent and the woman and between their offspring. But God also promised that the woman's offspring would crush the serpent's head (Gen 3:15). Embedded in this pronouncement is a prediction of perpetual warfare. Soon after, Cain killed Abel, and there has never been genuine and lasting peace since. Warfare – spiritual or earthly – will never stop until Jesus is entirely victorious.

The divine warrior motif tells us that in this perpetual fighting, God fights for his people. God has been fighting *for* his people and even *against* his people throughout history. While this *Chaoskampf* motif might have been drawn from ancient Near East myths, as Miller notes,

> Myth is humanity's social experience objectified. Myths address sociopolitical, psychological, and moral-pedagogical ends, both in their original contexts and in the power they retain, even when far removed from original contexts. And it is precisely the iconic element of myth, rather than the narrative, that gives myths this power, since the primary function of myth is evocation. . . . As a dramatic representation, the mythic image creates an "existential arena" wherein we encounter truth. Biblical myth, then, serves not mainly to communicate information but to engage us; it does not communicate elements of faith as much as it embodies the faith.[3]

Habakkuk expresses this divine warrior motif from the vantage point of the national crisis – both internal and external – of the sixth century BCE. Yahweh is presented as the cloud-riding storm God who battles the chaotic waters. Habakkuk's expression is but one in a long line of divine warrior motifs in the Bible, eventually leading us to Jesus Christ, the Son of God, who will crush Satan under his feet (Mark 12:36; Rom 16:20; 1 Cor 15:25, 27; Eph 1:22; Heb 2:8). And Jesus Christ will fulfill the Genesis 3:15 prophecy of judgment and salvation.

This statement by Miller made an impression on me: "Only in the biblical tradition do we get any myths where the dragon is reduced to a pet fish. Ultimately, the numinous God is omnipotent."[4] Although our own crisis may be taunting us right now – like a dragon or a chaotic flood – we trust that Jesus Christ will one day tame the forces of evil and put them in their place – like a goldfish in a fish tank.

---

1. Tremper Longman III, Daniel G. Reid, and Willem A. Van Gemeren. *God Is a Warrior* (Grand Rapids: Zondervan Academic, 1995).
2. James H. Charlesworth, ed., *The Old Testament Pseudepigrapha: Apocalyptic Literature and Testaments*, vol. 1 (Garden City: Doubleday, 1983), 34.
3. Emphasis mine. Miller, "Dragon Myths," 42.
4. Miller, "Dragon Myths," 55.

3:16–19C HABAKKUK'S TRANSFORMATION: I HEAR YOU, GOD!

Experiencing a theophany can be shocking and scary (Pss 99:1; 119:120). When God appeared at Sinai, the people trembled with fear (Exod 19:16; 20:18). When Ezekiel received a vision from God, he fell facedown (Ezek 1:28; 3:23). Daniel was deeply distressed and disturbed after seeing the visions from God (Dan 7:15; 8:17). When King Belshazzar saw fingers writing on the wall, he turned pale and was "so frightened that his legs became weak, and his knees were knocking" (Dan 5:5–6). By Habakkuk 3:16, Yahweh's theophany had ended, and the scene shifted back to the prophet, now grappling with the aftereffects of what he had experienced. Habakkuk had lost control of his entire body, even more shaken by this vision than by the earlier vision of the invading Chaldeans (1:5–11).

The author of Habakkuk strategically uses the phrases "I have heard" (3:2) and "I heard" (3:16) as bookends around the theophany. Like Job, Habakkuk had heard of God's fame, and having experienced God up close profoundly impacted him. Note that the same Hebrew word, "heard" (NIV "listen"), is also used at the beginning of the book (1:2) where Habakkuk accused God of not hearing. The verb "to hear" (*shama*) is found only in these three places in Habakkuk, making it an astutely placed rhetorical device. In 3:16, Habakkuk's accusation has turned a full 180 degrees. By the end of the book, *he* was the one who needed to hear.

While Habakkuk's reference to the invading Chaldeans (3:16) recalls chapter 1, we notice a shift in the prophet's attitude. His denial and resistance to the invading Chaldeans (1:13) has dissipated, and we see his calm acceptance of the Chaldean invasion, which the author makes clear by the use of the verb "quivered." This word is found only four times in the OT with this meaning, and every occurrence is in the context of a foreign invasion.[18] In Habakkuk 3:16, this word is used to communicate that the impending Babylonian invasion no longer has a disturbing effect on Habakkuk; instead, it is Yahweh's coming that has this effect. The prophet's impatience with injustice and violence at the beginning of the book has turned into a readiness to "wait patiently" (also translated "rest") for the distress that would befall the invaders.

This ability to endure in the face of the threat posed by the Chaldeans was due to the theophany. But what exactly was it about the theophany that brought about this shift in Habakkuk? I believe that Habakkuk had witnessed

---

18. The other three references are 1 Samuel 3:11; 2 Kings 21:12; Jeremiah 19:3.

a preview of the triumph of righteousness, justice, and victory of Yahweh – a vision of how God would bring retributive justice to the wicked, bloodthirsty, and treacherous by personally riding into war – which is the essence of the woe oracles in Habakkuk 2. The cosmic destructive forces would be overcome by Yahweh, the holy and victorious warrior. This anticipation of God's victory would strengthen the righteous to live by faith (2:4). In other words, the faith and faithfulness of the righteous depends on God's ultimate victory over his primordial enemy (the ancient Serpent).

Habakkuk 3:17 moves away from the prophet to a scene of ruin. Six failures of crops and livestock are expressed poetically using three parallel lines. Each pair of lines has a similar syntax: "though *x* does not *y*, and there is no *z*." While God's judgment often comes in "threes" (sword, famine, and pestilence or plague), the various destructions in this verse could be the result of the Chaldean invasion (sword). The invasion brings much destruction and death. Carcasses and corpses left to rot in the open turn the land into a breeding ground for pestilence. The failure of crops could have been due to plunder or a lack of tending.

Elsewhere, figs, vineyards, olives, and sheep are often used as metaphors for God's people (Ps 52:8; Isa 5:1–7; Jer 11:16; 24:3; Hos 9:10; Mic 2:12). Therefore, it is possible to interpret 3:17 as depicting the destruction of God's people along with the land itself. When the crops and cattle failed, the temple also suffered because these items were offered as tithes and used in the upkeep of the temple (Neh 13:12).

Figure 26: Old Olive Tree in Israel (photo by author)

Verses 18–19 shift the attention back to the prophet. These lines are written in an *I-He* format (as opposed to *I-You*), which has a grammatical distancing effect that expresses the temporal distance of the events Habakkuk was to patiently await. The contrast between 3:18–19 and 3:17 is intentional. Habakkuk's hope and joy were in Yahweh despite his immediate circumstances.

Verse 18 is chiastic, with a focus on joy. The underlying syntax is as follows:

A	Yet I,	[first person]
B	in the LORD,	[prepositional, third person]
C	[I] will rejoice;	[cohortative verb]
C′	I will be joyful,	[cohortative verb]
B′	in God,	[prepositional, third person]
A′	my Savior.	[first person]

Note the *I-He* subject-object in lines A-A′. This is followed by the prepositional phrases "in the LORD" and "in God" (B-B′). "God" and "LORD" are in the third person. At the center, we have the first-person "I will rejoice" and "I will be joyful" (C-C′). The symmetry highlights Habakkuk's confidence because of the theophany. Knowing how things would end was liberating and gave Habakkuk the strength to live through the difficulties. As the Bible says, "The joy of the LORD is your strength" (Neh 8:10).

The double first-person (imperfective) verbs at the center are in the cohortative mood, which is used to express volition. The only other place in the book where first-person cohortative verbs are used is 2:1, where Habakkuk willed himself to "stand" and "station" himself on the ramparts. Strikingly, this occurrence in 2:1 follows the same pattern – two cohortative verbs are featured in pairs at the symmetrical center of two cola. I have reorganized the translation of 2:1 (NIV) to reflect the underlying Hebrew syntax.

A	At my watch		[prepositional]
B		I will stand,	[cohortative verb]
B′		and [I] station myself	[cohortative verb]
A′	on the ramparts		[prepositional]

It is unlikely that such compositional features are random or coincidental. They were more likely strategically placed to frame chapters 2 and 3. The will of Habakkuk to hear from God at the beginning of chapter 2 finds closure as the prophet wills himself to rejoice at the end of chapter 3. From this perspective, chapter 3 is integral to the entire book. While there are literary features that tie chapters 1 and 2 together, there are also features that link chapters 2 and 3.

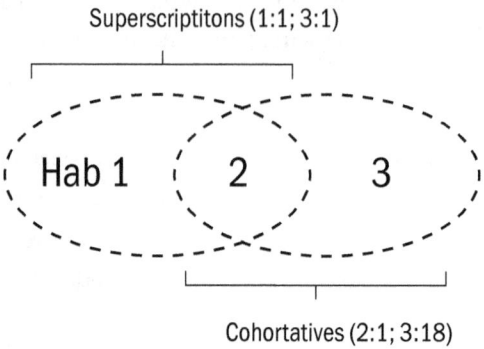

Figure 27: Habakkuk as a Unity

In this way, the message of the book of Habakkuk is unveiled, illustrating *how* "the righteous person will live by his faithfulness" (2:4) – through *hearing* (experiencing) and *trusting* in Yahweh, who will triumph over the enemy, administer justice, and restore the fortunes of his people. The book of Habakkuk shows that this will be accomplished through the appearance of Yahweh, the divine warrior. Experiencing God's power and knowing how it will all end make it possible to live by faith during this interim period.

In the book's last line (3:19), we see an essential aspect of living by faith and living faithfully. Perhaps Habakkuk was citing Psalm 140:7 – "Sovereign LORD, my strong deliverer, you shield my head in the day of battle" – or Psalm 118:14 – "The LORD is my strength and my defense; he has become my salvation."[19] Habakkuk might also have drawn inspiration from Isaiah 12:2: "The LORD, the LORD himself, is my strength and my defense; he has become my salvation." All these references speak of Yahweh as our strength and salvation on the day of battle. Having faith or being faithful does not remove our experience of pain or suffering because we, like Habakkuk, may still have to live through God's judgment in our time before that final "day." Faith presumes difficulty. The call to persist in suffering can be cognitively

---

19. The dating of Psalms 118 and 140 cannot be ascertained and could have been composed earlier than Habakkuk.

baffling. Yet God's purposes for his people are good and grants the grace of strength to those who trust in him.

Habakkuk's dependence on Psalm 18 was noted earlier. Verse 19, with minor modifications, is dependent on Psalm 18:33, as well as on 2 Samuel 22:34. God had made Habakkuk's feet like that of the deer, enabling him to tread on the high places. This imagery expresses the deer's agility, which enables it to navigate on the rocks, keeping it secure and safe from predators. The underlying Hebrew uses a grammatical form (Hiphil) to highlight God as the agent who caused Habakkuk to tread on the high places with agility and strength.

Finally, in these last three verses – which are the only "positive" verses in the book, from Habakkuk's perspective – the prophet praises God. Thus, the book of Habakkuk is shaped like the lament psalms with a movement from lament to laud, from haplessness to hope. Tears of pain will turn to tears of joy, and the last word belongs to Yahweh.

Figure 28: Deer Treading on High Places
Photo by Maglanist
Public Domain: https://commons.wikimedia.org/wiki/File:Yael2.jpg

3:19D POSTSCRIPT

Outside the book of Psalms, the phrase "for the director of music" (3:19d) – which is a single word in Hebrew – occurs only here in Habakkuk. Similarly, the second phrase, "on my stringed instruments" – which is also a single word in Hebrew – is a musical term that is often used in Psalms. The first-person possessive form – "*my* stringed instruments" (emphasis added) – is unique in the OT; moreover, none of the psalms use such attributions or musical notation at the end of a poem. This postscript, forming a frame with the superscript (3:1), is thus unique in the Bible and has inspired many studies.[20]

SUMMARY AND REFLECTION

The book of Habakkuk teaches us how we are to live by faith in a world where pain and injustice reign, and it does so with remarkable literary finesse. The book is a *triptych* – a picture drawn on three adjacent panels with the subject of interest often located at the central panel – that is designed and structured to focus on the vision and woe oracles at the center of the book. This center presents us with two main messages: first, the vision encouraging the righteous to persevere in faith and, second, the woe oracles condemning the wicked. These two thoughts – the theology of a righteous God (woe oracles) and what the righteous must do (vision) – are sandwiched between two awesome warfare scenes in the first and third chapters respectively (1:5–11; 3:3–15). The first battle describes the impending invasion of Judah by the Chaldeans; the second depicts the divine warrior riding into battle against the primordial chaos. These two battles tell us that as Judah (and Babylon) were judged, the spiritual and cosmic powers of the serpent and chaos will also be defeated by Yahweh for the salvation of his people. This vision of the final victory provides the confidence that earthly judgments, such as the woe oracles, will not be in vain. Yahweh will deal decisively with wickedness – and this is precisely what Habakkuk had initially sought when he cried out to God in chapter 1.

In the trajectory of Habakkuk, the theophany transformed Habakkuk's earlier attitude of lament into one of hope and praise. Habakkuk's personal experience with God not only unraveled a theological knot for him but also brought joy and optimism despite the unjust circumstances. The joy that proceeds from anticipating Yahweh's view of victory had become Habakkuk's strength, a strength which God himself had caused to rise within the prophet. This joy is the fuel that sustains our faith so that it will continue burning as we wait for God.

The ultimate divine warrior is Jesus Christ, who will defeat Satan and the primordial chaos – representing all the evil forces in the world. He has already done so by the cross – when he died, rose from the dead, and defeated death – and will do so completely when he comes again to judge the living

---

20. Bruce K. Waltke, "Superscripts, Postscripts, or Both," *JBL* 110, no. 4 (1991): 583–596.

and the dead. The Yahweh that Habakkuk saw, presented as a warrior like the ancient Near East storm god, points forward to Jesus Christ, the eschatological conquering king. This victory of Christ is our joy and strength. And, like Habakkuk, this victory is the basis of our faith and faithfulness.

Our times and contexts may not be too different from Habakkuk's. Writing toward the end of 2022, UN Chief Antonio Guterres warned that the world is "one miscalculation away" from a nuclear war.[21] ASEAN is facing collateral economic damage from the conflicts in Europe. Higher fuel prices and food scarcity fuel the fires of suffering in Myanmar.[22] In China, floods and droughts are happening simultaneously.[23] But the complacent care for themselves. The proud and the wicked oppress. Warfare, climate change, and pestilence, which rear their heads simultaneously, are precisely the kind of judgment God pronounced on sin and rebellion, both in the OT and the NT. Since these judgments prequel the final assize, suffering will increase, and God's people will not escape such suffering: "Everyone who wants to live a godly life in Christ Jesus will be persecuted" (2 Tim 3:12). Thus, the book of Habakkuk is profoundly significant and highly applicable in our generation as we wait for the promise of deliverance to be fulfilled.

I conclude with a story about a struggle faced by my colleague David Lang and his wife, Loo Geok. Each of their three children was diagnosed with a rare genetic disorder called Niemann-Pick Disease Type C. Two of the children have passed away. The following excerpt gives us a glimpse of what it means to live by faith and faithfulness as Habakkuk and Job did:[24]

---

21. "Nuclear Annihilation Just One Miscalculation Away, UN Chief Warns," *BBC News*, August 1, 2022, https://www.bbc.com/news/world-62381425.
22. "Fuel Price Hikes, Scarce Rice Add to Hardship in Myanmar," *Asia Today* (blog), August 19, 2022, https://asiatoday.co/2022/08/19/fuel-price-hikes-scarce-rice-add-to-hardship-in-myanmar/.
23. "China issues first national drought alert, battles to save crops in extreme heatwave," CNA News, August 19, 2022, https://www.channelnewsasia.com/asia/china-national-alert-drought-heatwave-crops-2888966; Yang Nick, "At Least 17 Dead and 17 Missing as Flash Flood Hits Northwestern China," South China Morning Post, August 18, 2022, https://www.scmp.com/news/china/article/3189304/flash-flood-hits-northwestern-china-leaving-4-dead-and-dozens-missing.
24. Rachel Phua, "Three Children with Fatal Genetic Disorder, yet David Lang Sees God's Sovereignty," *Salt&Light* (blog), 2018, https://saltandlight.sg/profiles/why-suffer-david-lang/; Gracia Chiang, "'We Have Much to Be Thankful for': Bible College Lecturer and Caregiver David Lang on the Death of His Daughter," *Thir.st* (blog), February 28, 2022, https://thirst.sg/we-have-much-to-be-thankful-bible-college-lecturer-and-caregiver-david-lang-on-the-death-of-his-daughter/.

Lang says he and Loo Geok went through different stages of grief throughout the entire process – denial, anger, bargaining, depression, and eventually acceptance.

Like Job, Lang cried out to God: "Why me?" (Job 7:20) during the initial years. He was angry with God. Why would a loving Father allow innocent children to suffer?

There was pressure on the couple to find the right treatment for their children: Put them on experimental therapy? Go for healing rallies? The pair often quarrelled with each other at the beginning, going to bed in tears, Lang says.

Like Job's friends, some of the couple's acquaintances, while well meaning, added to their burden.

"One of the problems we faced in the first two years of our daughter's degeneration was people telling us, 'The reason your children are not healed is because you lack faith.'"

"I told them, 'I believe God can heal, and I have asked that my children be healed. Now, I will just wait on the Lord.'"

"They told me, 'No, you have to be like the persistent widow (Luke 18:1–8). Keep going for rallies the way she went to the judge until God decides to heal them.'"

Lang began to question his faith, so he restudied the passage. "It refers to the justice God will bring, not answered prayers. It's about the second coming."

To cope, Lang dove into the book of Job, which brought immense comfort at times when he felt guilty for his outrage towards God.

"As a bible college lecturer, who am I to question God. Was I a hypocrite? I even thought of resigning," he says.

"But then Job also spoke against God. And God didn't fault him. His response was: 'Job has spoken of me what is right' (Job 42:7)."

Lang saw the beauty of God's sovereignty as well, in Job 38–39, when God finally answered Job through a long spiel of rhetorical questions. Some interpret it as God's rebuke of Job, but Lang found compassion and grace in God's words. He is in control over all existence.

And like the carefree ostrich (Job 39:13–18) and the willful horse (Job 39:19–25), God was going to give the Lang family the joy and courage to trudge on amidst the pain.

Lang saw his children degenerate in front of his own eyes, his young son died, his savings plummet. But he had found his answer in one of Job's final words in the chapter:

I have heard of You by the hearing of the ear,
But now my eye sees You. (Job 42:5 NKJV)

Despite what they have gone through, I often see David and Loo Geok smiling. I believe that is because they have *really* wrestled with God through their pain. Their God is bigger than their theology. Like Habakkuk, they can say, "Yet I will rejoice in the LORD, I will be joyful in God my Savior" (Hab 3:18).

ZEPHANIAH

OUTLINE

1:1	Superscription
1:2–3	Yahweh Gathers the Earth
1:4–16	Yahweh's Day of Judgment
1:4–6	Concerning the Idolaters of Judah/Jerusalem
1:7–13	Concerning the Rebellious Judah/Jerusalem
1:14–16	Concerning the Cities
1:17–18	Yahweh Consumes the Earth
2:1–3	Seek Righteousness before That Day
2:4–15	Woe against the Nations
2:4–7	Against the Philistines
2:8–11	Against the Ammonites and Moabites
2:12	Against the Cushites
2:13–15	Against Assyria and Nineveh
3:1–4	Woe against Jerusalem
3:5–7	Yahweh's Righteousness in the City
3:8–13	Yahweh's Day of Restoration
3:8–10	Yahweh Restores the Remnant of the Nations
3:11–13	Yahweh Restores the Remnant of Israel
3:14–20	Yahweh Gathers Zion and the Earth
3:14–17	Yahweh Takes Away Punishment and Saves
3:18–20	Yahweh Gathers Zion and All the Earth

ZEPHANIAH IN A NUTSHELL

At its heart, Zephaniah is about God's total rejuvenation of his people and city – a reversal of destiny of the horrors of Jerusalem's destruction, a return to God, and a spiritual cleansing from within. This trajectory of rejuvenation is presented through the historical settings of Josiah's reforms (640–609 BCE) and the Babylonian invasion as shown by the book's superscription.[1] When Zephaniah is read through an eschatological lens, the book envisions a future period of time signaled by the formulaic "day of the LORD [Yahweh]" or "at that time." These phrases are characteristic of the book of Zephaniah. The highest occurrence per thousand words of the expression "day of the LORD" – including variants such as "that day" or "on that day" – is in Obadiah, with Zephaniah ranking second.[2] As Baker notes, "Such devotion to a single theme [of the day of Yahweh] is not found in any other" prophetic book.[3] Zephaniah sometimes adopts universal language – such as "the whole earth" (1:18) – and pictures an ideal state of affairs without any fear of evil or trouble again (3:15).

In Zephaniah, we see Judah and the nations portrayed in a dark and sinful light, silhouetted against the bright and awesome manifestation of the day of Yahweh. There were two possible outcomes: either a day of distress and anguish because of God's fury or a day of peace and rejoicing for God's people. These contrasts were intended to drive Zephaniah's readers or hearers to consider their ways. The idolaters, the rebellious, the complacent, and those who rejected God and his laws would have to grapple with the consequences of their conduct (1:4–13).

Read immediately after Habakkuk (anticipation of exile) and before Haggai (return from exile), Zephaniah's position in the XII suggests that the judgment of Judah and the surrounding nations on the "day of the LORD" is to be understood in the context of the Babylonian invasion and Judah's exile (3:8, 19–20) at the turn of the sixth century BCE rather than at the time of Josiah's reforms. If Zephaniah was written earlier than Habakkuk, its placement after

---

1. Marvin A. Sweeney, *Zephaniah: A Commentary*, ed. Paul D. Hanson, Hermeneia (Minneapolis: Fortress, 2003), 1.
2. This search was done with Logos 10 software and the bundled *Lexham Hebrew Bible* module (Bellingham: Lexham, 2012).
3. Baker, *Nahum, Habakkuk, Zephaniah*, 84.

Habakkuk suggests that the Josianic reforms had not achieved the intended result and that the Babylonian invasion depicted in Habakkuk was now at hand.

The book of Zephaniah is vivid and intentional in its literary character. When its author wanted to highlight something, he repeated certain words or grammatical forms in close succession and proximity, and this was often done at strategic points in the book. For instance, we see eight repetitions of the phrase "day of" – which refer to the day of Yahweh – in 1:14–16 and the use of six infinitives in quick succession in 3:8–9.[4] The motif of people "gathering" is found at the beginning of chapter 2 and the end of chapter 3. Apart from named nations, Zephaniah calls out different people groups – "those who . . ." – by using participles. The book has the second-highest number of participles per thousand words in the XII (the top being Nahum).[5]

Like Habakkuk, the book of Zephaniah can be divided into three distinct constituent parts (a "triptych") according to its chapters. The book appears as a chiasmus, with the first and third chapters focusing on Judah and Jerusalem. The second chapter, which lies at the center of the book, focuses on God's judgment on the nations and the enemies of God's people.

Scholars have also pointed out that the Septuagint (LXX) reads slightly differently from the Masoretic Text (MT). While the MT adopts a more historical and exhortative perspective, by presenting Judah with a choice to return back to Yahweh, the LXX treats Judah's disobedience as a certainty and adopts the view that "restoration as an event . . . will take place throughout the world only after the punishment has been realized. Such a reading presupposes that choice is no longer possible."[6] However, I think that this perspective of the LXX is also present in the Masoretic version. This will become clear as we go along.

Chapter 1 begins with a superscription, tracing Zephaniah's genealogy a few generations back to King Hezekiah. This is followed by a universalistic depiction of Yahweh sweeping away the earth in eschatological and epic proportions (1:2–3), not unlike what happened with the flood in Noah's time. We then have God speaking in the first person and addressing the idolatry of Judah/Jerusalem (1:4–6). From verse 7 onward, we see references to the "day of the LORD [Yahweh]," interspersed with God's declarations about punishing officials, sons of kings, idolaters, and the complacent in Judah. In 1:14–16,

---

4. The six infinitives are: "[to] stand," "to assemble," "to gather," "to pour out," "[to] call," "[to] serve."
5. This search was done with Logos 10 software and the bundled *Lexham Hebrew Bible* module (Bellingham: Lexham, 2012).
6. Sweeney, *Zephaniah*, 3.

we see a striking eightfold repetition of the phrase "day of." Except for one main verb, these three verses of thirty-nine words are verbless sentences![7] The chapter ends with another universalistic description of God's punishment of sinners and his destruction of the earth (1:17–18). This chapter is framed by the word "earth," which is based on two different underlying Hebrew words – *adamah*, occurring twice at the beginning of this chapter (1:2–3) and *erets*, found twice at the end (1:18).

Following the pronouncement of judgment on sinners and the whole earth at the end of chapter 1, chapter 2 begins with a call to action. We hear an urgent demand for both the "shameful nation" and the "humble of the land" to "gather" and to "seek the Lord" before the coming "day." From verses 4–15, twelve named territories or peoples around Judah – nations in four directions around Jerusalem – are listed for condemnation: Gaza, Ashkelon, Ashdod, Ekron, Kerethites, Canaan, Philistines, Moabites, Ammonites, Cushites, Assyria, and Nineveh. Judah is portrayed as victorious over them because Yahweh will fight for his people. Although the interjection "woe" is used once in this chapter against the various nations listed for condemnation (2:5), this segment does not read like the woe oracles in Habakkuk (2:6–19).

In the final chapter, we have the final "woe," which is directed against Judah/Jerusalem, who is portrayed again as rebellious and decadent (3:1–4). In verse 2, the composer uses a series of negatively phrased verbs to describe the city: "she obeys *no one*"; "she accepts *no* instructions"; "she *does not* trust in the Lord"; and "she *does not* draw near to her God" (emphasis added). In verse 5, which speaks of Yahweh as being righteous in that city, the same negative phrased construction is used: Yahweh "*does no* wrong" and "*does not* fail" to dispense justice, in contrast to the unrighteous who "know *no* shame" (emphasis added).

The rest of the chapter continues this focus on Judah in two ways. First, Yahweh would gather Judah's external enemies, unleash his fury, and turn them to him (3:7–10). Second, Yahweh would remove the wickedness within Judah (3:11–15). Again, we see the repeated negatively phrased construction: Judah "will *never again* . . . be haughty," "will *do no* wrong," and "will tell *no* lies," and the people will "*never* again . . . fear any harm" (emphasis added). The last few verses highlight the transformed, positive state of Jerusalem (3:16–20). Here we have a series of first-person action verbs that convey the idea of God speaking personally and directly to the readers or hearers.

---

7. The warrior "shouts" (NIV), an indicative verb in English, is a Qal participle in the Hebrew.

THE SHAPE AND MESSAGE OF ZEPHANIAH

Unfortunately, there is little consensus on the exact shape of Zephaniah. Berlin exclaims, "The lack of agreement in dividing so small a body of the text is truly amazing."[8] The disagreements are the result of varying methodologies that scholars have used and whether or not a disjunctive literary device in the text is considered significant enough to mark a unit delimitation.[9]

Nonetheless, for purposes of interpretation, it is important to consider how various units within the entire book of Zephaniah come together coherently. The juxtapositions of these text units form the shape of the book, and it is this shape that communicates the logical thrust and message of the book. Not every scholar appreciates this approach. Some continue to focus on independent prophetic oracles and reconstruct redactional layers of the text. Rejecting this latter approach, Berlin notes,

> The primary task of the exegete is to explain the book, not only its pieces. The exegete will therefore assume coherence (as readers do for all texts), until all attempts to find it fail . . . I cannot prove that it was formed, *ab initio*, as a whole any more than Roberts can prove that it is a collection of separate oracles. I can only point to the fact that it exists now as a whole and there is no manuscript evidence that it ever existed otherwise; and that viewing it as a whole yield an interpretation much more interesting and compelling than viewing it as a collection of separate parts.[10]

Berlin's approach to reading the book reflects a stream of scholarship on prophetic books in the last three decades. As shown in my earlier analysis of Habakkuk, it is helpful to see how various juxtaposed subunits are read coherently within their contextual horizon.

In my view, the three chapters of Zephaniah follow a linear trajectory in which Jerusalem is judged but also promised a future restoration. At the same time, the book – like Habakkuk – has a concentric structure. At its center are two woe interjections – one addressed to the nations and the other to Judah/Jerusalem. Like the book of Habakkuk – which has two battles framing the woe oracles – we find two text units that sustain the motif of the day of Yahweh framing the central woe units in Zephaniah. The first day of Yahweh unit, in

---

8. Adele Berlin, *Zephaniah*, Anchor Bible (New York: Doubleday, 1994), 19.
9. Most scholars, e.g., Sweeney, have abandoned the Masoretic disjunctive *setumah* as unit delimitations. While Berlin maintains these Masoretic markers in her outline, she does not consider them as literary compositional units. Berlin, *Zephaniah*, 19.
10. Berlin, *Zephaniah*, 22–23.

Zephaniah 1, highlights Yahweh's judgment on both Judah and the nations. The second, in chapter 3, highlights Yahweh's restoration of both Jerusalem and the nations. However, Judah/Jerusalem are given the prime place in the book, and the references to nations and peoples provide the foil for God's chosen people and city. In this way, two things are held in tension in the book of Zephaniah: first, the tension between judgment and restoration; second, the tension between Jerusalem and the nations. And at its core, the woe sayings – the paraenetic or exhortative call to seek righteousness and God's work of righteousness (3:5–7) – emphasize persistent human weakness and God's determination to transform his people.

Before proposing a structure for Zephaniah, I will show how several literary features provide the impetus for unit delimitations. One of the major ways the composer has delimited texts is by *successive repetitions of words*. At the beginning of chapter 1 – after the superscription – the repetitions of "sweep" (Heb. *'sp*; 1:2–3) and "destroy" (1:3–4) immediately capture the attention of hearers or readers. Similarly, chapter 2 begins with a rapid-fire of repeated words such as "gather" (2:1), "before" (2:2), "day" (2:2), and "seek" (2:3). Chapter 3 uses five repetitions of the negative particle "not" in two verses (3:2–3).[11] The use of sustained repetitions to begin a text unit is found throughout the book.

The book also uses repeated *emphatic grammatical forms* (or less common stems or conjugations) at the beginning of these chapters. Chapters 1 and 3 begin with three successive participle forms. We see a Hebrew infinitive absolute form (*asop*) in 1:2 ("sweep") and an interjection in 3:1 (woe). The Hebrew infinitive absolute form (1:2) – which is used mainly to express the certainty of a verbal action – does not have an English equivalent. The infinitive absolute is a nonfinite verb; when paired with another finite verb with the same root, the combined effect intensifies the verbal action. English translations such as the ESV often add "certainly" or "surely" before the verb (1:2; note that the infinitive absolute is left untranslated in the NIV).

In addition, 2:1–3 uses an unusual series of five imperative (command) forms to establish a distinctive exhortative or paraenetic unit in the book, calling readers or hearers to "seek" Yahweh. This stands in contrast with the earlier mention of those who do *not* seek Yahweh (1:6). The emphatic repetition of these commands at the start of chapter 2 is designed to capture the audience's attention and demarcate a new text unit.

---

11. Note the phrases, "obeys no one," "accepts no correction," "does not trust," "does not draw," and "leave nothing for."

The use of *inclusio* (bookends) is also evident in the book. Note how at both ends of chapter 1, the whole earth is addressed (1:2–3, 18), framing Judah/Jerusalem as the primary addressee at the core of this chapter. The universalistic terms "all" and "whole," paired with "face of the earth" or "earth/land," are found at the beginning and end of chapter 1 (1:1:2–3, 18), the onset of chapter 2 (2:3), and at the end of the book (3:19–20).

While these markers identify each chapter's distinctive quality, other literary elements hold these three chapters together to form an integral whole. For instance, the "day" motif, introduced in chapter 1, links all three chapters (1:7–16; 2:2; 3:11, 16). This "day" is also connected to another temporal marker, "at that time" (1:12; 3:19–20), which defines events of both condemnation and restoration. Most significantly, the movement from condemnation to the restoration of Judah/Jerusalem, as well as the nations, binds the whole book together.

Repetition can function as a connecting device. A further division of repetition is *merism*, a poetic device where a writer uses two opposite terms to show completeness. For example, "he searched high and low" indicates searching everywhere and "God created the heavens and the earth" signifies that God created everything. Similarly, Zephaniah uses the "woe" interjection as God's indictment against "the nations" (2:5) and "Judah and Jerusalem" (3:1) to show that this judgment includes everyone who is unjust.

Consider the structural shape of Zephaniah and its various subsections as set out below.

A	Superscription	1:1	Superscription
B	Yahweh Gathers the Earth	1:2–3	Gathers Earth
C	Yahweh's Day of Judgment	1:4–16	Day of Judgment
B´	Yahweh Consumes the Earth	1:17–18	Earth
D	Seek Righteousness	2:1–3	Righteousness
E	Woe against the Nations	2:4–15	Woe
E´	Woe against Jerusalem	3:1–4	Woe
D´	Yahweh's Righteousness	3:5–7	Righteousness
C´	Yahweh's Day of Restoration	3:8–13	Day of Restoration
B´´	Yahweh Gathers Zion and All the Earth	3:14–20	Gathers Earth

Figure 29: Structural Design of Zephaniah

Zephaniah in a Nutshell

The literary techniques seen in the structural design of Zephaniah are not dissimilar to what we see in Habakkuk and other books of the Bible.[12] The use of word repetitions and distinctive grammatical forms help us identify a text unit. Cumulatively, these units can be seen linearly (a trajectory towards restoration) or concentrically to highlight a central idea (woe judgments), as Figure 29 above shows.

Taken as a whole, Zephaniah moves from God's condemnation to God's restoration. But the theme of the restoration comes across more forcefully from 3:5 onward, with expressions of Yahweh's sustained righteous actions in the city of Jerusalem (3:5–7, 11–19) and among the nations (3:8–10, 19–20). Yahweh's decisive and intentional actions are conveyed by the higher frequency of first-person verbal actions from verse 5 onward and in the quick succession of six infinitive forms that indicate purpose in 3:8–9.

This positive shift from 3:5 onward is abrupt, occurring immediately after Judah and Jerusalem are depicted as rebellious (3:1–4; compare 1:4–6). Read linearly, this implies that the paraenetic unit in 2:1–3 – exhorting readers or hearers to seek Yahweh – had not achieved its desired effect. In my view, 3:5–7 functions as a contrast to the paraenetic unit in 2:1–3 after the depictions of Jerusalem's stubborn and rebellious nature in 3:1–4. The call to repent was met with a persistent rebellion, and it was in such a deplorable situation that we see God decisively entering the scene.

Consider how the composer uses four negation particles in quick succession (3:2–3) to highlight Judah and Jerusalem's persistent refusal to heed Yahweh: "obeys no one," "accepts no correction," "does not trust in the Lord," and "does not draw near to her God." The composer then repeats this effect with the negation now applied to Yahweh, who "does no wrong" and "does not fail" to dispense justice, while the evildoers "know no shame" (3:5).

The contrast between Judah's wickedness in the city (3:1–4) and Yahweh's righteousness in the city (3:5–7) – highlighted through the use of the negative particle – is deliberate. We see this writing technique used elsewhere as well. For instance, the use of negatives associated with the names of Hosea's children (Hos 1:10–2:1) highlights how judgment turns to blessing.[13]

---

12. See also Peter C. W. Ho, *The Design of the Psalter: A Macrostructural Analysis* (Eugene: Pickwick, 2019); "The Macrostructural Design and Logic of the Psalter: An Unfurling of the Davidic Covenant," in *Reading the Psalms Theologically*, ed. David Howard Jr. and Andrew Schmutzer, Studies and Scripture and Biblical Theology (Bellingham: Lexham Academic, 2023), 35–62.
13. The punishment of "Jezreel," the judgment on God's people with "No-Mercy," and God's rejection of them as "Not-my-people," now turns into a great "day of Jezreel" when the people

In Zephaniah, the shift to restoration results from God's transformative work rather than the people's repentance. This is a significant point. The prophet's call for repentance did not bring about a fundamental change in his audience. It was God who ultimately brought about the transformation. Note how negation is used again in 3:11 and 3:13. By this point, the transformation brought about by God had been accomplished, and the result was a people who would "*never again* . . . be haughty," a remnant who would "do *no* wrong," "tell *no* lies," and in whom "a deceitful tongue will *not* be found" (emphasis added).

In the XII, the book of Zephaniah highlights God's transformational work despite human failures and rebellion. The prophetic call to seek Yahweh had not been heeded. Coming after Habakkuk, Zephaniah continues to use imagery depicting Jerusalem's decadence and barrenness. And the transformation in Zephaniah is shown by God's cleansing of Jerusalem through the Babylonian invasion. However, the repeated pairings of Judah/Jerusalem with the nations and God with humankind in contexts of judgment and restoration – using the "day of the Lord" trope – allow the book of Zephaniah to be read with an eschatological perspective, much like the last few chapters of Isaiah. Yet, the exhortation in the book of Zephaniah (2:1–3) remains relevant to readers in each new generation of God's people. God's punishment is prompted by humankind's wickedness, but restoration for humankind rests on God's own character, purpose, and determination.

---

will go up to the land. The brothers are now called "God's people," and the sisters have received "mercy."

ZEPHANIAH 1

The first chapter of Zephaniah seems to depict the state of dire circumstances in Judah/Jerusalem at the end of Habakkuk. The focus of Zephaniah 1 is Yahweh's judgment – expressed as the "day of the Lord" – which is unleashed on Zion (that is Jerusalem) and the nations. In this judgment, Yahweh is portrayed as a victorious warrior (compare Hab 3:3–15), while his enemies are depicted as the violent people, the idolatrous priests, the wicked leaders in Jerusalem, and the complacent wealthy upper-class, whose god was silver and gold (Zeph 1:4–18). The day of Yahweh is a day of both judgment and vindication, though the latter aspect is only seen clearly in Zephaniah 3. Chapter 1 is carefully structured, using a combination of grammatical repetitions, morphological shifts, inclusions, chiasmi, and temporal markers for transitions. Zephaniah's reuse and reapplication of motifs found elsewhere show that he was conversant with OT literature.

1:1 SUPERSCRIPTION

The phrase "the word of the Lord [Yahweh]," in various forms, occurs in about 250 verses in the OT. With more than eighty-five percent of its occurrences in the prophetic books, this formula is primarily prophetic in nature. It is found most frequently in Jeremiah and Ezekiel, with the latter having an extended formulation.[1]

In addition, this formula occurs in the superscriptions of only ten other books in the OT.[2] Within the XII, only four books – Hosea, Joel, Micah, and Zephaniah – link the prophet's ministry to Israelite or Judahite kings.

This opening superscription authenticates the book by stating the prophet's credentials. More importantly, the word of Yahweh that came to Zephaniah tells us that God had chosen to speak through Zephaniah at the time of King Josiah (640–609 BCE). A prophet was passive until God decided to speak through him at a time God deemed right. Yet, the words given to Zephaniah were written down at some point and transmitted as part of the XII. This means that the word of Yahweh remained relevant to the audiences of the XII even beyond the time of the composition of Zephaniah.

---

1. The extended formula, "And the word of YHWH came to me, saying," is most frequently found in Ezekiel.
2. Jeremiah 1:2; Ezekiel 1:3; Hosea 1:1; Joel 1:1; Jonah 1:1; Micah 1:1; Haggai 1:1; Zechariah 1:1; Malachi 1:1; Ezra 1:1.

Habakkuk and Zephaniah

In the Bible, there are at least four different people who bear the name "Zephaniah" (1 Chr 6:36; Jer 29:29; Zeph 1:1; Zech 6:10). The name means "Yahweh hid" or "Yahweh treasured." At the beginning of the book, the genealogy traces Zephaniah four generations back – which is unusual – to Hezekiah. In 2014, P. G. van der Veen and R. Deutsch published an article presenting a bulla (clay seal) from a private collection in Germany. The inscription on the bulla reads, "[Belonging to] Amaryahu, son of the King."[3] Based on the style of the script and decorative features, the bulla is dated between 725–675 BCE, around the time of Hezekiah's reign. What is interesting is that the name "Amaryahu" could have been Amariah, King Hezekiah's son, who was Zephaniah's great-grandfather (Zeph 1:1). If this connection is indeed true, Zephaniah would have been a royal personage. Since the epithet "king" is absent in this superscription, some discount an undisputed connection to King Hezekiah (compare Hos 1:1; Mic 1:1). However, it could be argued that King Hezekiah was so well-known that a reference to his kingship was unnecessary.

According to Talmudic traditions, this genealogy reflects favorably on the prophet simply as one who came from a righteous line (*b. Megillah* 15a). Others argue that the phrase "the son of Cushi" suggests foreign descent (Deut 23:7–8).[4] No consensus has been reached. Apart from this opening remark, the Bible tells us very little about the prophet Zephaniah.

The mention of Josiah and Hezekiah is significant in two ways in the context of this book. First, these two kings were famous and were rulers who did what was right in the eyes of Yahweh. Both had undertaken extensive religious reforms. King Hezekiah trusted in Yahweh, kept the commands of Moses, and was successful in all he did. Moreover, Hezekiah had defeated the Philistines, who were among those indicted in Zephaniah (2 Kgs 18:1–8; compare Zeph 2:4–5). Likewise, Josiah did what was right in the eyes of Yahweh. He renovated the temple, renewed the covenant, and eliminated idol worship in Jerusalem (2 Kgs 22:1–23:28).

The second reason that references to Hezekiah and Josiah are significant is that the reforms of both these kings were short-lived and, by the next generation, had failed (2 Kgs 21:1–9; 23:31–32). In fact, Hezekiah's son, Manasseh, had swung so far to the other end that his decadence and sin were

---

3. Pieter Gert van der Veen and Dr. Robert Deutsch, "The Bulla of 'Amaryahu Son of the King, the Ancestor of the Prophet Zephaniah?" in *Bible et Proche-Orient. Mélanges André Lemaire III*, eds. J. Elayi and J. M. Durand, *Transeu* 46 (Paris: Gabalda, 2014), 121–132, [Pl. IX].
4. Coggins and Han, *Six Minor Prophets*, 100–101.

singled out as reasons for God's destruction of Judah (2 Kgs 24:3).[5] Manasseh had erected altars for Baal and Asherah, while simultaneously building altars in Yahweh's temple (2 Chr 33:3–5). Even though the Josianic reforms were national and extensive, the reigns of subsequent kings proved that no real change had taken place.

The references to Hezekiah and Josiah in Zephaniah can thus be read both positively and negatively. Positively, in the sense that both kings did well in the eyes of God. If written just before the Josianic reforms, the book of Zephaniah might have been written to support these reforms. If so, the paraenetic unit in 2:1–3 would be a key exhortation of the book. But if written after the reforms, Zephaniah could be read negatively, suggesting that the reforms had failed, and that judgment awaited Judah.

What is important in Zephaniah is God's work of transforming Jerusalem and his people by his righteousness when all human efforts had failed. Zephaniah identifies a hope beyond any religious or national reforms: Only Yahweh's transforming righteousness truly saves. This transformation is seen from 3:5 onward, which stands in contrast to the rebellious city prior to 3:5. So, the superscription and the context of the book of Zephaniah invite hearers to read hope into Jerusalem's situation in and beyond the Babylonian invasion. Within the horizon of the XII, Zephaniah directs readers' attention to the theological hope that Yahweh alone can deliver.

1:2–3 YAHWEH GATHERS THE EARTH

These two verses form a unit because of their universality in scope, parallelism ("I will sweep"), and the use of the *inclusio* "face of the earth." We find a comprehensive list of creatures representing all biospheres – land ("man and beast"), air ("birds"), and sea ("fish").

As the book begins, Yahweh's speech is in the first person, a strong personal voice with an emphatic verbal construction: "I will sweep."[6] The underlying Hebrew lexeme (*'sp*) has a relatively wide semantic range – for example, gather,

---

[5]. The Chronicler's evaluation of Manasseh is more positive. See 2 Chronicles 33:13.
[6]. The construction is a Hebrew infinite absolute followed by an imperfective verb of the same root. The Hebrew infinitive absolute has no English equivalent. A similar phrasing in Micah 2:12 is more consistent grammatically with a clear Qal imperfect first-person verb following the infinitive absolute (*asop e-esop*). The one found here in Zephaniah 1:2 is grammatically difficult. Nonetheless, the Septuagint supports reading the imperfect verb with the same root as the infinitive absolute. Sweeney argues that the finite verbal form following the infinitive *asop* is of a different root: *swp* ("to destroy"), though he recognizes the use of another finite verb following an infinitive absolute is rare (Jer 8:13, Isa 28:28, and 2 Sam 1:6). Sweeney, *Zephaniah*, 58–61.

remove, destroy, and collect. These opening verses echo Jeremiah 8:13–14. When Zephaniah 1:2–3 is read immediately after the last few verses of Habakkuk, it seems that the editor of the text was aware that the book of Zephaniah follows Habakkuk in the XII. Compare the texts below:

> ¹⁷Though the fig tree does not bud
>   and there are no grapes on the vines,
> though the olive crop fails
>   and the fields produce no food,
> though there are no sheep in the pen
>   and no cattle in the stalls,
> ¹⁸yet I will rejoice in the Lord,
>   I will be joyful in God my Savior. (Hab 3:17)
>
> ²"I will sweep away [*asop asep*] everything
>   from the face of the earth,"
>   declares the Lord.
> ³"I will sweep away [*asep*] both man and beast;
>   I will sweep away [*asep*] the birds in the sky
>   and the fish in the sea –
>   and the idols that cause the wicked to stumble.
>
> When I destroy all mankind
>   on the face of the earth,"
>   declares the Lord. (Zeph 1:2–3)

¹ "At that time . . .
¹³I will take away [*asop asipem*[7]] their harvest,
  declares the Lord.
  There will be no grapes on the vine.
There will be no figs on the tree,
  and their leaves will wither.
What I have given them
  Will be taken from them."
¹⁴Why are we sitting here?
  Gather together! [*he-asepu*]
Let us flee to the fortified cities
  and perish there!

---

7. The underlying Hebrew is similar to Zephaniah 2:2, where there is first an infinitive absolute form followed by a first-person Qal imperfect verb of the same root.

> For the LORD our God has doomed us to perish
> and given us poisoned water to drink,
> because we have sinned against him. (Jer 8:1, 13–14)

Besides the use of the word "gather" and the motif of crop failure, Jeremiah 8:1 uses the formulaic "at that time" (compare Zeph 1:12; 3:19–20) and "declares the LORD" (compare Zeph 1:2–3, 10). Jeremiah 8 also emphasizes the sin and rebellion of the city of Jerusalem and her refusal to repent, thereby leading to crop failure and invasion by foreign powers, with Babylon in view. Thus, Jeremiah 8 parallels Zephaniah 1 semantically, seeing the inescapability of Jerusalem's destruction because of God's judgment.

The phrase "from the face of the earth" or "ground" – which occurs thirteen times (in its Hebrew form) in the OT[8] – is, in almost every instance, used in connection with God's judgment of his people or of sinners of the earth. And in every instance, Yahweh is the subject or indirect subject. It is especially poignant that this phrase, in this exact format, is found in the contexts of the judgment of Cain and the flood story in Noah's time. Within the prophetic books, all instances of this phrase occur in the context of God's judgment of the wickedness of Israel or Judah (Jer 28:16; Amos 9:8; Zeph 1:2–3). Zephaniah was clearly conversant with the language of universal judgment in OT texts.

A connection can be made to Genesis with the references to the biospheres of creation (sea, land, air). Three phrases, "birds in the sky," "fish in the sea," and "animals/beasts [on the face of the earth]" form a "merism" of sorts that indicates the totality of where life is sustained. These three realms, along with their representative creatures, refer to a) the total arena of life under human rule as entrusted by God (Gen 1:26, 28; 9:2), b) the totality of Solomon's knowledge (1 Kgs 4:33), c) the dominion of human beings (Ps 8:6–8), d) the extent of Yahweh's judgment of Israel (Hos 4:3) and her enemies (Ezek 29:5), and e) references to eschatological contexts (Ezek 38:20).

Such a merism, used together with the verb "swept" [*'sp*] in Hosea 4:3, is especially significant for our purposes since it suggests that Zephaniah or the composer of the XII was aware of Hosea's original indictment of Israel which, now applied to Judah, forms a second kind of literary totality – the judgment of the northern and southern kingdoms of Israel, representing the whole of God's people.

---

8. Hebrew: *me-al peeney ha-adamah*. See Genesis 4:14; 6:7; 7:4; 8:8; Exodus 32:12; Deuteronomy 6:15; 1 Samuel 20:15; 1 Kings 9:7; 13:34; Jeremiah 28:16; Amos 9:8; Zephaniah 1:2, 3.

³Because of this the land dries up, and all who live in it waste away; *the beasts of the field, the birds in the sky and the fish in the sea are swept ['sp] away.* (Hos 4:3, emphasis added)

So, right at the beginning of the book, the author of Zephaniah highlights the imminent judgment of God using the language of totality. Next, we have the statement, "the idols that cause the wicked to stumble," which is difficult to translate because the word *makeshelah* – one of the two underlying Hebrew words in this sentence – is a *dis legomenon* (a word occurring only twice in the entire Bible).[9] This word has been variously translated "rubble," "ruins," "heaps," "idolatrous images," or "stumbling block."[10] Consider several different renderings below:

"the idols that cause the wicked to stumble" (NIV)
"and the rubble with the wicked" (ESV)
"And the ruins along with the wicked" (NASB 1995)
"(The idolatrous images of these creatures will be destroyed along with evil people)" (NET)
"I will reduce the wicked to heaps of rubble" (NLT)

While *makeshelah* is difficult to translate, its association with the "wicked" – a word that follows soon after – allows us to render *makeshelah* as something unfavorable, such as stumbling or a ruin. Hence, God's removal of the creatures from the face of the earth is also a removal of ruinous things associated with the wicked.

1:4–16 YAHWEH'S DAY OF JUDGMENT

This large segment (1:4–16) details the day of Yahweh's *judgment* upon Judah/Jerusalem, followed by judgment of the world (1:17–18). This entire unit is a complement to the day of Yahweh's *restoration* in 3:8–20 (see the section above on "The Shape and Message of Zephaniah").

1:4–6 Concerning the Idolaters of Judah/Jerusalem

From verse 4, God's indictment narrows from a universal scope to Judah and "all who live in Jerusalem." The verbs "I will stretch out" and "I will destroy"

---

9. Isaiah 3:6 is the only other location where this lexeme is found. This phrase is missing in the Septuagint.
10. Clines, "הַמַּכְשֵׁלָה," *DCH* 5:275. The verbal form, *kshl*, occurs in Ezekiel 36:15, Malachi 2:8, and Proverbs 4:16. See also Renz, *Nahum, Habakkuk, and Zephaniah*, 461.

(1:4) are Hebrew perfective verbs used prophetically – that is, a future action so certain to happen that it is presented in the past tense.[11] Like verse 4, which uses the preposition "against" (*al*) twice to express God's opposition of Judah/Jerusalem, verse 6 uses the negative (*lo*, NIV, "neither/nor") to highlight the people's turning away from following God. Moreover, within Hebrew anticipatory discourses, the use of perfective verbs and negative particles often indicate unit boundaries.[12]

On further scrutiny, we see a literary symmetry in the choice and use of grammatical forms in these three verses. This symmetry reveals the composer's design or intent. The section begins by using first-person singular verbs to express God's judgment on those who live in Jerusalem (1:4) and ends with third-person plural verbs to express the refusal of those who were addressed to seek or inquire of God (1:6). With verbal forms at both ends, we see a series of five participles[13] at the center, characterizing the deeds of the people living in Jerusalem. The shape of these three verses can be represented as follows:

A		I will stretch out/I will destroy . . .
B		Those who bow down/those who swear/those who turn back . . .
A′		They do not seek/they do not inquire . . .[14]

---

11. In Hebrew grammar, the perfective or imperfective *aspects* are different from the past/future *tenses* as we know them in English. An imperfective aspect, for instance, refers to an ongoing action/event internal to the structure or in relation to the speaker within that particular text. Imperfectives usually make clear the "temporal constituency of the situation," whereas the perfective forms "view a situation as 'one single whole, regardless of its internal complexity.'" Max Rogland, *Alleged Non-Past Uses of Qatal in Classical Hebrew*, SSN 44 (Leiden: Brill, 2003), 7.

The non-perfective use of perfective verbs in Hebrew can sometimes be called the "gnomic," "performative," or "prophetic" use of perfect verbs. By "gnomic" it means an event is not bounded by time (e.g., Prov 31:12). By "performative," it means an "action that is [already] 'performed' by virtue of uttering a speech" (e.g., Deut 26:3). And by "prophetic," it means that future events are "represented as if they have already happened or are immanent" (e.g., Isa 5:13). Christo H. van der Merwe, Jacobus A. Naudé, and Jan H. Kroeze, *A Biblical Hebrew Reference Grammar*. Second Edition (London: T&T Clark, 2017), 159–160. Compare Ronald L. Troxel, "The Problem of Time in Joel," *JBL* 132, no.1 (2013): 77–96.

12. Duane A. Garrett and Jason S. DeRouchie, *A Modern Grammar for Biblical Hebrew* (Nashville: B&H Academic, 2009), 312.

13. A participle is a word that can function like a non-finite verb, noun, or adjective. For instance, consider the simple sentence: "John runs." The following examples include the participle forms of "run": "The running John" (as adjective), or "John is one who is running" (noun), "John is running" (present continuous verb).

14. The structuring reflects the Hebrew text.

The shape of these three verses contrasts what *God would do* to Judah with what *Judah was doing*. The repeated use of participles functions to emphasize the idolatrous Judah/Jerusalem, on which the rest of the chapter expands.

The phrase "I will stretch out my hand" portrays God as a warrior who fights against his enemies. Such terminology, which is found in several significant battles that Israel had fought against foreign nations, might have originated in liturgical texts (Exod 6:6; Deut 4:34; Ps 136:12). In the book of Exodus, Yahweh fights against the Egyptians to deliver Israel from Egypt (14:14–31). The motif of stretching out the hand is also used when Yahweh fought against the Babylonians (Jer 51:25). In Ezekiel, Yahweh promises to "stretch out" his hand for Israel against the Edomites (25:13; 35:3) and the Philistines (25:16). But God's hand is also stretched out against his people when they continue to sin and rebel against him (Jer 6:12). What we see below in Ezekiel 6:13–14 ties in with the historical context underlying Zephaniah 1:4.

> [13]"And they will know that I am the Lord, when their people lie slain among their idols around their altars, on every high hill and on all the mountaintops, under every spreading tree and every leafy oak – places where they offered fragrant incense to all their idols.
>
> [14]And I will stretch out my hand against them and make the land a desolate waste from the desert to Diblah – wherever they live. Then they will know that I am the Lord."

God's wrath was unleashed on his people as they persisted in their worship of idols. Baal and Asherah were Canaanite-Phoenician deities of fertility and weather. Baal was represented by a calf or smiting figure and Asherah by a pole or a feminine figurine with large breasts. These deities were worshiped for crop harvest and reproduction (see my comments on *Baal as a warrior god in Habakkuk 3:3–15*). Israel's worship of Baal and Asherah is found as early as Numbers 25, when Israel had barely left Egypt.[15] Such worship peaked during the time of the Judges (2:11–13) and during the preexilic periods of 1–2 Kings.

After Joshua's time, during the period of the Judges, Israel forgot Yahweh, assimilated the beliefs of the locals, and worshiped Canaanite deities. From a cultic point of view, it is hard to differentiate between Yahwistic and Canaanite worship practices of that time. Some scholars argue that "Baal and Asherah were part of Israel's 'Canaanite' heritage, and the process of the emergence of

---

15. Day, *Yahweh and the Gods*, especially chapter 2.

Israelite monolatry was an issue of Israel's breaking with its own 'Canaanite' past and not simply one of avoiding 'Canaanite neighbors.'"[16] Put differently, at one point, the Israelite religion might have overlapped so much with pagan worship that Yahweh was seen merely as one among El, Baal, Asherah, and other gods.

The Canaanites adopted theophoric (bearing the name of a deity) elements of their local deities into their names and the names of their towns. Baal was worshiped as a localized deity – identified by names such as "Baal-Zebub, the god of Ekron" (2 Kgs 1:2) or "Baal Peor"[17] (Deut 4:3). In the Amarna Letters of the fourteenth century BCE, we find Egyptian-Canaanite governors and princes in the Levant sporting names bearing the names of their gods (technically called "theophoric"), Baal and El. The prince of Pella in the northern Jordan Valley was called "Mut-ba'lu" (meaning "Man of Baal").[18] Even kings were called "Baal." In the seventh century BCE treaty between Esarhaddon and Baal of Tyre, the vassal king of Tyre was named "Baal."[19] Edomite kings also had names with theophoric elements of Baal – for example, "Baal-Hanan" (1 Chr 1:49–50).

The use of theophoric elements in names was also seen among the Israelites. The famous Gideon, who cut down the altar of Baal, was later called "Jerub-Baal" (Judg 6:32).[20] After Gideon's death, people began to set up "Baal-Berith" (literally, "Baal-covenant" or "Lord of the covenant") as their god and built temples for Baal (Judg 8:33; 9:4).[21] Within the horizon of the book of Judges, idol worship flourished whenever a judge died and, at some point, Baal worship gradually developed into a national religion.

---

16. Smith, *The Early History of God*, 7.
17. Mount Peor is in the land of Moab. Other references to Baal as locality deity include Baal Gad (Josh 11:17), Baal Hamon (Song 8:11), Baal Hazor (2 Sam 13:23), Baal Meon (Num 32:28), Baal Perazim (2 Sam 5:18–20), Baal Shalishah (2 Kgs 4:42), Baal Tamar (Judg 20:33–36), and Baal Zephon (Num 33:7).
18. EA No. 256. See Pritchard, *Ancient Near Eastern Texts Relating to the Old Testament*, 486.
19. Pritchard, *Ancient Near Eastern Texts Relating to the Old Testament*, 533–534.
20. Smith argues that at the time of Judges, the cult of Baal was "deemed tolerable by some Israelites." He notes, "In the second millennium, Baal was an epithet of Haddu. Like the name Jerubbaal, the name Rib-Addi means 'may Addu contend.' Judges 7:32 reinterprets the name of Jerubbaal negatively as an anti-Baal name: 'let Baal plead against him because he has thrown down his altar.' The negative interpretation of the name as anti-Baal shows the tradents' assumption that the theophoric element refers to the god Baal." Smith, *The Early History of God*, 45.
21. While "Baal Berith" had been considered a local title for Yahweh, Judges 8:33–34 clearly distinguished Baal and Yahweh. Scott A. Williams "Baal-Berith." *The Lexham Bible Dictionary* (Bellingham: Lexham, 2016).

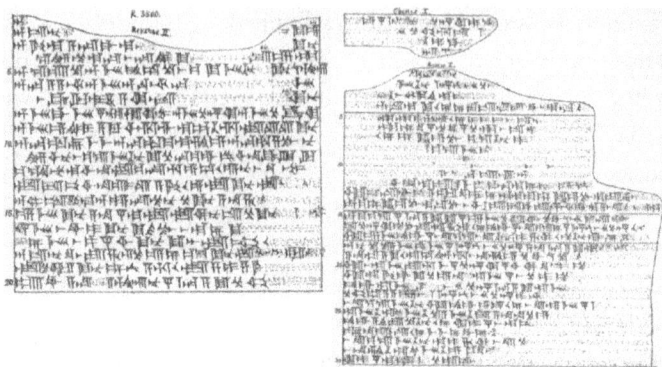

Figure 30: Treaty of Esarhaddon of Assyria and Baal of Tyre
Source: *Altorientalische Forschungen, II* (1898); Transcription by Hugo Winckler; https://commons.wikimedia.org/wiki/File:Treaty_of_Esarhaddon_with_Baal_of_Tyre_(K_3500_%2B_K_4444_%2B_K_10235).png

By the time of Saul, names with theophoric elements of Baal and Yahweh were seen even within the same family – for example, "Esh-Baal," "Merib-Baal," "J[eh]o-nathan," or "Micah," a shortened form of Micha-el (1 Chr 5:5, 8; 8:30, 33, 34; 9:39–40). But "Baal" could also mean "lord" or "master," and this term was sometimes applied to Yahweh. For instance, "Esh-baal" can mean "a man of the LORD [Yahweh]."

King Ahab married Jezebel, a Baal worshiper, and served and worshiped Baal and even built a temple for Baal (1 Kgs 16:31–32), thereby violating Yahweh's command not to serve other gods (Deut 7:1–4). Under Ahab, there were organized prophets of Baal (1 Kgs 18:22–25).[22] If the phrase "remnant of Baal worship in this place" (Zeph 1:4) is indicative of the situation of Judah and the Jerusalem temple *after* the Josianic reforms, we have a more negative reading of Zephaniah since this means that the reforms had failed and the book thus sought to prepare readers for the impending judgment.

The expression "starry host" in 1:5 (literally, "hosts of the heavens") does not occur very often in the Bible. This term is associated primarily with a) Yahweh's creation and control over the constellations of stars (Neh 9:6; Ps 33:6; Isa 34:4; 40:26; 45:12) or b) the worship of Baal and Asherah (2 Kgs 17:16;

---

22. Some scholars suggest that the indictment and condemnation of Baal worship is a late phenomenon at the time of the kings, and in earlier references, such as the book of Judges, one must consider earlier/later redactional layers. Smith argues that a late redaction of Judges puts Baal/Asherah worship in a negative light. Smith, *The Early History of God*, 47.

21:3–5; 23:4–5; 2 Chr 33:3–5; Jer 19:13), with the latter taking place mainly during the time of the Assyrian invasion (2 Kgs 17:3–6), the decadent reign of Manasseh of Judah (2 Kgs 21:1–18), and at the time of Josiah's reform (2 Kgs 23:1–28; Jer 19:13; Zeph 1:5).

"Milcom" (*milekom*) or "Molek" (1:5)[23] refers to the national god of the Transjordanian Ammonites (compare 1 Kgs 11:5, 33; 2 Kgs 23:13), though some scholars suggest that Molek was the name of a sacrifice.[24] Molek was clearly associated with the child sacrifice practiced at Tophet and the valley of Hinnom, a cultic practice that God vehemently condemned (Lev 18:21; 20:2–5; 2 Kgs 23:10; Jer 7:31–32). The worship of Molek as a deity of the underworld had already been established by the time of King Ahaz and continued until the exile. Like Baal, Molek (Milcom) also appeared as a theophoric element in names.[25]

In 1:4–6, we see two phenomena at work. Not only is there a condemnation of those who had turned away from Yahweh to the worship of Baal and Molek (also to Asherah and the starry hosts), but the condemnation was also of those who worshiped Yahweh among other gods in a syncretistic manner. Verse 6 shows that people were no longer seeking or inquiring of Yahweh. The two verbs ("seek," "inquire") used in 1:6 are in the negative. This is likely intentional as they contrast with the same two main verbs in Deuteronomy 4, where a new generation of Israel was to "seek" (*bqsh*, *drsh*) Yahweh:

> [29]But if from there you seek [*bqsh*] the LORD your God, you will find him if you seek [*drsh*] him with all your heart and with all your soul. [30]When you are in distress and all these things have happened to you, then in later days you will return to the LORD your God and obey him. [31]For the LORD your God is a merciful God; he will not abandon or destroy you or forget the covenant with your ancestors, which he confirmed to them by oath. (Deut 4:29–31)

---

23. There are debates on whether 1:5 can be translated as "who are sworn to YHWH and who are sworn by their king." Jason Radine, "The 'Idolatrous Priest' in the Book of Zephaniah," in *Priests and Cults in the Book of the Twelve*, ed. Lena-Sofia Tiemeyer, ANEM 14 (Atlanta: SBL Press, 2016), 131–148, [134]. For more information about the forms of the names of Molech/Milcom, see George C. Heider, *Cult of Molek: A Reassessment*, eds. David J. A. Clines, Philip R. Davies, JSOTSup 43 (Sheffield: JSOT Press, 2009), especially chapter 4.
24. Day, citing Otto Eissfeldt, in *Yahweh and the Gods*, 209.
25. Inscribed on an Ammonite seal, we find the name, "Milkomur," a servant of King Baalis (Jer 40:14). Millard, *Peoples*, 312.

Deuteronomy 4:29 recalls the Shema and the greatest commandment to "love the LORD your God with all your heart and with all your soul and with all your strength" (Deut 6:5). This was also the instruction that David, as he lay on his deathbed, gave Solomon (1 Chr 28:9). There are impressive intertextual connections between Zephaniah and Deuteronomy.[26] Zephaniah might have had Deuteronomy 4:29 in mind since his use of the negative forms of "seek" and "inquire" in verse 6 highlight the covenantal unfaithfulness of Judah/Jerusalem and their rejection of Yahweh.

Significant Deuteronomic references (especially Deuteronomy 28) in Zephaniah suggest that the latter is a prophetic evaluation and indictment of the people's culpability. In the Deuteronomic History (an academic proposition that the books of Deuteronomy, Joshua, Judges, and Kings are a single work), the verb "inquire" or "consult" (*drsh*) has been used to evaluate kings and people of Israel and Judah. A king who inquired (*drsh*) of Yahweh – rather than of other gods – was doing what was right in the eyes of God (2 Chr 6:4–5). But a king who consulted other gods was guilty of evil (2 Kgs 1:16). Thus, we can say that Zephaniah's use of "inquire" (*drsh*) sought to highlight the negative assessment of Judah/Jerusalem at the time of Josiah, just as the kings of Israel and Judah had done what was evil in the eyes of God.

1:7–13 Concerning the Rebellious Judah/Jerusalem

In Zephaniah, the call to be "silent" (*has*) is a call to submissive anticipation of God, who would come to judge and punish. This same word is used at the end of Habakkuk 2, just before God's appearance in chapter 3 as a warrior who fights for his people. In Zephaniah 1:7, the silent anticipation is for a specific "day," though this is more like an unspecified period of time than a 24-hour day. This command to be silent should probably be interpreted as a call to reverence and attention in view of the impending arrival of a king. All actions, especially unbridled decadent revelry, must cease.

I recall my time as a recruit during my national service in the Singapore Armed Forces. Whenever a senior officer or trainer entered the trainees' room, the first person who noticed him would shout, "Room!" Everyone in the room would have to freeze and remain silent regardless of what they were

---

26. Consider the parallels noted by Robertson: Zephaniah 1:13 // Deuteronomy 28:30; Zephaniah 1:13 // Deuteronomy 28:39; Zephaniah 1:15 // Deuteronomy 28:53, 55, 57; Zephaniah 1:17 // Deuteronomy 28:29; Zephaniah 1:18 // Deuteronomy 32:21–22; Zephaniah 3:5 // Deuteronomy 32:4; Zephaniah 3:17 // Deuteronomy 28:63; 30:9; Zephaniah 3:19–20 // Deuteronomy 26:19. Robertson, *The Books of Nahum, Habakkuk, and Zephaniah*, 254–255.

doing until permission was given to "carry on!" No matter how awkward our posture, we had to stay perfectly still while the officer inspected the room. The officer would call out any recruit who did something unauthorized, and that recruit – and sometimes all the recruits in the room – would be punished. Perhaps Zephaniah's call for silence was similar to this call "Room!" When Yahweh arrives, he will call to attention everyone and question those who have transgressed his commands.

The day of Yahweh, introduced in verse 7, is the focus of the rest of the chapter. This special "day" has been studied extensively, and scholars believe that its origins are connected to Jewish feasts, which included the autumn festival of the Day of Atonement (*Yom Kippur*) – which marks God's forgiveness – and the Festival of Booths or Tabernacle (*Sukkot*)[27] – which commemorates Israel's wilderness wanderings and their entry into the promised land. Coinciding with the annual rainy season, these appointed times also symbolized the period of renewal and transition as the harvest season ended and new crops were planted. The combination of the acts of offerings, consecration, and feasting on such festivals could explain the connection between that "day" and the sacrifices in 1:7–8.[28]

In this text unit (1:7–10), there are four references to a specific "day" and one reference to "time" (1:12), which is another temporal marker. Each of these temporal references functions as a *transition marker* that opens a subunit of text. Five such subunits describe five different groups of people who are addressed either positively or negatively. In verse 7, we have the first reference to the "day of the Lord" (1:7b) – and these are the only addressees who are mentioned positively. They were those whom Yahweh had "consecrated" and "invited" (1:7d). This group consisted of those who would feast on the sacrifice that Yahweh had prepared. The second "day" is found in verse 8.[29] Here, the addressees are the officials, the king's sons, and those dressed in foreign clothes. These people belonged to the upper echelons of Judean society. "Those who dressed in foreign clothes" probably refers to foreigners who ruled over or traded with Judah.[30] By their social status, the second group were supposedly participants at the feasts, but they had rejected Yahweh. Therefore, instead of feasting with Yahweh, they would be punished.

---

27. Sweeney, *Zephaniah*, 52.
28. Sacrifices are also connected with idol worship (Hos 4:14).
29. The "to-be" verb, *wehayah*, at the beginning of verse 8, functions as a transition marker. The same verb functioning as a transition marker also occurs in 1:10 and 12.
30. Sweeney, *Zephaniah*, 76.

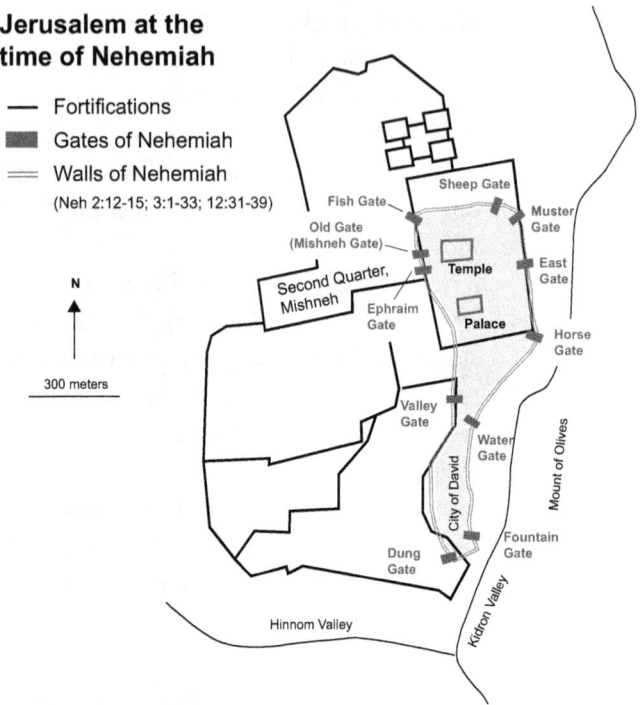

Figure 31: City Walls and Gates at the Time of Nehemiah

The third "day" is found in verse 9, which parallels verse 8. The subject of these two verses is Yahweh and the object are those who were identified by masculine plural participles ("all who" or "who") – is those who were idolaters, violent, and deceitful. The unusual phrase "avoid stepping over the threshold" might be a reference to adoption of the foreign practice of the priests of Dagon, who did not step on the threshold of the temple of Dagon as a sign of respect. The background of this practice can be traced to 1 Samuel 5:4–5, where the image of Dagon lay fallen before the ark of God, and Dagon's head and arms were broken off and laid on the temple's threshold.

The fourth "day," in verse 10, identifies the inhabitants and merchants of Jerusalem and the surrounding hills. The "Fish Gate" was a city gate at the northwestern corner of Jerusalem, mentioned only in three other places in the Bible. It was rebuilt by Manasseh (2 Chr 33:14) and rebuilt again at the time of Nehemiah (Neh 3:3) and was located along the route where the procession of thanksgiving passed through at the dedication of the Jerusalem walls (Neh 12:39).

The "New Quarter" – also known as the "Mishneh" – was possibly a residential district for court officials and the elite, and it was situated to the west of the temple and the city of David. The prophetess Huldah and her husband, Shallum, had lived in the New Quarter (2 Kgs 22:14; 2 Chr 34:22).

Zephaniah 1:10–11 has a parallel and symmetrical structure and centered by an imperative "wail" at 1:11a (see below). The first half of this structure (A-B-C) has three parallel clauses, each carrying a sound from a specific location (for example, "wailing from the New Quarter"). These three clauses are all verbless, and the locations are all introduced with the preposition "from." In the second half of the structure (A′-B′-C′), three verbs are applied to three groups of people.

A	A cry will go up	from the Fish Gate,
B	Wailing	from the New Quarter,
C	A loud crash	from the hills.

A′	Wail	you who live in the market district;
B′	[they] will be wiped out	all your merchants,[31]
C′	[they] will be destroyed	all who trade with silver.

The parallel construction of these lines suggests that they were composed as a unit under the fourth "day." As a parallel unit, these two verses confirm the delimitation for text units introduced by the markers "day" or "time," which were referred to earlier. Note that the locations and addressees refer to the same *kind* of people – those who were economically prosperous through trade and had become complacent. Despite living beside the temple, these people no longer depended on Yahweh but relied on silver and gold as their gods.

The last unit begins with the transition marker "time" rather than "day." Like the previous unit, these two verses (1:12–13) are carefully shaped, forming two subunits, each with a pair of syntactical parallel lines. A visual depiction is given below.

A	I will search	Jerusalem with lamps
A′	and [I will] punish	those who are complacent,
B		who are like wine left on its dregs,
B′		who think,

---

31. Note that this is the literal syntax in Hebrew, where the verb comes first. Note that B′ and C′ use passive (Niphal) verbal forms.

C	'The LORD will	do nothing, either good or bad.'
D	<u>Their</u> wealth	will be plundered,
D′	<u>their</u> houses	demolished.
E	<u>Though</u> they build houses,	they will <u>not</u> live in them;
E′	<u>though</u> they plant vineyards,	they will <u>not</u> drink the wine.

The first half (1:12) consists of five clauses (AA′BB′C) and collectively speaks of what God would do to those who dwelled in Jerusalem – that is, those who were complacent and reveled in debauchery. In lines A-A′, Yahweh is the first-person subject of the verbs "search" and "punish." The second half (1:13) refers to "Jerusalem" and "those who are complacent" (1:12) as the object of the verbs. In this way, lines A-A′ are syntactical parallels.

Lines B-B′-C, which are verbless, expand on the object – "who are like wine left on its dregs" (B)[32] and "who think" (B′) that "the LORD will do nothing, either good or bad" (C). Besides being the only reported statement in this chapter, line C deviates from the surrounding lines in word length and its use of a negative. These deviations are intended to create an asymmetrical element in otherwise consistent parallel lines. This asymmetry functions as the pivoting center of the entire unit (1:12–13), where the focus is on the people's nonchalant indulgences.

In the second half of the text unit (1:13), we see two more pairs of parallel lines (D-D′-E-E′). These four lines, as a whole, describe the outcomes of those referred to by the third person pronouns ("their," "they") because of God's punishment. Lines D-D′ are syntactical and semantic parallels. The noun "wealth" parallels "houses," while the passive verbs "plundered" and "demolished" are situated at the end of the lines.[33] Lines E-E′ are syntactic and semantic parallels. Each half-line has a verb and begins with a Hebrew conjunction – translated here as a concessive "though" (NIV) in the first half of the line or a contrastive "but" (NASB 1995) in the second half of each line. Note also that the second half of lines E-E′ consist of parallel negative particles.

In these four lines (1:13), we see a pronouncement of judgment on the wealthy and complacent identified above. The pivoting center at the end of 1:12 highlights the reason for this. These complacent and wealthy people in

---

32. This phrase is difficult because of a rare word in the phrase. NASB has "who are stagnant in spirit," NLT has "in their sins," and ESV left it untranslated altogether.
33. In the Hebrew, the second half of each line has a prefix preposition *lamed*.

Jerusalem thought that life was "business as usual." Because of their economic wealth and their proximity to the temple and the Davidic city, they wrongly believed that they were unshakable. But this complacency had turned them away from Yahweh. All that they had would be taken from them "at that time."

> ## WHO WILL GOD CONDEMN ON THAT DAY?
>
> It is helpful to pause at this point to reflect on how this chapter has developed and consider how it relates to us. In Zephaniah 1, we see a shift in how the indicted are characterized – from a more general "wicked" and "all mankind" (1:3) to more specific descriptions such as worshipers of Baal or Molech, idolatrous priests, and backsliders (1:4–6). From our vantage point, we may find it difficult to relate to such people since they are culturally and religiously far from us. But we can relate to those described in 1:7–13. Judgment will fall on those who are complacent, those who revel in drunkenness, and those who arrogantly assume that they are economically and socially secure.
>
> These descriptions are closer to home since we are familiar with such situations. We may know people who think they are saved because they have it all – a solid bank account and a freehold property. They may think they are secure and assume that God "will do nothing either good or bad." God only matters to them on Sundays.
>
>
>
> **Figure 32: The Developing Scope of God's Judgment**

This development in Zephaniah 1 of the characterization of God's judgment and indictment is important because it gradually uncovers our rebellion of the heart – taking us from a distant and hard-to-grasp description to a more recognizable but still "others-but-not-me" category and then, finally, to seeing that "I am like one among them." In other words, the more we read Zephaniah, the more we can relate to the prophet's indictments and condemnations. Few of us can name a worshiper of Baal or Molek among us, but almost everyone knows someone who is complacent about their faith because of their economic or social standing.

> Paul says, in 1 Corinthians 10:12, "So, if you think you are standing firm, be careful that you don't fall!" This is a much-needed reminder today as we repeatedly see prominent Christian figures fall from grace.[1]

Do we have leaders or members who live in the "New Quarter" (see our earlier discussion of Mishneh, Zeph 1:10) of our time? Is church something we do on one day of the week? Do we, too, think that "the LORD will do nothing, either good or bad"?

Singapore ranks fifth on the list of the world's wealthiest cities. It has 249,800 millionaires, the second-highest number after Tokyo.[2] And this tiny nation was caricatured in the movie "Crazy Rich Asians," with a scene portraying several rich Singaporean women studying the book of Ephesians.[3] As a critique, the scene juxtaposed opulent prosperity and surface piety in a storyline where the rich disdained the have-nots (of course, what is typical in a movie is that the protagonists are the antithesis of this stereotype). But all caricature is based on some form of reality. Guna Raman, a pastor of Agape Baptist Church, had this to say when interviewed by *The Gospel Coalition*:

> Singapore has become very affluent in the last 30 years, largely due to the government's pragmatic thinking. By and large, Singaporeans don't care for what is of intrinsic value as opposed to what works and can bring in more money, more success, more comfort, and more convenience. This approach has spilled into the church. Churches in Singapore tend toward the easy and comfortable life. The nation has not seen a major catastrophe (except for SARS for a brief period in 2003) or a major economic downturn. As result, many Christians here are averse to suffering. Many believe God is a god of love but not of wrath. There is little understanding of the doctrine of sin and, therefore, little appreciation for the work of the cross and the grace that comes

to us from the finished work of Christ. Christians are often more interested in a god of healing and a god of blessing than the God of the Bible.[4]

While there are exceptions to these characterizations, Raman's reflection on the affluence of the Singaporean church is spot-on. When we are wealthy, we tend to become complacent. We find it hard not to flaunt our wealth. Such odious flaunting is often *rationalized* as being a matter of personal tastes. We *rationalize* it as enjoyment we deserve.

When we have ample resources, we fool ourselves into believing that these are a mighty fortress that will protect and provide for us (Prov 18:11). But the righteous, whether rich or poor, find safety in the name of Yahweh, the only true fortified tower (Prov 18:10). If we look to wealth – or anything else apart from God – for our protection, we turn to it as an idol. Soon that idol becomes the instrument we use to justify our moral lapses and, eventually, God becomes irrelevant. To be sure, complacency need not be contingent on one's wealth. Anyone can be complacent. And complacency, like religious hypocrisy, is odious to God.

Whom will God condemn on "that day"? Zephaniah's focus on the aristocracy of Jerusalem, the ruling elite of Judah, priests, and royal personages is telling. The day of Yahweh is a day of judgment for those who appear to be blessed by God but no longer walk humbly with God. Outwardly, these people may look good to the community, but their hearts are far away from God (Jer 12:2). As Isaiah says: "These people come near to me with their mouth and honor me with their lips, but their hearts are far from me. Their worship of me is based on merely human rules they have been taught" (Isa 29:13; see also Jer 12:2). The complacent among us must take note!

When the rich young man came to Jesus asking how he might inherit eternal life, Jesus mentioned five of the six commandments related to relationships with others that are found in the Ten Commandments: "You shall not commit adultery, you shall not murder, you shall not steal, you shall not give false testimony, honor your father and mother" (Luke 18:20). The only commandment among the six that Jesus did not cite was, "You shall not covet" (Exod 20:17). As the conversation continued, Jesus told the young man, "Sell everything you have and give to the poor, and you will have treasure in heaven. Then come, follow me" (18:22). But the rich young man went away sad. He could not do what Jesus asked. And Jesus remarked, "How hard it is for the rich to enter the kingdom of God" (18:24). It is striking that so many of us have tried to become richer on earth without acknowledging that this may also make it harder to enter the kingdom of God. The lie we choose to believe is that we can serve both God and money. But the heart of the gospel is, essentially, this: "For whoever wants to save their life will lose it, but whoever loses their life for [Jesus Christ] and for the gospel will save it" (Mark 8:35).

---

1. "A fall from grace: These pastors resigned, were fired or accused of 'unholy' acts," USA Today, March 25, 2022, https://www.usatoday.com/picture-gallery/news/nation/2022/03/25/pastors-accused-of-bad-things/7141693001/.
2. Andrew Amoils, "The 20 Wealthiest Cities in the World for 2022," Henley & Partners, https://www.henleyglobal.com/publications/henley-global-citizens-report/2022-q3/global-insights/20-wealthiest-cities-world-2022.
3. The house in that scene is actually in Malaysia. Eleanor Gibson, "Crazy Rich Asians house represents region's changing taste, says architect," dezeen, September 21, 2018, https://www.dezeen.com/2018/09/21/interview-crazy-rich-asians-movie-architect-stephanie-maignan-be-landa-house/.
4. Brett McCracken, "How the Gospel Takes Root in 'Crazy Rich' Singapore," Faith & Work, TGC, September 24, 2018, https://www.thegospelcoalition.org/article/gospel-takes-root-crazy-rich-singapore/.

1:14–16 Concerning the Cities

The day of Yahweh – introduced in verse 7 – is the main topic in this unit (1:14–16). These three verses contain an impressive series of eleven verbless clauses that focus on the day of Yahweh.[34] Verse 14 is made up of two poetic bicolons (a bicolon is two short clauses that form a unit) that introduce the day of Yahweh. Based on how these verses are structured, the emphasis is on the *nearness* and the *outcry* on the day of the LORD, which will be imminent and horrifying. Yahweh, portrayed here as a warrior in battle (1:14), recalls Habakkuk 3:3–15, where God is described as a warrior. But who was Yahweh fighting against? Given the context, Yahweh was leading a battle against the people indicted in the earlier verses (compare 1:12–13 and 1:16–18).

The vivid descriptions in the text are accompanied by aural ones. The text invites the reader to hear the tumult of an army closing in. The call to silent anticipation of that day (1:7) is a contrast to the bitter uproar on the arrival of that day (1:14). We can almost hear the battle cries, the shouts of

---

34. There is only one active participle at the end of verse 14 that describes the continuous action of the "Mighty Warrior." NIV's capitalization of the words "Mighty Warrior" means that the translators had interpreted the warrior as Yahweh, in parallel to the "LORD" of the previous clause.

the soldiers, trumpet blasts, thunder, the rumble-tumble of troop movements, the shattering of fortifications, destruction of city walls, clanging of swords, spears, and shields, and human beings howling in fear, anguish, pain, and death (1:10–11). There will also be the crackling fires of destruction. Perhaps we can also smell the stench of sweat, blood, soil, rust, and rotting death (1:15–16). This is the day of Yahweh!

As noted earlier, the book of Zephaniah has the second highest frequency of the phrase "the day of the LORD" (including its variants) per thousand words in the Bible. Zephaniah 1:15–16 alone contains seven references to that "day," each linked to a descriptive noun or pronoun.[35] These descriptions have been chosen to tingle the ears of those who could hear the phonological and syntactical parallels. The "day of [God's] wrath" (*eberah*) in verse 15 has several parallels in the OT, including the day of "anger" (Lam 2:21–22; Zeph 2:3), "fierce anger" (Isa 13:9; Lam 1:12; Zeph 2:2; 3:8), "a cruel day" (Isa 13:9), "jealousy" or "jealous anger" (Zeph 1:18; 3:8), "day of vengeance" (Jer 46:10), "day of wrath" (Ezek 22:24), "panic" (Ezek 7:7), and a "dreadful day" (Mal 4:5).[36] These images highlight the physical, psychological, and emotional misery that come with the destruction of God's enemies.

Consider an example of phonological and syntactical parallel lines below:[37]

A day (*yom*) of distress (*tsarah*)[38] and anguish (*u-metsuqah*),[39]
A day (*yom*) of trouble (*shoah*)[40] and ruin (*u-meshoah*).[41]

The next pair of parallel lines – "a day of darkness and gloom, a day of clouds and blackness" – reflect, verbatim, the text of Joel 2:2.[42] This imagery of the cloud of blackness recalls the theophany of Yahweh at Mount Sinai (Deut

---

35. Grammarians call such constructions the genitive-construct state, where the supporting noun modifies the "day" (e.g., "day" + "wrath" = "the day of wrath").
36. Ralph W. Klein, "Day of the Lord," *CTM* 39, no. 8 (1968): 517–525, [517, 521].
37. For the Hebrew enthusiasts note that the Hebrew construct noun (supported) governs two absolute nouns (supporting). So, in 1:15, we have, "a day [*yom*, construct noun] of trouble [*shoah*, absolute noun] and ruin [*umeshoah*, second absolute noun]." This is uncommon. Merwe, Naudé, and Kroeze, *Biblical Hebrew Reference Grammar*, 224.
38. On the word, "distress," see Isaiah 37:3; Jeremiah 16:19; Obadiah 12, 14; Nahum 1:7; Habakkuk 3:16.
39. On the word "anguish," see Job 15:24; Psalm 107:28.
40. On the word, "trouble," see Isaiah 10:3; 47:11. The Jewish Holocaust is based on the same Hebrew word with the prefixed article, *HaShoah*. We can also use the translation, "catastrophe."
41. On the word, "ruin," see Job 30:3; 38:27. This word is rare, occurring only twice elsewhere.
42. See also Job 15:23; Ecclesiastes 11:8.

4:11; 5:22; Ps 97:2). In the Bible, the word "blackness" is always associated with Yahweh's theophanies.[43]

Finally, verse 16 refers to a "day of trumpet" and "battle cry," which recall God's appointed times for special days or feasts, as well as calls for the tribes to move in the wilderness and to battle – for example, the blowing of the trumpet and the fall of Jericho (Josh 6:1–22).[44] The "trumpet" and "cry" were also connected to festal celebrations for victory, the reestablishment of the temple, and the praise of God (Ezra 3:11, 13; Pss 27:6, 89:16; 150:6). Zephaniah speaks of a war cry that would accompany the warrior God when he went into battle – and like the ark that went ahead at Jericho – Yahweh led the troops.

Toward the end of this text unit, we see two parallel clauses – "against the fortified cities" and "against the corner towers" (1:16). High walls enclosed fortified cities, and entry into the city was only possible through heavily defended gates. The "corner towers" in Jerusalem were strategic high fortifications along the walls and provided a good view. These places were an excellent vantage point for watchmen and archers, thereby providing leverage against siege invaders. These towers also housed devices and contraptions that could hurl great stones (2 Chr 26:15). Extended outward from the walls, these towers offered additional angles of attack in a siege. On the day of Yahweh, he would move against these constructions, though it is unclear whose fortifications these were – while they could belong to foreign nations, it seems more likely, in the immediate context, that these were Judah's.

The day of Yahweh will be a day of both judgment and vindication. Judgment is emphasized here in chapter 1, while chapter 3 focuses on vindication. God's judgment will not be directed only against Judah/Jerusalem but also against all who sin against Yahweh (1:17–18). Therefore, the day of Yahweh can be interpreted as both near and far, past and future. That is, the destruction can be seen either as the imminent invasion of Judah and surrounding cities by Babylon as a past event (Lam 1:12; 2:1–3); it could also include Babylon's judgment at some point in the future.

---

43. See Exodus 20:21; Deuteronomy 4:11; 5:22; 2 Samuel 22:10; 1 Kings 8:12; 2 Chronicles 6:1; Job 22:13; 38:9; Psalms 18:10; 97:2; Isaiah 60:2; Jeremiah 13:16; Ezekiel 34:12; Joel 2:2; Zephaniah 1:15.
44. Klein, "Day of the Lord," 517.

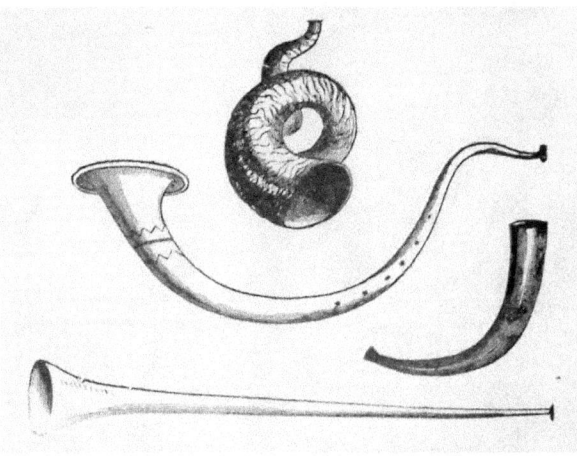

Figure 33: Trumpets of Numbers 10
By illustrators of the 1890 Holman Bible
Public Domain: https://commons.wikimedia.org/wiki/File:Holman_Trumpets.jpg

Figure 34: The Great Day of His Wrath (ca. 1851)
Painting by John Martin
Public Domain: https://commons.wikimedia.org/wiki/
File:MARTIN_John_Great_Day_of_His_Wrath.jpg

Figure 35: Northeastern Corner Tower of David
(Phasael or Hippicus) in Jerusalem
Photo by Pazit Polak
Wikimedia Common: https://commons.wikimedia.org/
wiki/File:Jerusalem_047_(2458082819).jpg

In the OT, Yahweh's manifestations to his people brought judgment or deliverance (Amos 5:18–20).[45] According to Aernie and Hartley, these manifestations of Yahweh were

> a typological pattern pointing to the final eschatological day of the Lord, when God would return and ultimately set things right

---

45. Martin Leuenberger, "Day of the Lord," in *Oxford Encyclopedia of the Bible and Theology*, S. E. Balentine, ed. (Oxford: Oxford University Press, 2015), 200–203.

once and for all. Consequently, the day of the Lord will either be a day of celebration that God's people should joyfully anticipate or will be a day of great fear and trepidation, when God will enact final vengeance on those who oppose him.[46]

In the NT, Paul's encounter with the risen Jesus on the road to Damascus helped him to understand "that Jesus fulfills the role as consummate Judge to whom all must give an account at the final assize. The day of the Lord Jesus is the final court day when all will appear before his judgment bench, where he will render the final verdicts (2 Cor 5:10)."[47] For Paul, the "day of the Lord" had become the coming "day of our Lord Jesus Christ" (1 Cor 1:8; see also 2 Cor 1:14; Phil 1:6, 10; 1 Thess 5:4; 2 Thess 2:1) because all God's fullness dwells in bodily form in Christ (Col 1:19; 2:9). This eschatological understanding of the coming day of Jesus Christ is also a key message in the General Epistles (1 Pet 1:7, 13; 2 Pet 1:16) and Revelation (22:20). The proclamation of the day of Yahweh in the OT and the day of Jesus Christ in the NT thus has a critical and exhortative function.

Klein's concluding reflection on the day of Yahweh puts this into perspective:

> It is not enough to be Israelites or Christian in name. When justice in the community is not the goal of the people of God, when war, poverty, prejudice, and other sins are accepted as inevitable, when security is predicated on an ethnic or ecclesiastical heritage that endeavors to lock the saving God in a box, then the confrontation with the living God is as horrible to contemplate as the martial pictures of the prophetic day of Yahweh – and so we must proclaim. But, contrariwise, *the unalloyed hope which we offer to people today springs neither from a melioristic philosophy nor from our own goodness, but it is our faithful reaction to the impending new day of Yahweh when He, going forth like a mighty man and stirring up His fury like a man of war (Is. 42) reaps the promises of His resurrection triumphs.*[48]

---

46. Matthew Aernie and Donald Hartley, "The Day of the Lord in Paul's Theology," in *The Righteous and Merciful Judge: The Day of the Lord in the Life and Theology of Paul* (Bellingham: Lexham, 2018), 94–103, [94].
47. Aernie and Hartley, "Day of the Lord," 97.
48. Emphasis mine. Klein, "Day of the Lord," 525.

The rhetoric of the day of Yahweh and the day of Jesus Christ is no mere saber-rattling. It is a day of cosmic judgment for the wicked and redemption for all who turn to God. This coming day – held back only by God's mercy on and patience with his creation – demands courageous trust and obedience.

1:17–18 YAHWEH CONSUMES THE EARTH

The last two verses picture the devastating effects of the day of Yahweh's wrath. From 1:17, we see a shift from a series of verbless to verbal clauses. There is also an expanding target audience beyond those who dwell in Judah/Jerusalem. Here, the text uses "all people," "the whole earth," and "all who live on the earth." The word *adam* translated as "mankind/people" is found in Zephaniah at the beginning and end of the first chapter alone (1:3, 17). The occurrence of the root form of the word "wicked" (*rasha*) in 1:3 and "sinned" (*chata*) in 1:17 is also found nowhere else in Zephaniah. These select repetitions reflect a compositional intent to bookend the chapter, a technique we have seen repeatedly in this book.

The expression "grope about like those who are blind" is the language of divine curse, especially toward people who have sinned. Within the Bible, there is a typical contextual development of this motif that moves from a context of prophetic curse to lamentation, and then to an evaluation of that deplorable state. The prophetic curse of blindness is seen in the list of covenantal blessings and curses in Deuteronomy 28. When the people of God disobeyed God's commands, they would be overtaken by a string of curses, one of which was that

> at midday you will *grope about like a blind person* in the dark. You will be unsuccessful in everything you do; day after day you will be oppressed and robbed, with no one to rescue you. (Deut 28:29, emphasis added)

Note that the word "like" is used. This means that the "blindness" is figurative. Within the context of Deuteronomy 28:15–67, the curse on the disobedient is such that their sight had no positive bearing on them. Their vision was as good as the darkness of disappointment and disillusionment. This prophetic curse, set within a covenantal framework, was realized when Jerusalem was horrifically destroyed in the sixth century BCE. In Lamentations, this figurative blindness is put into poetry:

> Now they *grope through the streets as if they were blind*. They are so defiled with blood that no one dares to touch their garments. (Lam 4:14, emphasis added)

Having sight but devoid of any vision of hope and goodness, the people of God could no longer see life ahead and were as good as the dead. Now, if the context underlying Isaiah 59 expresses a state of foreign oppression or internal unrest within Israel in the postexilic period, then we find an evaluation of those who looked for light and yet walked in the shadows.

> *Like the blind we grope along the wall, feeling our way like people without eyes.* At midday we stumble as if it were twilight; among the strong, we are like the dead. (Isa 59:10, emphasis added)

The words of Isaiah and Zephaniah remain true for all those who are spiritually blind and deaf – the walking dead. This evaluation is reinforced by Jesus's altercation with the Pharisees after he healed a blind man.

> [39]Jesus said, "For judgment I have come into this world, so that the blind will see and *those who see will become blind*." [40]Some Pharisees who were with him heard him say this and asked, "What? Are we blind too?" [41]Jesus said, "If you were blind, you would not be guilty of sin; but now that *you claim you can see, your guilt remains*." (John 9:39–41, emphasis added)

This warning is for us as well. It is possible to see yet grope about like a blind man. The blindness that we need to avoid is the blindness *to* Jesus Christ. As Paul warns, "The god of this age has blinded the minds of unbelievers, so that they cannot see the light of the gospel that displays the glory of Christ, who is the image of God" (2 Cor 4:4). Jesus Christ is revealed to us, first and foremost, in Scripture. A nonchalant attitude toward Scripture is blindness to Christ. When we no longer seek Jesus Christ in the Bible, we grope about like the blind.

The pouring out of blood "like dust" and entrails "like dung" (1:17) evoke the retching uncleanness of human defilement (1 Kgs 14:10) and slain soldiers on the killing fields (Isa 63:6). The reference to the futility of "their silver" and "their gold" (1:18) recalls the complacent in Jerusalem, who had made wealth their god (1:11).

Zephaniah 1:17–18a focuses on the outcome for these sinners. The rest of verse 18 explains the result of fighting against Yahweh, whose jealousy would totally consume the whole earth. No one can escape God's judgment.

SUMMARY AND REFLECTION

The overarching message of Zephaniah 1 is the overwhelming power of Yahweh's judgment directed at the wicked both in Jerusalem and in all the earth. On the one hand, this judgment can be interpreted as an exhortation to support the Josianic reforms. On the other hand, it might imply that the reforms had failed, and that God's judgment now had to run its course with the Babylonian invasion. The second view lines up better with the latter chapters of Zephaniah, to which we now turn.

ZEPHANIAH 2

Standing at the center of the book, this chapter focuses on Yahweh's judgment of the nations around Jerusalem. The first three verses are a call to contrition in order to avoid condemnation. Then, under the umbrella of a single woe interjection (2:4–15), the rest of the chapter comprises oracles against foreign nations located in four directions around Jerusalem: the Philistines and the coastal regions to the west; Ammon and Moab to the east; Cush to the south; and Assyria to the north.[1] The outcome of the wicked among the nations (and in Judah) is the poetic foil to the destiny of the *remnant* of Judah/Jerusalem and the nations.

2:1–3 SEEK RIGHTEOUSNESS BEFORE THAT DAY

The main motif of this unit is urgent repentance, conveyed through the use of several repeated words and phrases. As noted earlier, repetition is a technique used to mark textual units. In 2:1, the repetition of the imperative form of "gather" (root: *qshsh*)[2] is meant to parallel, first, the similar but different word "sweep" (root: *'sp*) in 1:2–3 and, second, another pair of similar words, "assemble" and "gather" (roots: *'sp* and *qbts*), in 3:8. The use of a common semantic motif ("gather in these three places marks the three major textual units of Zephaniah (see the earlier discussion in "The Shape and Message of Zephaniah"). The phrase "you shameful nation" is rare, and its passive construction (in Hebrew) is unique. With a negation before the verb, the phrase can be translated as "O nation that is not ashamed!" And the singular "nation" probably refers to Judah, which was the subject of the preceding chapter (1:4).

In 2:2, we see three repetitions of the conjunction "before," each introducing a line of text. Besides this temporal marker, this verse is distinct from the preceding and following verse in three other ways. First, "day" occurs twice. This "day" is the subject of all the singular verbs in this verse. Second, verse 2 does not use any imperative verbs. This stands out as 2:2 is set within a unit

---

1. This totality of judgment of the earth around Jerusalem is also found in Isaiah 24, specifically the east-west reference in 24:15.
2. The root occurs in two different stems. This root is found only eight times in the OT, and the two occurrences in Zephaniah 2:1 are the only instances in the XII.

that consists of five imperatives. Third, there are two (almost) verbatim phrases in 2:2, causing scholars to debate whether a copying error had occurred:[3]

before	the decree takes effect and *that day*	*passes* like windblown chaff,
before	the LORD's *fierce anger*	*comes* upon you,
before	the *day of* the LORD's *wrath*	*comes* upon you.

Regardless, these two phrases identify the imminent coming of the day of Yahweh. Note that in this chapter, references to the day of Yahweh are found only in this textual unit. Three commands follow, urging all the "humble" (or "afflicted") of the land to "seek": a) Yahweh, b) righteousness, and c) humility. This triple call to "seek" should be read against the phrase "neither seek the LORD nor inquire of him" in Zephaniah 1:6. The command to seek is directed not only to the humble, poor, or afflicted of all the earth but also to those who had kept God's judgments or commands (*mishpat*).

In contrast to the charge to "gather" (2:1), these references to the day of Yahweh suggest that the entire unit is not really a call to avoid God's wrath. Rather, those already yearning for God and obeying his commands were to persist in the same direction of seeking "righteousness" and "humility." In contrast, the "shameful," who rejected Yahweh, were to be gathered – like the gathering of tares – to be burned!

Significantly, all other occurrences of the lexeme "gather" (root: *qshsh*) in the Bible (Exod 5:7, 12; Num 15:32–33; 1 Kgs 17:10, 12), apart from Zephaniah 1:1, are associated with the gathering of stubble or wood *for burning*, whether for firing bricks or cooking.

So, the opening unit (2:1–3) is as much a pronouncement of the judgment that will take place on the day of Yahweh as it is a paraenetic call to persevere in him. Verse 2 stands out (as an emphatic clause) in this unit, giving it a sense of urgency, while also effecting a dramatic pause before the arrival of the day of Yahweh.

A	Gather! Gather! You, nation (Judah)!
B	Before . . . Before . . . Before . . . comes upon you
A'	Seek! Seek! Seek! All you humble of the land.

---

3. The possible copying error is called an "homoeoarcton" (literally, "same beginning"). This error explains the omission or addition of texts from the copyist's eye tracking back to the same word on the source text (for omissions, the eye tracks to the same word occurring a few lines down) and copying the line again. However, the textual differences in the two lines in 2:2 suggest that both lines could have been present in the original text.

Figure 36: Gather Tares for Burning
Illustration by M. Bihn and J. Bealings
Public Domain: https://commons.wikimedia.org/wiki/
File:El_trigo_y_la_ciza%C3%B1a_2.PNG

WE ARE CALLED TO SEEK YAHWEH, HIS RIGHTEOUSNESS, AND HUMBLE OURSELVES

Zephaniah has called to the people to seek Yahweh and his righteousness, and to walk humbly before God. This echoes Micah's call to do justice, love mercy, and walk humbly with Yahweh. But God, too, has humbled himself, as seen in the prophet Isaiah's words about God's willingness to accommodate and live with those who are contrite and lowly in spirit.

> He has shown you, O mortal, what is good. And what does the LORD require of you? To act justly and to love mercy and to walk humbly with your God. (Mic 6:8)

> For this is what the high and exalted One says – he who lives forever, whose name is holy: "I live in a high and holy place, but also with the one who is contrite and lowly in spirit, to revive the spirit of the lowly and to revive the heart of the contrite." (Isa 57:15)

It is also possible to see a connection between Zephaniah's call to humility and Josiah's contrition when he heard the Book of the Law being read, inquired of Yahweh, and wept in God's presence. Note the several similar lexemes (italicised) between Josiah's response and Zephaniah 2:1–3.

> [18]Tell the king of Judah [Josiah], who sent you to *inquire* [root: *drsh*] of the LORD, "This is what the LORD, the God of Israel, says concerning the words you heard: [19]Because your heart was responsive and you *humbled* [root: *kn*] yourself before the LORD when you heard what I have spoken against this place and its people – that they would become a curse and be laid waste – and because you tore your robes and wept in my presence, I also have heard you, declares the LORD. [20]Therefore I will *gather* [root: *sp*] you to your ancestors, and you will be buried in peace."
> (2 Kgs 22:18–20, emphasis added)

What does it mean to walk humbly before Yahweh? Humility – which is defined as one having "a) accurate self-appraisal (e.g., awareness of one's strengths and weaknesses), b) a receptive orientation toward others, including an appreciation for differences, c) the capacity for self-regulation of emotions, particularly shame and pride, d) teachability, and e) low concern for social status" (Phil 2:6–8) – is one of the metavirtues of Christian spirituality and a predictor of the well-being of seminary students![1]

Our best model is Jesus, who walked humbly before God (Phil 2:6–8). Humility involves a denial of our own will and the right to be delivered in times of danger. It may involve rejection, ridicule, and even repudiation from our family or friends. To walk humbly before Yahweh is to be obedient to God and his will and to live a life devoted to this long obedience.

The heart of humility is the willingness to surrender the right to save ourselves. This is what the Bible means when it speaks of carrying our cross each day and dying to ourselves. George Müller ((sometimes spelled Mueller), when asked about the secret of his service, had this to say:

> There was a day when I died, *utterly* died; . . . died to George Mueller, his opinions, preferences, tastes, and will; died to the World, its approval or censure; died to the approval or blame even of my brethren and friends; and since then I have studied to show myself approved only to God.[2]

Humility is forsaking a thousand audiences we can see for the sake of the God whom we cannot see. Surprisingly, in the book of Zephaniah, this call to humility comes to those who were already "humble." This means that the call to humility is a persistent one – *the perseverance of the saints*.

The expressions of one's humility may be an outward behavior or action, visible in the eyes of others, but whether that humility is genuine is something that cannot escape the eyes of God, who looks at the hearts.

Growing up in a traditional Chinese independent church in Singapore in the 1980s and 1990s, I have often found this concept of humility problematic within the structural-relational dynamics of the church. The respect that older church leaders expected of younger ones often did not sit well with the generation growing up in the 1980s. This was the generation that had experienced the effects of a number of massive rallies in Singapore – for example, those led by Billy Graham, David Yonggi Cho, Reinhard Bonnke, and Luis Palau – which resulted in a rapid growth in the number of Protestant churches in Singapore.[3]

My peers no longer accepted by default the authoritative demands within the church. Having grown up during a period of three decades of rapid advancement of education and technology, the younger generation was more educated and exposed to Western ideas of freedom, emancipation, and leadership, and they looked for consensus rather than unchallenged fiat expressions.[4] They did not want church leaders to lead from their seats of authority or traditions. The rise of such a generation in Chinese-speaking churches collided with the preferences of the more senior members within those congregations. Dissatisfied with the status quo, many younger believers sought membership elsewhere or started their own congregations, and perhaps this was what led to churches increasingly splitting into English- and Chinese-speaking congregations in the 1990s.[5]

The point I am emphasizing here is humility. Older Christian leaders sometimes hold on to their experience and status, seeing themselves as superior to the younger generation. Younger Christians, on the other hand, see themselves as the light-bearers of twenty-first-century education and consider themselves superior. Humility runs thin on either side, and the result is often a parting of ways. Peter's call is extremely helpful: "In the same way, you who are younger, submit yourselves to your elders. All of you, clothe yourselves with humility toward one another because 'God opposes the proud but shows favor to the humble'" (1 Pet 5:5). Zephaniah's repudiation of complacency and his exhortation to the humble and the righteous to persevere are a warning for us as we wait for the day of Yahweh. "For those who exalt themselves will be humbled, and those who humble themselves will be exalted" (Matt 23:12).

---

1. Elizabeth G. Ruffing et al., "Humility and Relational Spirituality as Predictors of Well-Being among Christian Seminary Students," *Journal of Psychology and Theology* 49, no. 4 (2021): 419–435, [420].
2. Arthur T. Pierson, *George Mueller of Bristol*, reformatted by Joanne Kimble, Biblical Studies Ministries International (New Jersey: Fleming H. Revell, 1899), 188, http://www.bsmi.org/download/mueller/GeorgeMuellerOfBristol.pdf.
3. Bobby E. K. Sng, *In His Good Time: The Story of the Church in Singapore 1819–2002*, 3rd ed. (Singapore: Bible Society of Singapore, 2003), 314.
4. Robbie B. H. Goh, "Christian Identities in Singapore: Religion, Race and Culture between State Controls and Transnational Flows," *Journal of Cultural Geography* 26, no. 1 (2009): 1–23, https://doi.org/10.1080/08873630802617135; Barna Group, "Six Reasons Young Christians Leave Church - Article," BioLogos, June 5, 2017, https://biologos.org/articles/six-reasons-young-christians-leave-church/.
5. There was an increase in English congregations in Singapore, at least in the Presbyterian circles in the 1990s. "The Presbyterian Church in Singapore – History."

2:4–15 WOE AGAINST THE NATIONS

Distinct from earlier text units, the rest of chapter 2 captures judgment oracles against several nations. These oracles are introduced in verse 4, and they fall under the woe interjection umbrella in verse 5. This segment, like the second woe segment in 3:1–4, wholly avoids the use of the expression "the day of the LORD." Additionally, these two woe units are different in form and character compared with the woe sayings in Habakkuk 2:6–19, where each oracle against a foreign city carries a woe interjection.

In Zephaniah, there are only two woe interjections (2:5; 3:1) – one against foreign nations as a whole (2:4–15) and the other reserved for Judah/Jerusalem (3:1–4). Woe oracles against nations are common in the prophetic books.[4] We find at least two common features in these oracles: a) condemnation of the pride and arrogance of these nations, and b) indictment for the atrocities committed against Israel or Judah. These features will be explained in our discussion below.

---

4. Against Philistines (Jer 47:1–7; Ezek 25:15–17; Amos 1:6–8); Moabites (Isa 15–16; Jer 48:1–47); Ammonites (Jer 49:1–7); Cushites (Ezek 30:2–12); Assyria (Isa 31:8–9; Ezek 31:3–15).

2:4–7 Against the Philistines

There are debates on whether 2:4 should belong to the earlier text unit. Sweeney, for instance, argues that 2:4 functions as a link between 2:1–3 and the rest of the chapter.[5] Others, like Berlin and Renz, combine 2:4 with the earlier verses because of the Masoretic closed-paragraph marker (*setumah*) at the end of verse 4. Moreover, woe interjections tend to open new text units (see 3:1–4). Nonetheless, for several reasons, it is better to see verse 4 as the beginning of a new unit. First, this verse functions as an introduction, summarizing God's indictment of the foreign nations, beginning with the Philistines. There is a clear shift in topic in verse 4. Second, as we have seen in Habakkuk 2:6, a woe unit need not always begin with an interjection. Third, the Masoretic *setumah* marker is an interpretive signal for reading – introduced later, during the first to the sixth centuries CE – rather than a compositional one.

Historically, the Philistine Pentapolis cities were listed as Gaza, Ashdod, Ashkelon, Gath, and Ekron (Josh 13:2–3). The fact that "Gath" is missing here need not alarm us because several indictment passages in the prophetic literature also do not include Gath (Jer 25:20; 47:4–7; Amos 1:6–8; Zech 9:5–7). There could be historical reasons for the absence of Gath. However, there might also be a literary reason why Gath is excluded here in Zephaniah 2:4.[6] Consider the striking syntactical and phonological literary feature of four Hebrew cola (a colon [singular] functions like a clause, which carries a subject and predicate, and is the smallest sense unit) in a pair of bicolons below.[7] Each bicolon depicts the destruction of two cities.

In the Hebrew, the names of these four cities and their verbal forms – as shown below – have been deliberately chosen to rhyme (see underlined letters).[8]

---

5. Sweeney, *Zephaniah*, 9.
6. Baker notes that Gath had "faded into insignificance by Zephaniah's time." Baker, *Nahum, Habakkuk, Zephaniah*, 82.
7. I have used the term, "line," quite loosely. A poetic "line" can correspond to an entire Masoretic verse or a bicolon. The levels of poetic sense unit are given here: colon (clause), bicolon, line, strophe, canto, stanza, and poem. In general, each of these increasing sense units generally consists of two (to four or more) of the earlier sense units. So, a line may consist of a bicolon or two bicolons. Some lines are a single tricolon (e.g., Ps 67:4 is the only tricolon in a psalm that consists of bicolons). A strophe can include two or three poetic lines. A canto may include two or more strophes and so on. The movement of sense units, often marked by specific transitional forms, often coincides well with semantic shifts.
8. Note the consonances of the Hebrew letters of the cities as well as the assonances in the vowels.

Gaza [*azzah*] will	be abandoned [*azuvah*]	} bicolon
and Ashkelon [*asheqelon*]	left in ruins [*lyshemamah*];	
Ashdod [*ashedod*], at midday,	will be emptied [*legareshuha*].	} bicolon
and Ekron [*eqeron*]	uprooted [*teaqer*].	

In Hebrew, the first letters of the names of the four cities form a chiasmus.[9] The addition of Gath would break the literary parallelisms of form and phonology. And these literary features functioned as a technique to grab the audience's attention for what is to follow – the woe indictments against the nations and what this meant for Judah.

The following map, which lists cities in Zephaniah 2, gives us a sense of where these cities are located in relation to Jerusalem:

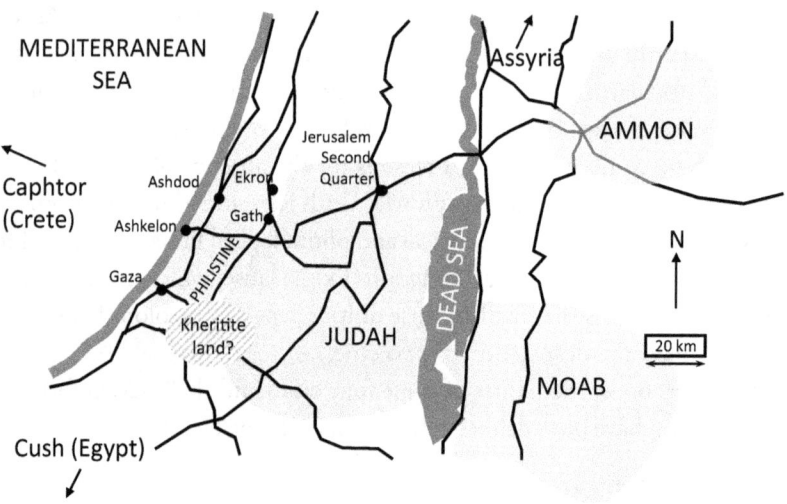

Figure 37: Foreign Nations in the Book of Zephaniah

The woe interjection (2:5) introduces two regions: the land of the Kerethites (also spelled "Cherethites"), who lived by the sea, and Canaan, the land of the Philistines. The Kerethites could have lived south or southeast of Gaza. Biblical references to the Kerethites are mostly linked to David and his armed guards (1 Sam 30:14; 2 Sam 8:18; 15:18; 20:7, 23). Their origin is unclear.

---

9. The first letters of the names of the four cities form an *ayin-aleph-aleph-ayin* chiasmus. Gath begins with the letter *gimel*.

Perhaps the Kerethite-Philistine juxtaposition in Ezekiel 25:16 associates them geographically. And since the Philistines' origin was linked to Caphtor (Amos 9:7; compare Gen 10:14), it is possible that the Kerethites originated from the Aegean region.[10]

The Philistines are mentioned as early as Genesis 10, and then at the time of Abraham (Gen 21:34). God himself prevented the Israelites from going to Canaan through Philistine country (Exod 13:17). By the time Israel came out of Egypt, the Philistines were already there along the southwestern coast of Israel. The Philistines were Israel's nemesis throughout the conquest and during the early monarchical period. Nonetheless, by the time of the Babylonian captivity in the sixth century BCE, the Philistines had faded away from the story.

At the end of verse 5, there is, for the first time, a shift to a first-person verb, marking a development in the text. Yahweh, speaking in the first person, declares his fight *against* those who had sinned against him, whether among foreign nations or in Israel. There is another shift in 2:6–7, moving from Yahweh's destruction of the Philistine and Kerethite cities to Yahweh's goodwill toward the remnant of Judah. The reference to the restoration of the fortunes of the remnant of Judah (2:7) seems to suggest that Judah/Jerusalem was in a worse state at the time of composition, which could have been due to the Assyrian invasion about a century before. What is significant in this unit and in the rest of the chapter is Yahweh's role as the victor (against the nations) and restorer (for the remnant of his people).[11] The concept of the remnant of Judah

> is centered on the principle that God is a moral and just being. As such it would be inconceivable that Yahweh would destroy both the righteous and the unfaithful without first warning them of the danger with which they are faced. This warning might come from God or, more usually, from a messenger (angel) or representative of God (prophet). It is then up to the audience of this message to take steps to ensure their preservation . . . Once God has completed the destruction act aimed at eliminating the corrupt elements in the nation or the world, the righteous remnant stands forth as the seed from which the covenantal community is restored.[12]

---

10. Carl S. Ehrlich, "Cherethites," *The Anchor Yale Bible Dictionary* (New York: Doubleday, 1992), 898–899.
11. Kenneth Mulzac, "The Remnant Motif in the Context of Judgment and Salvation in the Book of Jeremiah" (PhD Diss., Andrews University, Seventh-day Adventist Theological Seminary, 1995), https://digitalcommons.andrews.edu/dissertations/100.
12. Victor H. Matthews, *Old Testament Themes* (St. Louis: Chalice, 2000), 41.

Yahweh, a just and holy God, is not indifferent either to the exploitation, wickedness, and sin of human beings, or to the predicament of the remnant of his people.

2:8–11 Against the Ammonites and Moabites

In this unit, we have Yahweh, as the first-person subject, responding to the insults and taunts of Moab and Ammon. The Moabites and Ammonites were the descendants of Lot, conceived by his daughters in a cave after escaping the destruction of Sodom and Gomorrah (Gen 19:30–38). Moab and Ammon were situated east of Jerusalem across the River Jordan and were deemed outside of the circle of God's chosen people. During the period of the divided monarchy, Moab was under the rule of Omri and Ahab for a time (2 Kgs 3:4–27), and Moab was later ruled by Jehoram and Jehoshaphat after a quashed Moabite revolt. The Mesha Stele (c. 840 BCE) records that Moab was being oppressed by Omri. Lines 5–6 on the Mesha Stele note: "[5] Omri was king of Israel and oppressed Moab during many days, and Chemosh was angry with his [6] aggressions. His son succeeded him and said, 'I will oppress Moab.'"[13]

Not much is recorded about the relationship between Judah, Moab, and Ammon after the period of Omri and Jehoshaphat except for a few reports of Moabite or Ammonite incursions in the regions of Judah and similar attacks by Judah against these regions (2 Kgs 13:20; 2 Kgs 24:2; 2 Chr 20:1; 27:5).

Zephaniah 2:9, which describes Yahweh's judgments on Ammon and Moab, is the longest verse in the book. The characterization of these two nations as "Sodom" and "Gomorrah" and as "a place of weeds and salt pits" is uncommon. We are familiar with the Dead Sea, where high salinity inhibits life. The scattering of salt over a captured city to render it unproductive was a practice in the ancient world (Judg 9:45). In the OT, references that connect salt to a geographic location almost always depict unproductive life, where nothing sprouts or grows (Deut 29:23). The indictment of Moab and Ammon comes full circle in 2:10. The root forms of the nouns and verbs (or lexemes) "insult" (2:8, 10), "taunt" (2:8),[14] and "threat" (2:8, 10) form bookends with 2:8. This scoffing will be opposed by Yahweh, who is described as "awesome" (*nora*). This descriptor is used overwhelmingly of Yahweh, his deeds, and the day of Yah-

---

13. James King, *Moab's Patriarchal Stone: Being an Account of the Moabite Stone, Its Story and Teaching* (London: Bickers and Son, 1878), 55–58. King has adapted the translations of Ganneau and Ginsburg. Full translation available online: http://archive.org/details/moabspatriarcha01fundgoog.
14. This noun, *gidduf* (scorn), is rare and occurs elsewhere only in Isaiah 43:28.

weh ("dreadful" in Joel 2:11, 31; Mal 4:5).[15] The term "distant nations" (or *iye hagoyim*, "islands/coastlands of the nations") occurs primarily in the prophetic texts, especially Isaiah and Jeremiah, and are commonly used in contexts where Yahweh is exalted among the nations (Isa 11:11; 66:19; Jer 47:4; Ezek 39:6).

In short, Moab and Ammon would become places devoid of life and flourishing. Other descriptions elsewhere in the Bible also confirm that an orientation *away* from God is an orientation toward death. In contrast, an orientation toward God brings life and flourishing.

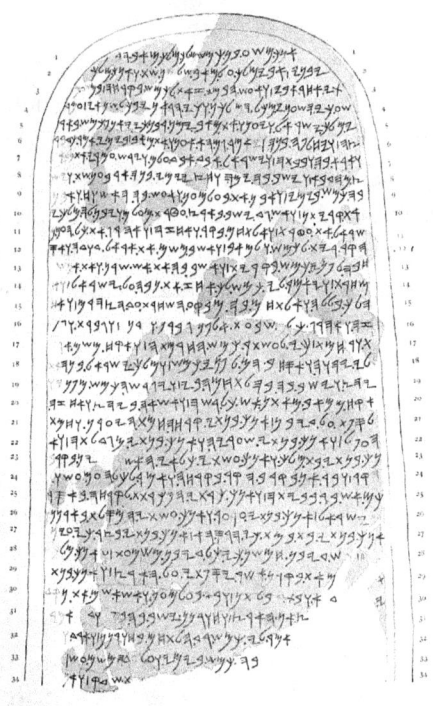

Figure 38: Drawing of the Mesha Stele by Mark Lidzbarski (published 1898)
Discovered in 1868–70, the Stele is currently housed at the Louvre
Source: *Handbuch der nordsemitischen Epigraphik nebst ausgewählten Inschriften*
Public Domain: https://commons.wikimedia.org/wiki/File:Mesha_Stele_drawing.png

---

15. From the root, "to fear," and in the passive Niphal participle form, there are only a handful of references where it is used to describe something else apart from Yahweh (e.g., angelic being, wilderness, Babylon/Cush).

2:12 Against the Cushites

"Cushites" (2:12) is translated as "Ethiopians" in several Bible versions including the NASB 1995 and the NET (compare Jer 13:23 NIV).[16] Cush, as a place, may function as a "synecdoche" – a literary device in which a part represents the whole – referring to Egypt. Historically, Cush, also known as Nubia, was connected to Arabia (note that "Cushan" is usually understood to be situated in Arabia, see Hab 3:7).[17] Cush had been a formidable military force (2 Kgs 19:9–10; 2 Chr 14:9; Isa 18:1–7). If the Ethiopian connection can be sustained, then the NT tells us that the gospel of Jesus Christ, as preached by Philip the evangelist to the eunuch on the road from Jerusalem to Gaza, had reached Cush (Acts 8:26–39).

At the time of Zephaniah, it is unlikely that the indictment of Cush referred to the Babylonian invasion since the city of Cush (Ethiopia) had already been destroyed in 663 BCE by the Assyrians. Hence, Baker argues that Cush (2:12) probably referred to Egypt as a whole.[18] This proposition is possible because Zephaniah was not simply writing from a historical point of view, but he was likely listing the nations around Jerusalem as the total arena of God's judgment (see Figure 37). The indictment of Cush follows the pattern of that of other nations mentioned in chapter 2.

2:13–15 Against Assyria and Nineveh

We come now to the final representative nation in this unit. The reference to the direction "north" (2:13) suggests that Zephaniah was completing the list of representative nations around Jerusalem. The Philistines and the land by the sea were on the west, Moab and Ammon lay east of Jerusalem, Cush represented the south, and Assyria or Nineveh represented the north. This has Jerusalem – or Zion – situated at the center of the world, and this is a significant feature of Zion theology. Levenson notes that

> Zion is the place from which the world was created, as the point from which the primal ray of light emanated, and as the only mountain to stand above the deluge, is also the highest point in

---

16. Cush is a descendant of Ham (Gen 10:7). The Septuagint translates both the noun and adjectival form for the lexeme "Cush" as "Ethiopia" or "Ethiopian" in Zephaniah 2:12 and 3:10.
17. John D. Currid, *Ancient Egypt and the Old Testament* (Grand Rapids: Baker Books, 1997), 233–235.
18. Baker, *Nahum, Habakkuk, Zephaniah*, 83.

the highest land, the center of the center, from which all the rest of reality takes its bearings.[19]

As the locus of God's action and attention, we have a clearer vision of how Jerusalem relates to the nations, with the latter functioning as a complement to the former. We have also discussed the stretching out of Yahweh's hand (1:4) as a formula that portrays Yahweh as a man of war, fighting for his people against the nations.

This last text unit does not have Yahweh speaking in the first person. Instead, we see the use of a third-person subject ("he"). The root form of the word "desolate" (*shemamah*) is used three other times in Zephaniah to describe the predicament of the complacent elite in Judah/Jerusalem ("demolished," 1:13), the Philistines ("ruins," 2:4), and Transjordanian cities ("wasteland," 2:9).

As in Moab's and Ammon's destruction (2:9), Assyria's desolation is pictured as a dry, deserted wasteland where wild creatures reside. The motif of dryness is usually associated with Yahweh's judgment of cities (see Isa 35:1; Jer 50:12; 51:43; Hos 2:3). Such judgment is sometimes described as abandoned fortresses and deserted ruins that are overgrown with thorns and thistles that only delight wild animals like donkeys (Isa 32:14). These were the dwelling places of unclean animals and birds such as the desert owls (Isa 14:23). Zephaniah's description of Assyria is similar to Edom's fate as depicted in Isaiah:

> [11]The desert owl and screech owl will possess it;
> the great owl and the raven will nest there.
> God will stretch out over Edom
> the measuring line of chaos
> and the plumb line of desolation.
> [12]Her nobles will have nothing there to be
> called a kingdom,
> all her princes will vanish away.
> [13]Thorns will overrun her citadels,
> nettles and brambles her strongholds.
> She will become a haunt for jackals,
> a home for owls.
> [14]Desert creatures will meet with hyenas,
> and wild goats will bleat to each other;

---

19. Jon D. Levenson, *Sinai and Zion: An Entry into the Jewish Bible* (Minneapolis: Winston, 1985), 135.

> there the night creatures will also lie down
>   and find for themselves places of rest.
> ¹⁵The owl will nest there and lay eggs,
>   she will hatch them, and care for her young
>   under the shadow of her wings;
> there also the falcons will gather,
>   each with its mate. (Isa 34:11–15)

The last verse (2:15) describes a poetic reversal. The city that was supposedly strong, secure, and full of pride would be turned into a ruin.[20] The city's arrogance is evident in the reported speech, "I am the one! And there is none besides me" (2:15b). Underlying this phrase are three Hebrew words that are found in this exact format only in Isaiah, where they record Babylon's boast about herself (Isa 47:8, 10). This self-appraisal mimics how God revealed himself, and in the salvation in Jesus Christ (Deut 4:35; 1 Kgs 8:60; Isa 45:5, 6, 14, 18, 22; compare Mark 12:32; John 1:14; Acts 4:12). In this way, the biblical writers wanted us to see the misplaced pride of Babylon and Assyria.

Assyria's self-aggrandizing pride is also contrasted with the appraisals of the onlookers: "All who pass by her scoff and shake their fists" (2:15b). This imagery is common in the Bible, often describing passersby who "scoff" (root: *shrq*; 1 Kgs 9:8; Lam 2:15–16) or shake their "fist" (Job 15:25; Isa 10:32) or their "head" (Pss 22:7; 44:14; 64:8; 109:25; Jer 18:16; 48:27; Lam 2:15) in disdain.

SUMMARY AND REFLECTION

Chapter 2 focuses on Yahweh's judgment of the nations around Jerusalem. The first three verses are a call to contrition in order to avoid condemnation. The indictment of the wicked is certain. They would be gathered like chaff to be burned on the day of Yahweh's anger. But the humble and obedient are called to persevere in Yahweh. The rest of the chapter consists of oracles against foreign nations, which are depicted as arrogant and prideful. These nations serve as a type for the arrogant enemies of Yahweh and God's people. And because Yahweh would restore the fortunes of his remnant and be victorious over the nations, the afflicted and humble among his people must wait in hope.

---

20. This "city of revelry" ("proud city" in NET; or "boisterous city" in NLT) is used elsewhere on Jerusalem (22:2; 32:13) and Tarshish (23:7).

ZEPHANIAH 3

This chapter is a critical point in the XII – a climactic firework of God's powerful deliverance of his people despite their decadence. This chapter also shows Yahweh's determination to bring about righteousness in Zion on the day of Yahweh. It comprises three main units, beginning with a severe indictment of Jerusalem for her persistent wickedness (3:1–4). The second unit (3:5–7) shows that because of God's faithfulness to his covenantal promises, he himself becomes the righteousness of the city. The final unit (3:8–20) speaks of a day and a time when God will utterly transform the city. He will also gather and restore, from all the earth, a remnant who will no longer commit wickedness. On that day, this remnant will dwell securely in Zion, and Jerusalem will rejoice and receive a great name. There will be a reversal of fortunes – their brokenness will be healed, their shame will be replaced by honor, and they will be restored.

3:1–4 WOE AGAINST JERUSALEM

This chapter is linked to the previous one by the second woe interjection in the book (3:1). This "woe" is directed at the "city," which, although unnamed, is Jerusalem – as seen from references to "the Lord," the "sanctuary," and the "law" (3:2, 4). This unit (3:1–4) consists of fourteen descriptors of the city and its people, displaying an impressive literary effect, and even employing the use of symbolic numbers in the underlying Hebrew text morphology.[1]

Verse 1 is verbless and consists of three participle forms: a city of "oppressors" (*hayyonah*), who are "rebellious" (*moreah*)[2] and "defiled" (*nigealah*). Not only are the verbal constructions rare but, in Hebrew, the participles also rhyme. In the OT, oppression often takes the form of the abuse of the weak, especially the poor, orphans, widows, and foreigners. What made these acts of oppression particularly odious is that they were committed by the officials and leaders of Israel (Ezek 45:8), who were specifically commanded not to oppress these groups (Exod 22:21; Lev 19:33; Deut 23:15–16, 19). The actions of the oppressors in Zephaniah 3:1–4 recall Israel's repeated failure to be God's holy people and a kingdom of priests. The defilement mentioned here (3:1) conjures

---

1. The Hebrew adopts seven feminine forms and seven perfective verbs, with five negative particles, five masculine and five participle forms. There are also ten verbs in the Qatal stem.
2. Another Hebrew word, *meri*, also translated as "rebellious one/rebellion," is found repeatedly in Ezekiel's book describing Judah's house (Ezek 2:5–8; 12:2–3, 9).

up images of uncleanness associated with blood violence and treachery (Isa 59:3), contempt of Yahweh (Mal 1:7, 12), and pagan debauchery (Dan 1:8).

Verse 2 consists of two bicolons with flipped syntaxes. Note how the subject "she" and negative verbs (underlined) occur at the beginning of the first bicolon and in the latter half of the second bicolon. Also, only in B-B′ do we have Yahweh and God as the object of the verbs.

A	She <u>does not</u> listen[3]	to anyone [any voice],	} bicolon
A′	she <u>does not</u> accept	correction.	
B	In the LORD [Yahweh],	she <u>does not</u> trust	} bicolon
B′	to her God,	she <u>does not</u> draw near.	

These four cola highlight the city's rebellious and unteachable nature. The city had been profoundly disloyal to Yahweh. In the OT, trusting in Yahweh is a significant concept, especially in Psalms and Jeremiah.[4] The person who trusts in Yahweh trusts him primarily for deliverance from enemies and for vindication and justice, as King Hezekiah did (2 Kgs 18:5). Judah, however, was guilty of misplaced trust, placing her trust in human institutions, traditions, deceptive words, and in her own riches (Jer 7:4, 8; 28:15; 48:7). The word "trust" (root: *bth*) occurs infrequently in the XII, but every occurrence[5] describes a failure to trust in Yahweh. Zephaniah's indictment also echoes Amos 6:1, where the complacent in Zion had placed their security (trust) in their own strength rather than in Yahweh.

In the next two verses (3:3–4), we see four kinds of people set apart for condemnation: a) officials, b) rulers, c) prophets, and d) priests. "Officials" is a broad term that can include military commanders (Deut 1:15; 2 Sam 18:1), sanctuary ministers (1 Chr 24:5), royal princes or rulers (Ps 148:11), secretaries (Jer 36:12), and even angelic princes (Dan 10:13). The second term, "rulers" – commonly translated as "judges" – refers here to those with authority, who execute the law.

The combined use of these four terms represents the pillars of the entire Judean leadership – the shepherds of Israel. These terms are also used in Jeremiah's condemnation of the collective leadership of the entire Judean commu-

---

3. I have translated literally from the Hebrew text to illustrate the literary effect. NIV has "She obeys no one, she accepts no correction." Note that these four verbs, "listen," "accept," "trust," and "draw near," are in the perfective Qatal form. Perhaps we have a gnomic Qatal here, offering an atemporal, universal perspective, a general truth of a situation verified by facts.
4. See Psalms 22:4–5; 56:4, 11.
5. Hosea 10:13; Amos 6:1; Micah 7:5; Habakkuk 2:18; Zephaniah 3:2.

nity for forsaking Yahweh and practicing wickedness even as the Babylonian invasion loomed (Jer 32:32).

Besides the king, officials and rulers were entrusted with the authority to shepherd God's people. Instead of carefully shepherding the people, they had become predatory lions and wolves who devoured the very sheep they were supposed to protect. Similarly, the prophets and priests – who were supposed to keep the law, teach it to the people, and maintain God's house – had despised their charge and forsaken their responsibilities. As the prophet Habakkuk had said (Hab 1:4), instead of being the guardian and executor of Yahweh's righteous law, they had perverted the law. Thus, those given the privilege of upholding and mediating the righteousness and sanctity of Yahweh's law and temple were the most violent and debased perpetrators.

In July 2022, Gershon Galil – Professor of Biblical Studies and Ancient History at the University of Haifa published a translation of a 63-letter Proto-Canaanite inscription on a stone dated 3,300 years ago. Galil claims that this is the earliest inscription found in the city of David, near Gihon Spring in Jerusalem.[6] The inscription reads:

> Cursed, cursed, you will surely die;
> Cursed, cursed, you will surely die;
> Governor of the city, you will surely die;
> Cursed, you will surely die;
> Cursed, you will surely die;
> Cursed, you will surely die.[7]

This is a fascinating yet uncomfortable find. This inscription has poetic features similar to what we see in the Bible (Gen 3:14–19; Num 5:21–24; Deut 28:15–68). At the time of writing this commentary, there has been no consensus about Galil's translation, but, if his proposition is upheld, what we have is the earliest record of the Hebrew script – and this script is a condemnation of the governor or "official" (*sar*) of Jerusalem!

As with Galil's translation of Jerusalem's earliest inscription, Zephaniah's indictment of the leaders of Jerusalem reminds us of Peter's warning that "it

---

6. "Prof. Gershon Galil Presents Translation of 'Jerusalem's Earliest Inscription,'" Armstrong Institute of Biblical Archaeology, July 14, 2022, https://armstronginstitute.org/737-prof-gershon-galil-presents-translation-of-jerusalems-earliest-inscription.
7. A hand-drawn image of the inscription is available here: https://armstronginstitute.org/enlarge_image?data=eyJpZCI6IjE2MzQiLCJjYXB0aW9uIjoiSGFuZC1kcmF3biBvdXRsaW5lIG-9m%0AIHRoZSBpbnNjcmlwdGlvbiIsImNyZWRpdCI6IkdlcnNob24gR2FsaW-wifQ%3D%3D%0A.

is time for judgment to begin with God's household" (1 Pet 4:17). Pastors, elders, and leaders of the church must shepherd the church carefully and with godly fear.

Although the complete list of charges against the city sealed her condemnation, the city of Jerusalem remained chosen for God's name and as his dwelling place. God had singled out the city of Jerusalem to keep his promises to David (1 Kgs 11:32–39). At this point in Zephaniah, the fate of Jerusalem seems ambiguous. On the one hand, she would be punished for her explicit rejection of Yahweh, as stated in chapter 1. One the other hand, God was unwilling to give up on the city because of his promises. In the next text unit (3:5–7), we see God's determination to keep his promises for his own name's sake.

3:5–7 YAHWEH'S RIGHTEOUSNESS IN THE CITY

There is no evidence that Judah/Jerusalem had repented in response to the exhortation of 2:1–3. Judah had been headstrong in her rebellion and sin. Yet, it is in this persistent unfaithfulness that we begin to see Yahweh's faithfulness. This unit marks the transition to the third segment of the book (from 3:8–20), where God begins his transformative work in Jerusalem. The transition here (3:5–7) shows both God's magnanimity and his vulnerability. There is also a perceptible shift in the subject of the verbs. Here, we see a tension within Yahweh, who must punish Jerusalem for her sins without completely destroying her. This dilemma is particularly apparent when compared to 3:1–4, where the city is portrayed as hopelessly wicked. But 3:5–7 portrays Yahweh as determined to do good to the city, choosing to remain "within her" as her righteousness and extending opportunities for his people to turn to him. Yahweh, like a good parent, demonstrates long-suffering and patience toward his children. Verse 5 speaks of his generous mercy to Jerusalem in the face of her stubborn rebellion.

Although Yahweh's patience persisted and tarried, the sin of Judah/Jerusalem worsened. The transformation of God's people could not be achieved by Judah's own efforts and would only come about because of God's determination. Zephaniah reveals that God refused to destroy his chosen people entirely and sought to accomplish their transformation himself. The spatial reference "within her" (literally, "in the midst of her") – which occurs only in chapter 3 of the book – is significant. Zephaniah uses this phrase to develop the motif of Jerusalem's transformation, moving from the condemnation of the wicked and complacent officials of Jerusalem to God's determination to act for the good of Zion, to Yahweh's transformation of Zion on "that day," and, finally, to Yahweh's dwelling in a righteous and humble Zion.

3:3	The [wicked] officials *within her*	(1) Condemnation of the wicked
3:5	Yahweh *within her* is righteous (in spite of her wickedness)	(2) God's determination for Zion's righteousness
3:11	On that day, Yahweh removes the arrogant boasters *within you* [Jerusalem][8]	(3) God's transformation of Zion
3:12	Yahweh will leave *within you* [Jerusalem] the meek and humble	
3:15	Yahweh, the King of Israel, is *with you* [Jerusalem]	(4) God dwells with his people in Zion
3:17	Yahweh your God is *with you* [Jerusalem], the Mighty Warrior who saves	

This unit maintains an uncomfortable tension. Although Yahweh continued to do "no wrong" (*awelah*) in the city and dispensed his justice day after day, the "unrighteous" (*awel*) remained shameless in their deeds (3:5). But on that day, the transformed remnant in the city would do "no wrong" (*awelah*, 3:13).

Even after Yahweh had destroyed Jerusalem's enemies, the tension remained. Yahweh had hoped that Jerusalem would fear him and "accept correction" (3:7). The destruction of the cities (3:6) recalls our earlier discussion on the destruction of the foreign nations around Jerusalem. Now, the shift to first-person speech in verse 6 is poignant because it emphasizes the relational aspect – how Yahweh felt about the city he loved, which was also the city that persisted in decadence. Despite these affectionate motifs, Jerusalem continued to act treacherously. Her eagerness (literally, "she rises early") to act corruptly (3:7) forms a striking contrast to – and an *inclusio* with – verse 5, which refers to Yahweh doing no wrong "morning by morning" and dispensing justice "every new day" (literally, "dawn" or "daylight").

---

8. I have translated this literally from the Hebrew. NIV has "I will remove from you."

GOD'S DETERMINATION TO LOVE AND TRANSFORM HIS PEOPLE STEEPED IN THEIR DECADENCE

The idea of God's grace is easily abused as a self-serving argument. This happens when the focus is turned from God as the subject from whom the grace originates, to the recipient as the object who receives that grace. When the attention of God's grace is focused on the goodness or benefit received by us, we become blind to God's determination and patience on the one hand and our stubborn wickedness on the other. This grace of God becomes the "get-out-of-jail" card we pull out each time we sin. The wicked keep hedging on grace.

Zephaniah presents the grace of God in tandem with the requirement for righteousness. Punishing sins was not enough; God was determined to transform his people so that Jerusalem could be righteous. The easier way would have been for God to destroy Judah/Jerusalem, just like the other foreign nations. It is easier to mold and fire new pottery than to repair a shattered pot. But we see God determined to create a new jar from the broken shards, even if that means hurting himself in the process. This idea is beautifully illustrated in the Japanese philosophy of *kintsugi* – the art of repairing broken pottery with powdered gold – which is about embracing an object's brokenness rather than hiding it.[1]

Figure 39: Bowl, Restored by Kintsugi
Photo by Haragayato (2016)
Wikimedia Commons: https://commons.wikimedia.org/wiki/File:Kintugi.jpg

Often requiring far more effort and craftmanship to produce than the original, the mended pottery is even more valuable than the original. The desire to preserve the original creation, the honesty to embrace the shame of brokenness, and the determination of the craftsman to mend every broken piece makes *kintsugi* a helpful object lesson in understanding the message of Zephaniah. That is the real face of the grace of God from his vantage point – the determination to transform his people steeped in their iniquity. This vantage point is a perspective we selfishly miss.

In Zephaniah 3, we see this expression of grace at work. The first four verses establish the culpability and condemnation of Jerusalem (3:1–4). The next three verses reveal God's vulnerability (3:5–7). As Paul notes, God struggles as he bears with great patience the objects of his wrath: "What if God, although choosing to show his wrath and make his power known, bore with great patience the objects of his wrath – prepared for destruction?" (Rom 9:22).

In July 2018, 12 boys and their football coach were trapped deep in the Tham Luang cave when heavy rainfall flooded the cave and blocked their exit. A massive and frantic operation began to locate them. British divers eventually found the boys on an elevated dry pocket almost 2,950 meters from the cave's entry.[2] Then followed an even more elaborate plan to rescue them from the cave. The rescue operation involved more than 10,000 people, comprising hundreds of divers, thousands of soldiers, police officers, and volunteers. An entire town was there to lend support, pray, and cheer the work. Although the rescue operation was ultimately successful, it cost the life of Saman Gunan – a 37-year-old Royal Thai Navy Seal – who died when his air tank ran out of air after delivering air tanks into the flooded cave. Another Thai Navy Seal diver, Petty Officer Beirut Pakbara, died a year later from a blood infection he had contracted during this rescue operation.[3]

This successful rescue story is one of the most heartwarming and memorable stories aired on global news in the last few years. People from all over the world gathered and worked together toward the single goal of saving the lives of 12 boys and their coach at the risk of their own. John Volanthen, one of the British divers, said in an interview, "The boys were in this strange situation where, if we did nothing, they were going to die. That makes difficult decisions, which you wouldn't even normally consider, much more justifiable."[4]

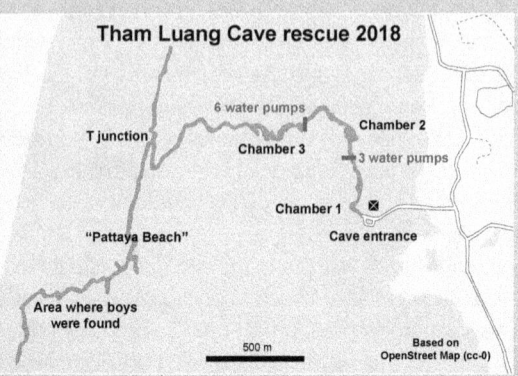

Figure 40: Tham Luang Cave System
Picture by Per Meistrup
Public Domain: https://commons.wikimedia.org/wiki/
File:2018_Tham-Luang-cave-map-cropped.png

In this rescue operation, human beings acted selflessly to accomplish what seemed impossible and saved many lives. God has done even more to save his people, who had been condemned to destruction. Zephaniah 3 portrays a holy God, determined to preserve his people by becoming the righteousness that his people – who would otherwise perish – lacked. This determination resulted in God sending his Son to be the righteousness we all need. This is the grace of God from the vantage point of God, the determination of God to love and transform his people steeped in their iniquity.

---

1. I would like to thank Janis Lim, who shared with me this connection to *Kintsugi*, which is quite a beautiful illustration for our point here.
2. The full story is now available as a National Geographic documentary, *The Rescue*, available on Netflix, https://films.nationalgeographic.com/the-rescue.
3. "Thai Cave Rescuer Dies from Year-Long Blood Infection," *BBC News*, December 28, 2019, https://www.bbc.com/news/world-asia-50931695.
4. Frances Carruthers, "'Within Minutes You're in a Different World': An Interview with Cave Diver John Volanthen," loveexploring.com, February 3, 2022, https://www.loveexploring.com/news/128346/john-volanthen-cave-diver-interview-thai-cave-rescue.

Zephaniah 3

3:8–20 YAHWEH'S DAY OF RESTORATION

This third and final segment of the book of Zephaniah describes God at work on that future day of restoration. This unit (3:8–20) can be divided into four subunits, each introduced by the expression "day" or "time." The entire unit is framed by the motif of God's gathering the people (3:8, 20) at the appointed day or time. In 3:8–10, God's restoration is focused on the nations. In 3:11–13, God will remove the wicked from Jerusalem. In 3:14–17, God will restore the remnant of Israel. And, finally, in 3:18–20, God will gather Zion and all the earth. The universal scope of these last few verses forms a frame with the universal nature of God's wrath at the beginning of the book (1:2–3).

3:8–10 Yahweh Restores the Remnant of the Nations

The command to "wait" for the appointed day of Yahweh (3:8) occurs elsewhere in the OT only in Habakkuk 2:3. The second-person imperative masculine plural used here does not make it clear who is being asked to wait. The most likely referents are the "humble" who did Yahweh's will (2:3) and Daughter Zion, who is asked to "sing" and "shout aloud" (3:14), as these two groups again appear in the text.

The fierce anger of Yahweh will be unleashed on the nations that Yahweh gathers for destruction (3:8). We have discussed how the word "gather" opens the three main units in Zephaniah and is used in connection to "chaff" that is gathered for burning (see discussion on 2:1–3). In 3:8–9, Zephaniah uses the Hebrew infinitive six times in rapid succession to highlight Yahweh's intention to consume these nations.[9]

However, it is difficult to differentiate between the earlier identification of the "nations" – who are referred to as "them" in verse 8 – with the "them" in verse 9. The "them" in verse 9 are not "consumed" by God's anger but are identified as "my worshipers." This distinction is also evident in the two infinitives "to call" and "to serve" in verse 9, which has a different subject. In other words, this latter group is a subset of the "whole world" (3:8), the *remnant* of God's chosen people among the nations.

Interestingly, the result of God pouring out his wrath is the preservation of Yahweh's worshipers scattered throughout the earth. The use of the conjunction "then" (literally, "for then" or "at that time") at the beginning of verse 9 is

---

9. The Hebrew infinitive construct occurs six times, of which five are prefixed with the preposition *lamed* to indicate intent. They are translated into English as: "to stand," "to assemble," "to gather," "to pour out," "to call," and "to serve."

suggestive of a future time that follows logically from verse 8.[10] The use of the first-person verb "I will purify" (3:9) indicates that these transformations are the work of Yahweh. The burning anger of God will achieve seven things for a specific group of God's people: a) their lips will be purified; b) they will call on the name of Yahweh; c) they will serve Yahweh shoulder to shoulder; d) they will worship God; e) they will gather at Zion (and not be scattered);[11] f) they will bring offerings to Yahweh; and by extension g) they will not be consumed.

These transformations might have been drawn from the woe oracle against Cush in Isaiah 18:1–7 – where we find the only other occurrence of the phrase "the rivers of Cush" in the Bible (Isa 18:1) – and expanded on here in Zephaniah. Note the common motif of people who are scattered in the world bringing "gifts" to "Zion" and the emphasis on "the Name of the LORD Almighty" (Isa 18:7). Moreover, the oracle against Cush in Isaiah 18 also shows the harvest of Cush before the ingathering of the people. Zephaniah's woe oracle in 2:12 is oddly curt compared to the oracles against other foreign nations (2:4–15). This could be due to the composer's adaptation and expansion of Isaiah 18 in Zephaniah 3:9–10, which coheres well with our interpretation of this unit.[12]

3:11–13 Yahweh Restores the Remnant of Israel

In this second subunit that begins with that "day," the focus shifts to Jerusalem. As noted earlier, the Hebrew phrase "in the midst of you" (NIV has "from you") develops the idea of Yahweh removing the arrogant but leaving the humble and the meek in Jerusalem. Notice the reversal at work: The arrogant and complacent will be shamed and removed, but the meek and humble will remain and not be ashamed.

As in the previous unit, we see a remnant in Judah/Jerusalem after the destruction of the wicked. The word "because" (3:11) has the exact underlying Hebrew phrase *ki az* (literally, "for then" or "at that time") that is found in verse 9. These phrases, which are found nowhere else in Zephaniah, were probably used for parallelism. Also, as in the previous unit, there is a description of what the remnant of Jerusalem will do: a) they will trust in the name of Yahweh; b)

---

10. The Hebrew *ki az* ("for then") has a logical dependence and is not necessarily temporally sequential. See Clines, *DCH* 1:167–168.
11. The motif of scattering picks up the Tower of Babel tradition in Genesis 11:1–9.
12. Sweeney argues that "the Egyptian/Ethiopian oracles in Isaiah 18–19 was available in the mid-seventh century. Indeed, the assignment of 20:1–6, which is linked literarily to Isaiah 19, to the time of Josiah, indicates an effort to read these oracles in relation to Josiah's reform." Sweeney, *Zephaniah*, 183.

they will do no wrong; c) they will tell no lies; d) they will not be deceitful; e) they will eat; f) they will lie down; and g) they will not be afraid. Note the references to the "name of the LORD" in both units (3:9, 12) and the parallel between the purification of "lips" in 3:9 and the "tongue" and "mouths" that carry no deceit in 3:13.

Images of eating, lying down, and not being afraid recall the earlier description of the flock of God grazing in good pasture (2:6–7; compare 2:14). This conveys the idea that Yahweh's people will trust in him as the good shepherd and follow him obediently. This contrasts with the depiction of the Judean shepherds, who were like "roaring lions" and "evening wolves," ravaging and devouring the inhabitants of Jerusalem.

This image of pastoral tranquility reflects the domestic herder's life in ancient Israel. The shepherd would lead the flock to pasture in the morning. After feeding, the flock would lie down to rest before returning to the pen in the evening.[13] This tranquil imagery relates to texts such as Isaiah 11:6–9, Ezekiel 34:14, and the Zion tradition that carried significant messianic and eschatological overtones.[14] The good shepherd imagery of the NT is well-known. Jesus Christ is the good shepherd who seeks and cares for the lost (John 10:11–18). Overseers of the early church – also known as pastors – were called to care for the flock of God (1 Pet 5:1–4). Finally, in Revelation 17, we see "the Lamb at the center of the throne," our chief shepherd, who will lead those who have "washed their robes and made them white in the blood of the Lamb" to "springs of living water," where "God will wipe away every tear from their eyes" (17:14, 17).

3:14–17 Yahweh Takes Away Punishment and Saves

It is possible to see verse 14 as the beginning of a new text unit, especially since it follows the Masoretic disjunctive marker – though this need not always be the case. The use of imperative (volitive) forms is commonly found at the beginning of text units (1:7; 2:1; 3:8).[15] The verbs related to rejoicing – "sing," "shout aloud," "be glad," and "rejoice" (3:14) – are all in the imperative form.

---

13. John D. W. Watts, *Isaiah 1–33*, WBC 24 (Waco: Word Books, 1985), 173.
14. On the Zion tradition, Levenson, *Sinai and Zion*; See also John N. Oswalt, *Isaiah: The NIV Application Commentary* (Grand Rapids: Zondervan, 2003), 188–189; John B. Taylor, *Ezekiel: An Introduction and Commentary*, ed. Donald J. Wiseman, TOTC 22 (London: Tyndale, 1971), 222–224.
15. "Be Silent!" – Piel imperative/interjection (1:7), "Gather . . ., gather . . ." – Hitpael and Qal imperatives (2:1), and "Wait" – Piel imperative (3:8).

Zephaniah 3:14–17 is made up of two subunits (3:14–15 and 3:16–17). Together, this entire unit forms a transition to 3:18–20, which is the finale describing the work of restoration on the day of Yahweh. The call to sing, shout aloud, be glad, and rejoice is connected with Yahweh's deliverance of his people (Pss 5:11; 9:2; 27:6). And the combination of these actions is especially prominent in Israel's singing a *new song* to Yahweh (compare Pss 33:1–3; 40:3; 96:1; 98:1; 144:9; 149:1; Isa 42:10–13) – an act that leads to Yahweh's consummative work. The singing of a new song often comes before God's ultimate work of consummation:

> Theologically, this characteristic penultimate location of the 'new song' marks an important point in the trajectory from Lament to Praise. Their locations may be understood as follows: the 'new song' of the psalmist (and the readers) is situated after witnessing Yahweh's power in history. This calls for trusting and waiting in spite of the fall of the Davidic kingship and the Zion-temple. Yahweh's victorious kingship is the climactic turning point. He will bring about the utopic life in the ideal city and execute just revenge on his enemies and the oppressors of his people. The place of the 'new song' is situated just before that consummative end. It anticipates the realization of a new era in the eschaton. The 'new song' is the psalmist's song for an impending new world order that is dawning.[16]

This same kind of penultimately-located rejoicing is seen in Revelation 5:9 and 14:3, again before God's final consummative work. Hence, it is possible to see Zephaniah 3:14–17 as the penultimate call to sing to Yahweh before the ultimate expression of God's work of consummation in 3:18–20.

---

16. Ho, *Design of the Psalter*, 181–182.

Zephaniah 3

Having said this, consider the shape of 3:14–17.[17]

A		[14]Sing [1, root: *rnn*], Daughter Zion; shout aloud [2, root: *rw*], Israel! Be glad [3, root: *smh*] and rejoice [4, root: *lz*] with all your heart, Daughter Jerusalem!
A*		[15]The LORD has taken away your punishment, he has turned back your enemy.
	B	The LORD, the King of Israel, is with you ["in your midst"]; never again will you fear any harm.
		C [16]On that day they will say to Jerusalem, "Do not [*al*] fear, Zion; do not [*al*] let your hands hang limp.
	B′	[17]The LORD your God is with you ["in your midst"], the Mighty Warrior who saves.
A′		He will take great delight [5, root: *sws*] in you [6, NIV lacks "joy," root: *smh*];[18]
A*		in his love he will no longer rebuke you, but will rejoice [7, root: *gyl*] over you with singing [8, root: *rnh*]."

In these verses, Zephaniah speaks to Daughter Zion and Daughter Jerusalem, and Yahweh is addressed only in the third person. Consider how verse 14 (A) and the latter part of verse 17 (A′) form an *inclusio*. First, there is the

---

17. See Baker's structural consideration below. Baker, *Nahum, Habakkuk, Zephaniah*, 87.

A   Zion singing (3:14a)
B   Israel's shouts (3:14b)
C   Jerusalem's joy (3:14c)
D   Yahweh's deliverance (3:15a, b)
E   Presence of Yahweh the king (3:15c)
F   No more fear (3:15d)
G   Jerusalem's future message (3:16a)
F′   No more fear (3:16b, c)
E′   Presence of Yahweh the God (3:17a)
D′   The mighty deliverer (3:17b)
C′   God's joy (3:17c)
B′   Yahweh's silence (3:17d)
A′   Yahweh's singing (3:17e).

18. It is unclear why NIV has left the word "with joy" untranslated. But ESV translates the line as, "he will rejoice over you with gladness," and NLT has it as "he will take delight in you with gladness."

feminine portrayal of Zion and Jerusalem, who are portrayed as a bride in whom her husband, Yahweh, takes great delight in his love (compare Hosea 2). In the OT, such phrasing is common in describing the people of a city – for example, "Daughter Babylon" (Isa 47:1) or "Daughter Sidon" (Isa 23:12). Second, the parallels in A-A′ are evident in the use of eight different words related to joy, four on either end (3:14, 17).

Unfortunately, the NIV translation obscures this literary beauty by leaving out the word "joy" in verse 17. Remarkably, these eight Hebrew words related to joy are each used just once in Zephaniah. Third, just as Zion – the subject in A – is called to rejoice, Yahweh – the corresponding subject in A′ – will also rejoice in her. Fourth, Yahweh's wrath and rebuke of Jerusalem is removed in the parallel lines (A*). This motif is not found elsewhere in this unit. The day of Yahweh's anger does not apply to the remnant of Judah who trust in the name of Yahweh and do no wrong (3:12–13).

Moving inward from the frames, we see the reason for the rejoicing in lines B-C-B′. Here, the parallel lines B-B′ reiterate the presence of Yahweh in the midst of Jerusalem or Zion. They will be delivered from their enemies and will not fear harm again! At C, the center – which also marks the beginning of the second half of the unit – we have the temporal marker "on that day." To mark the center, the composer uses two negations in 3:16 – "do not" (*al*) – with a form that differs from all other negations (*lo*) used in Zephaniah.

It is also significant that, after this temporal marker in 3:16 at the center, the seven verbs in the rest of 3:16–17 (the second half of this unit) are all grammatically future (imperfective). Nowhere else in Zephaniah do we see a series of seven consecutive future verbs. It is also interesting that only in 3:14 and 3:16 – the front end and pivot of the chiasmus – do we see references to Zion and Jerusalem as a pair. Jerusalem, at this point, is described as "Zion" and not simply as "the city" (3:1). It is rhetorically significant that Zion is not used anywhere else in the book, possibly as a way to emphasize the shift in the trajectory of Zephaniah.

The point of this unit, given its shape, is the transformation of Jerusalem or Zion on that day. This transformation is characterized by the removal of Yahweh's wrath and his deliverance of Jerusalem from her enemies, signifying that the wrath of God has passed over his people. Most importantly, we see the dwelling of Yahweh in the midst of his people. All these things call for a new song and an outburst of praise by God's people.

3:18–20 Yahweh Gathers Zion and All the Earth

This closing unit of Zephaniah is designed to parallel the opening section (1:2–4). At 3:18, we see another shift – from addressing Yahweh as the third-person subject to Yahweh's first-person speech (3:14–17). This first-person emphasis highlights a key rhetorical thrust of the book – Yahweh is the one who will take action – and draws our attention directly to Yahweh's will and words. To some extent, the first-person speech is unmediated retelling. The stakes are clear: Yahweh has spoken. If he fails to do what he says, he is not God.

The extended series of first-person verbs used in 3:18–20 is impressive,[19] comparable only to 1:2–4. The repetitions of synonyms such as "remove" or "gather" (root: *'sp* in 3:18, root: *qbts*) between 3:19–20 and 1:2–3 ("sweep," *'sp* and *swp*) form bookends for the whole book of Zephaniah. Moreover, temporal markers ("when," "before the day," "at that time") used in conjunction with the act of Yahweh's gathering are designed to draw these texts together (1:3; 2:1–3; and 3:19–20).

The shape of the last three verses is set out below:[20]

A	[18]"I will remove from you all who mourn over the loss of your appointed festivals, which is a burden and reproach for you.
B	[19]*At that time* I will deal with all who oppressed you. I will rescue the lame; I will gather the exiles. I will give them praise and honor in every land where they have suffered shame.
B′	[20]*At that time* I will gather you; at that time I will bring you home. I will give you honor and praise among all the peoples of the earth when I restore your fortunes before your very eyes," says the LORD.

Zephaniah 3:18 introduces this unit with many remarkable reversals of Judah's idolatrous condition. But this verse is considered "one of the most difficult statements in the book of Zephaniah, and it has provoked a wide variety of readings among the ancient versions of the book and its modern interpreters."[21] The underlying Hebrew is terse – literally, "those who are grieved over the appointed feasts I shall remove/sweep away." It is possible to interpret this

---

19. There are five finite, one participle, and two infinitive construct forms in the first-person. The use of first-person finite verbs with the participle is also a transition marker (as we have seen in 1:2; 1:4; 1:8; 1:12; 2:5).
20. See also the structural considerations of Baker, *Nahum, Habakkuk, Zephaniah*, 88.
21. Sweeney, *Zephaniah*, 203.

verse as referring to the idolatrous mourning for the goddess Tammuz (Ezek 8:14).[22] If this interpretation is accepted, then the mourning for an appointed feast – that is, the ritual mourning of Tammuz, the fertility god – parallels the worship of the other fertility god, Baal, at the beginning of Zephaniah (1:4). Either way, the reference to "burden and reproach" indicates that the act of mourning at the appointed festivals (or at the loss of these festivals) is to be understood in a negative sense and that Yahweh would "remove" or "gather" (ESV) them.[23]

Consider the parallel lines B-B'. Both begin with the modified temporal marker "at that time" instead of "on that day," thereby setting the last three verses apart from the earlier units. Notice also that both B and B' convey the idea of God giving "honor" (literally, "name") and "praise" to Zion in all the earth. Both verses contain the motif of the ingathering of those scattered or exiled. The collocation of antonyms "gather" (*qbts*) and "the exiles" (*hanidakah*, or "scattered") from all the earth, is found only in the prophetic literature (Isa 11:12; 56:8; Jer 49:5).[24]

Consider what Yahweh will do to and for Zion (3:18–20). He will: a) remove (sweep away) all who mourned the appointed festivals; b) deal with all who have oppressed them; c) rescue the lame (compare Mic 4:6–7) and outcasts;[25] d) turn their shame into praise and honor; e) gather the exiles ("you" in 3:20);[26] f) make them praiseworthy and renowned among the peoples; g) bring them home; and h) restore their fortunes. This list presumes that before "that time," Daughter Zion or Daughter Jerusalem was idolatrous, oppressed, weakened, scattered, exiled, ashamed, dishonored, and plundered.

But this list is not to be read in isolation. Altogether, there are at least thirty first-person forms where Yahweh is the (inferred) subject in Zephani-

---

22. Tammuz is connected to the Sumerian pastoral deity, Dumuzid, the god of sheep and lamb. Tammuz is said to die and depart to the underworld during the hot and dry period of the year. And the mourning of Tammuz is the cultic act of bringing him back to life, which signals the return of rain and the harvest season.
23. The phrase, "I have removed/gathered" (root: *sp*), can be taken positively or negatively. In this case, it should be in the negative sense. Renz, *Nahum, Habakkuk, and Zephaniah*, 635.
24. In Jeremiah 49:5, note that Yahweh is the one who scatters (root: *ndh*) the Ammonites.
25. The lines, "I will rescue the lame; I will gather the exiles" is close to Micah's "I will gather the lame; I will assemble the exiles" (Mic 4:6–7).
26. We can trace the referent of the second person pronoun "you" (singular, feminine/masculine) in Zephaniah 3:18–19 to the characterization of Jerusalem whose judgment has been taken away (3:14–20). In 3:20, there is a shift to the plural "you," which is used on Judah's enemies elsewhere in Zephaniah. From the immediate context, this plural form in 3:20 refers to the same but emphasizes the multitude nature of God's people gathered from all nations. Sweeney, *Zephaniah*, 207.

ah,[27] and chapter 3 alone consists of almost sixty percent of such forms. The high concentration of references to Yahweh in the first person intensifies the emotional appeal of the text. It highlights the immediacy, intent, ownership, and connection between Yahweh and the audience at a significant point in this book – Yahweh will *personally* reverse Zion's negative predicament and restore all the good that he had purposed for her. By reading Zephaniah immediately after Habakkuk and before Haggai, during the transitional or liminal time of the Babylonian exile, the message of Zephaniah is a call to trust in Yahweh in times of devastation, a call especially to the "humble of the land . . . who do what he commands" (2:3).

At this time, two thousand years after Jesus, we, too, need to hear Jesus's words spoken to us in the same first-person voice as we wait for our ingathering and restoration by God:

> "I am coming soon. Hold on to what you have, so that no one will take your crown." (Rev 3:11)
>
> "Look, I am coming soon! Blessed is the one who keeps the words of the prophecy written in this scroll." (Rev 22:7)
>
> "Look, I am coming soon! My reward is with me, and I will give to each person according to what they have done." (Rev 22:12)

SUMMARY AND REFLECTION

The final chapter of Zephaniah begins with a severe indictment of Jerusalem. She was rebellious, defiled, and oppressive. Her princes and priests were idolatrous. Instead of shepherding the people carefully, her leaders acted like lions and wolves who terrorized the flock. As a result, Yahweh's laws were perverted. From the text, there is no evidence that the city had repented. Yet, because of God's faithfulness to his promises, he was patient with Jerusalem, even as he sought to destroy the wicked nations around her. But Jerusalem remained unrepentant and wicked. Therefore, God determined that he himself would become the city's righteousness and unilaterally transform the city on a particular "day" and "time." He will gather and restore the remnant from all the earth. This remnant who trusts in God will not engage in wickedness, and they will dwell secure in Zion. On that day, Jerusalem will rejoice and receive honor and praise. There will be a reversal of fortunes – their brokenness will be healed, shame will be replaced by honor, and they will be restored. Zephaniah

---

27. These first-person forms include participles (with text critical issues) and infinitive suffixes.

is both the dark tunnel *and* the light at the end of the tunnel for all who have suffered that darkness; it is both the cold *and* the spark that lights the fire of warmth in the cold camp; the dungeon *and* the sound of keys to the jail; the pain *and* the song we need in times of tears. The book of Zephaniah is the desert *and* the oasis in the desert.

CONCLUSION

Habakkuk, Zephaniah, and other voices in the XII proclaim that God is trustworthy and call his people to remain faithful despite their difficult situations. In Zephaniah, God says, "Therefore wait for me" (3:8). In Habakkuk, the Lord says, "Though it linger, wait for it" (2:3). "I will wait patiently," says Habakkuk (3:16). "Wait for your God always," says Hosea (12:6). "As for me, I watch in hope for the Lord, I wait for God my Savior; my God will hear me," says Micah (7:7).

In the Song, Yuan, and Ming dynasties, there was great interest in virtues that foster human relationships.[1] The top five virtues were called the "Five Constants" (五常): goodness (仁),[2] righteousness (义),[3] ritual propriety (礼),[4] wisdom (智),[5] and faithfulness (信). The last in this list, faithfulness, is considered the most fundamental because it attests to the genuineness and consistency of all other virtues.

The character of this final virtue, *xin* (信) – meaning, "trust" or "faithfulness" – is made up of two separate parts, with ren 亻 ("human") on the left and 言 ("word") on the right.[6] The combination of these parts suggests that *xin* ("trust" or "trustworthiness") is the integration of the person and his or her words. Its importance in the *Analects* is shown in the areas of rule, governance, and relationships with others. *Xin* is one of the two fundamental principles of ruling a large nation (*Analects* 1:5).[7] Compared to the military and food, *xin* is the least dispensable (*Analects* 12:7).[8] *Xin* is a necessary ingredient in

---

1. Justin Tiwald, "Song-Ming Confucianism," in *The Stanford Encyclopedia of Philosophy*, ed. Edward N. Zalta, Summer 2020 (Metaphysics Research Lab, Stanford University, 2020), https://plato.stanford.edu/archives/sum2020/entries/song-ming-confucianism/.
2. This includes selfless acts of love and kindness, like taking care of someone in need.
3. This includes a refusal to violate laws and regulations, and the fait administration of justice.
4. This term is wide-ranging and includes many social protocols, such as bowing or shaking hands.
5. Wisdom includes the ability to understand someone else's quality and character and their effectiveness in achieving a goal. In this latter, the Chinese "wisdom" is similar to the Hebrew *hokma*, or "skill" (Exod 31:3).
6. For a fascinating philosophical discussion on this word, see Winnie Sung and Philosophy Documentation Center, "Xin: Being Trustworthy," *International Philosophical Quarterly* 60, no. 3 (2020): 271–286.
7. C. C. Tsai, *The Analects: An Illustrated Edition*, trans. Brian Bruya, *The Analects*, vol. 4. The Illustrated Library of Chinese Classics (Princeton: Princeton University Press, 2018), 49, https://doi.org/10.23943/9781400890408.
8. Tsai, *Analects*, 128.

friendships (*Analects* 5:26) and an indispensable element in the interactions between superiors and subordinates (*Analects* 19:10).

It is significant that Yahweh epitomizes all the five virtues noted above (Dan 2:20; 9:14; Joel 2:13; Luke 18:19; Rom 1:17; 1 Cor 1:9; 1 John 4:8). But if we were to read *xin* along the grain of OT relationships – especially the relationship between Yahweh and his people – we see that the faithfulness of God connects with the expressions of the other four virtues in his dealing with his people. How is God good, righteous, and wise, and how does he deal appropriately with his people? The concerted voice of Scripture says that even in the darkest of times – as seen in Habakkuk and Zephaniah – God is faithful: "Know therefore that the LORD your God is God; he is the faithful God, keeping his covenant of love to a thousand generations of those who love him and keep his commandments" (Deut 7:9).

Let me end as I have begun: The retribution principle is effective – both for the wicked and the righteous – on that day when the Lord Jesus Christ is revealed.

> [6] God is just: He will pay back trouble to those who trouble you [7] and give relief to you who are troubled, and to us as well. This will happen when the Lord Jesus is revealed from heaven in blazing fire with his powerful angels. [8] He will punish those who do not know God and do not obey the gospel of our Lord Jesus. [9] They will be punished with everlasting destruction and shut out from the presence of the Lord and from the glory of his might [10] on the day he comes to be glorified in his holy people and to be marveled at among all those who have believed. This includes you, because you believed our testimony to you. [11] With this in mind, we constantly pray for you, that our God may make you worthy of his calling, and that by his power he may bring to fruition your every desire for goodness and your every deed prompted by faith. (2 Thess 1:6–11)

The books of Habakkuk and Zephaniah demonstrate that God's people can never achieve the righteousness required to stand before God without God's mercy. At the lowest point in their history, they remained unrepentant. Yet in such a situation, God's grace was shown in the face of his people's persistent godlessness. More than that, God supplied the merit of righteousness for his unrepentant people, and showed that he was determined to love them in spite of their sin and wickedness. It can be said that God suffered to become their righteousness and for the transformation of his people. Nonetheless, these books require their readers to wait patiently for that "day" when God would act decisively. An ultimate transformation awaits.

In the same way, as we wait for God's final judgment and deliverance in our day and time, we must remember that God is determined to love and transform us by his faithfulness and for his own glory. He will do so by supplying his righteousness to us through Jesus Christ, whose death and resurrection provide the atonement for our sins and the surety of our victory over death. Meanwhile, like Habakkuk and Zephaniah, our predicaments may remain dire as we wait for a more complete deliverance. When God does not seem to hear our cries to him at a time when his laws are perverted, or when evil continues like a horde against us, God's delay in delivering us may be precisely because he is making us more like him. The righteous shall live by faith, just as God is faithful – therein lies our hope and salvation.

SELECTED BIBLIOGRAPHY

Aernie, Matthew and Donald Hartley. "The Day of the Lord in Paul's Theology." In *The Righteous and Merciful Judge: The Day of the Lord in the Life and Theology of Paul*. Bellingham: Lexham, 2018.

Arnold, Bill. "Babylonians." In *Peoples of the Old Testament World*. Edited by Alfred J. Hoerth, Gerald L. Mattingly, and Edwin M. Yamauchi. Cambridge: Baker Academic, 1998.

Baker, David W. *Nahum, Habakkuk, Zephaniah*. TOTC. Leicester, UK: Inter-Varsity Press, 1988.

Barker, Kenneth L. and Waylon Bailey. *Micah, Nahum, Habakkuk, Zephaniah: An Exegetical and Theological Exposition of Holy Scripture*. NAC 20. Nashville: B&H, 1998.

Barna Group. "Six Reasons Young Christians Leave Church - Article." BioLogos, June 5, 2017. https://biologos.org/articles/six-reasons-young-christians-leave-church/.

Barré, Michael L. "Newly Discovered Literary Devices in the Prayer of Habakkuk." *CBQ* 75, no. 3 (2013): 446–462.

BBC News. "Nuclear Annihilation Just One Miscalculation Away, UN Chief Warns," August 1, 2022. https://www.bbc.com/news/world-62381425.

BBC News. "Thai Cave Rescuer Dies from Year-Long Blood Infection," December 28, 2019. https://www.bbc.com/news/world-asia-50931695.

Ben Zvi, Ehud and James D. Nogalski. *Two Sides of a Coin: Juxtaposing Views on Interpreting the Book of the Twelve/the Twelve Prophetic Books*. Piscataway: Gorgias, 2009.

Berlin, Adele. *Zephaniah*. Anchor Bible. New York: Doubleday, 1994.

Bloom, Jon. "Should You Earnestly Desire to Prophesy?" *Desiring God* (blog), September 21, 2018. https://www.desiringgod.org/articles/should-you-earnestly-desire-to-prophesy.

Boda, Mark J. *Exploring Zechariah, Volume 2: The Development and Role of Biblical Traditions in Zechariah*. ANEM. Atlanta: SBL Press, 2017.

———. "Freeing the Burden of Prophecy: Maśśā' and the Legitimacy of Prophecy in Zech 9–14." *Bib* 87, no. 3 (2006): 338–357.

Boda, Mark J. and J. G. McConville, eds. *Dictionary of the Old Testament: Prophets*. IVP Bible Dictionary Series 4. Downers Grove: IVP Academic, 2012.

Bohstrom, Philippe. "Israelites in Biblical Dan Worshiped Idols – and Yahweh Too, Archaeologists Discover." *Haaretz*, October 31, 2018.

Bruce, Frederick Fyvie. *The Epistle of Paul to the Romans: An Introduction and Commentary*. TNTC 6. London: Inter-Varsity Press, 1974.

Carruthers, Frances. "'Within Minutes You're in a Different World': An Interview with Cave Diver John Volanthen." loveexploring.com, February 3, 2022.

Chalmers, Aaron. *Interpreting the Prophets: Reading, Understanding and Preaching from the Worlds of the Prophets.* Downers Grove: IVP Academic, 2015.

Charlesworth, James H., ed. *The Old Testament Pseudepigrapha: Apocalyptic Literature and Testaments*, vol. 1. Garden City: Doubleday, 1983.

Chiang, Gracia. "'We Have Much to Be Thankful for': Bible College Lecturer and Caregiver David Lang on the Death of His Daughter." *Thir.st* (blog), February 28, 2022.

Childs, Brevard S. *Biblical Theology of the Old and New Testaments: Theological Reflection on the Christian Bible.* Minneapolis: Fortress, 2011.

———. *Introduction to the Old Testament as Scripture.* Philadelphia: Fortress, 1979.

Clendenen, Ray. "Salvation by Faith or by Faithfulness in the Book of Habakkuk?" *Bulletin for Biblical Research* 24.4 (2014), 505–513.

Coggins, Richard and Jin H. Han. *Six Minor Prophets through the Centuries: Nahum, Habakkuk, Zephaniah, Haggai, Zechariah, and Malachi.* Chichester: Wiley-Blackwell, 2011.

Crown, Alan D. "Tidings and Instructions: How News Travelled in the Ancient Near East." *Journal of the Economic and Social History of the Orient* 17.3 (1974): 244–271.

Currid, John D. *Ancient Egypt and the Old Testament.* Grand Rapids: Baker Books, 1997.

Day, John. *Yahweh and the Gods and Goddesses of Canaan.* Edited by David Clines and Philip R. Davies. JSOTSup 265. London: Sheffield Academic, 2002.

Dorsey, David A. *The Literary Structure of the Old Testament: A Commentary on Genesis-Malachi.* Grand Rapids: Baker Academic, 2004.

Ephʿal, Israel. "Nebuchadnezzar the Warrior: Remarks on His Military Achievements." *IEJ* 53, no. 2 (2003): 178–191.

Floyd, Michael H. "Basic Trends in the Form-Critical Study of Prophetic Texts." In *The Changing Face of Form Criticism for the Twenty-First Century.* Edited by Marvin A. Sweeney and Ehud Ben Zvi. Grand Rapids: Eerdmans, 2003.

———. "Introduction." In *The Book of Twelve & The New Form Criticism.* Edited by Mark J. Boda, Michael H. Floyd, and Colin M. Toffelmire. ANEM 10. Atlanta: SBL Press, 2015.

———. "New Form Criticism and Beyond: The Historicity of Prophetic Literature Revisited." In *The Book of Twelve & The New Form Criticism.* Edited by Mark J. Boda, Michael H. Floyd, and Colin M. Toffelmire. ANEM 10. Atlanta: SBL Press, 2015.

———. "The אַשָּׂמ (Maśśāʾ) as a Type of Prophetic Book." *JBL* 121, no. 3 (2002): 401–422.

Selected Bibliography

Freedman, David Noel, Gary A. Herion, David F. Graf, John D. Pleins, and Astrid B. Beck, eds. *The Anchor Yale Bible Dictionary*. New York: Doubleday, 1992.

Frye, Northrop. *Anatomy of Criticism: Four Essays*. Princeton: Princeton University Press, 1957.

Garrett, Duane A. and Jason S. DeRouchie. *A Modern Grammar for Biblical Hebrew*. Nashville: B&H Academic, 2009.

Gentry, Peter J. *How to Read and Understand the Biblical Prophets*. Wheaton: Crossway, 2017.

Gerstenberger, Erhard. "The Woe-Oracles of the Prophets." *JBL* 81, no. 3 (1962): 249–263.

———. "Twelve (and More) Anonyms: A Biblical Book without Authors." In *Priests and Cults in the Book of the Twelve*. Edited by Lena-Sofia Tiemeyer. ANEM 14. Atlanta: SBL Press, 2015.

Goh, Robbie B. H. "Christian Identities in Singapore: Religion, Race and Culture between State Controls and Transnational Flows." *Journal of Cultural Geography* 26, no. 1 (2009): 1–23.

Gunkel, Hermann. *Creation and Chaos in the Primeval Era and the Eschaton: A Religio-Historical Study of Genesis 1 and Revelation 12*. Translated by William Whitney Jr. Biblical Resource Series. Grand Rapids: Eerdmans, 2006.

Heider, George C. *Cult of Molek: A Reassessment*. Edited by David A. Clines and Philip R. Davies. JSOTSup 43. Sheffield: JSOT Press, 2009.

Hilber, John, Tremper Longman III, Duane Garrett, J. Glen Taylor, Mark W. Chavalas, Philip S. Johnston, Alan R. Millard, et al. *The Minor Prophets, Job, Psalms, Proverbs, Ecclesiastes, Song of Songs*. Edited by John H. Walton. Zondervan Illustrated Bible Backgrounds Commentary 5. Grand Rapids: Zondervan Academic, 2009.

Hiramatsu, Kei. "The Structure and Structural Relationships of the Book of Habakkuk." *Journal of Inductive Biblical Studies* 3, no. 2 (2016): 106–129.

Ho, Peter C. W. *The Design of the Psalter: A Macrostructural Analysis*. Eugene: Pickwick, 2019.

———. "The Macrostructural Design and Logic of the Psalter: An Unfurling of the Davidic Covenant." In *Reading the Psalms Theologically*. Edited by David Howard, Jr. and Andrew Schmutzer. Studies in Scripture and Biblical Theology. Bellingham: Lexham Academic, 2023.

House, Paul R. *The Unity of the Twelve*. BLS 27. Sheffield: Sheffield Academic, 2009.

Jacobsen, Thorkild. *The Sumerian King List*. AS 11. Chicago: University of Chicago Press, 1939.

Janzen, J. Gerald. "Eschatological Symbol and Existence in Habakkuk." In *When Prayer Takes Place*. Edited by Brent A. Strawn and Patrick D. Miller. Cambridge: The Lutterworth Press, 2012.

Jeyaraj, Daniel. "The Struggle of Dalit Christians in South India for Their Identity and Recognition." *Theology* 100, no. 796 (1997): 242–251.

King, James. Palestine Exploration Fund. *Moab's Patriarchal Stone: Being an Account of the Moabite Stone, Its Story and Teaching*. London: Bickers and Son, 1878.

Klein, Ralph W. "Day of the Lord." *CTM* 39, no. 8 (1968): 517–525.

Klingbeil, Martin. *Yahweh Fighting from Heaven: God as Warrior and as God of Heaven in the Hebrew Psalter and Ancient Near Eastern Iconography*. Vol. 169. OBO. Göttingen: Vandenhoeck & Ruprecht, 1999.

Klopper, Frances. "Aspects of Creation: The Water in the Wilderness Motif in the Psalms and the Prophets." *OTE* 18, no. 2 (2005): 253–264.

Lambert, W. G. "The Babylonians and Chaldeans." In *Peoples of Old Testament Times*. Edited by Donald J. Wiseman. Oxford: Clarendon, 1973.

Lecureux, Jason T. *The Thematic Unity of the Book of the Twelve*. HBM 41. Sheffield: Sheffield Phoenix, 2012.

Leichty, Erle. *The Royal Inscriptions of Esarhaddon, King of Assyria (680–669 BC)*, vol. 4. Royal Inscriptions of the Neo-Assyrian Period. Winona Lake: Eisenbrauns, 2011.

Leuenberger, Martin. "Day of the Lord." In *Oxford Encyclopedia of the Bible and Theology*. Edited by Samuel E. Balentine. Oxford: Oxford University Press, 2015.

Levenson, Jon D. *Sinai and Zion. An Entry into the Jewish Bible*. Minneapolis: Winston, 1985.

Loeffler, James. "The Problem With the 'Judeo-Christian Tradition.'" *The Atlantic*, August 1, 2020. https://www.theatlantic.com/ideas/archive/2020/08/the-judeo-christian-tradition-is-over/614812/.

Lohfink, Norbert. *The Covenant Never Revoked: Biblical Reflections on Christian-Jewish Dialogue*. Translated by John J. Scullion. New York: Paulist, 1991.

Longman III, Tremper, Daniel G. Reid, and Willem A. Van Gemeren. *God Is a Warrior*. Grand Rapids: Zondervan Academic, 1995.

Lyons, Michael A. "Standards of Cohesion and Coherence: Evidence from Early Readers." *Hebrew Bible and Ancient Israel* 9, no. 2 (2020): 183–208.

Magome, Mogomotsi. "South Africa's Response to Pandemic Hit by Corrupt Contracts." *AP NEWS*, January 25, 2022. https://apnews.com/article/coronavirus-pandemic-health-pandemics-africa-covid-19-pandemic-9a0afd37e14d2a707f7785822b21eba7.

Matthews, Victor H. *Old Testament Themes*. St. Louis: Chalice, 2000.

Selected Bibliography

McConville, J. Gordon. "Retribution in Deuteronomy: Theology and Ethics." *Interpretation* 69, no. 3 (2015): 288–298.

McDermid, Charles. "Christians in Asia: Persecuted, Oppressed . . . but Keeping the Faith." *South China Morning Post*, January 18, 2019. https://www.scmp.com/week-asia/politics/article/2182800/christians-asia-persecuted-oppressed-keeping-faith.

Merwe, Christo H. van der, Jacobus A. Naudé, and Jan H. Kroeze. *A Biblical Hebrew Reference Grammar*. Second Edition. London: T&T Clark, 2017.

Miller, Robert D. "Dragon Myths and Biblical Theology." *TS* 80, no. 1 (2019): 37–56.

———. "Tracking the Dragon across the Ancient Near East." *ArOr* 82 (2014): 225–245.

Mulzac, Kenneth. "The Remnant Motif in the Context of Judgment and Salvation in the Book of Jeremiah." PhD Dissertation, Andrews University Seventh-day Adventist Theological Seminary, 1995. https://digitalcommons.andrews.edu/dissertations/100.

Nick, Yang. "At Least 17 Dead and 17 Missing as Flash Flood Hits Northwestern China." *South China Morning Post*, August 18, 2022. https://www.scmp.com/news/china/article/3189304/flash-flood-hits-northwestern-china-leaving-4-dead-and-dozens-missing.

Nogalski, James D. *Literary Precursors to the Book of the Twelve*. BZAW 217. Berlin: de Gruyter, 1993.

———. *Redactional Processes in the Book of the Twelve*. BZAW 218. Berlin: de Gruyter, 1993.

———. *The Book of the Twelve: Hosea–Jonah*. Smyth & Helwys Bible Commentary. Macon: Smyth & Helwys, 2011.

———. "Where Are the Prophets in the Book of the Twelve?" In *The Book of Twelve & The New Form Criticism*. Edited by Mark J. Boda, Michael H. Floyd, and Colin M. Toffelmire. ANEM 10. Atlanta: SBL Press, 2015.

Nogalski, James D. and Marvin A. Sweeney, eds. *Reading and Hearing the Book of the Twelve*. SBL Symposium 15. Atlanta: Society of Biblical Literature, 2000.

O'Neal, G. Michael. *Interpreting Habakkuk as Scripture: An Application of the Canonical Approach of Brevard S. Childs*. StBibLit 9. New York: Peter Lang, 2006.

Oswalt, John N. *Isaiah: The NIV Application Commentary*. Grand Rapids: Zondervan, 2003.

———. *The Holy One of Israel: Studies in the Book of Isaiah*. Eugene: Cascade Books, 2014.

Petrovich, Craig S. "Toward the Originally Authored Book of the Twelve: Testing the Coherence of the Variant Shapings of the Twelve Prophets." Masters of Arts, Talbot School of Theology, Biola University, 2015.

Phua, Rachel. "Three Children with Fatal Genetic Disorder, yet David Lang Sees God's Sovereignty." *Salt&Light* (blog), 2018. https://saltandlight.sg/profiles/why-suffer-david-lang/.

Prinsloo, G. T. M. "Habakkuk 2:5a: Denouncing 'Wine' or 'Wealth'? Contextual Readings of the Masoretic Text and 1QpHab." *HTS Theological Studies* 72, no. 4 (2016): 12.

———. "Reading Habakkuk 3 in Its Literary Context: A Worthwhile Exercise or Futile Attempt?" *Journal for Semitics* 11, no. 1 (2002): 83–111.

Pritchard, James, ed. *Ancient Near Eastern Texts Relating to the Old Testament: Third Edition with Supplements*. Princeton: Princeton University Press, 1969.

Radine, Jason. "The 'Idolatrous Priest' in the Book of Zephaniah." In *Priests and Cults in the Book of the Twelve*. Edited by Lena-Sofia Tiemeyer. ANEM 14. Atlanta: SBL Press, 2016.

Rajkumar, Peniel. *Dalit Theology and Dalit Liberation: Problems, Paradigms and Possibilities*. London: Routledge, 2016.

Ramantswana, Hulisani. "Conflicts at Creation: Genesis 1–3 in Dialogue with the Psalter." *OTE* 27, no. 2 (2014): 553–578.

"Recasting Justice: Securing Dalit Rights in Nepal's New Constitution." Center for Human Rights and Global Justice. New York: NYU School of Law, 2008.

Redditt, Paul and Aaron Schart, eds. *Thematic Threads in the Book of the Twelve*. BZAW 325. Berlin: De Gruyter, 2012.

Renz, Thomas. "Habakkuk and Its Co-Texts." In *The Book of the Twelve: An Anthology of Prophetic Books or The Result of Complex Redactional Processes?* Edited by Heiko Wenzel. Göttingen: V&R Unipress, 2017.

———. *The Books of Nahum, Habakkuk, and Zephaniah*. NICOT. Grand Rapids: Eerdmans, 2021.

Rickett, Brian R. "Temple of Idol Worship Found Near Jerusalem." *Patterns of Evidence* (blog), February 20, 2020. https://patternsofevidence.com/2020/02/20/temple-of-idol-worship-found-near-jerusalem/.

Roberts, Edgar V. *Writing about Literature*. 8th edition. Englewood Cliffs: Prentice Hall, 1995.

Robertson, O. Palmer. *The Books of Nahum, Habakkuk, and Zephaniah*. NICOT. Grand Rapids: Eerdmans, 1990.

Rogland, Max. *Alleged Non-Past Uses of Qatal in Classical Hebrew*. SSN 44. Leiden: Brill, 2003.

Ruffing, Elizabeth G., Dottie Oleson, James Tomlinson, Seong Hyun Park, and Steven J. Sandage. "Humility and Relational Spirituality as Predictors of Well-

Being among Christian Seminary Students." *Journal of Psychology and Theology* 49, no. 4 (2021): 419–435.

Smith, Mark S. *The Early History of God: Yahweh and the Other Deities in Ancient Israel*. Second Edition. Grand Rapids: Eerdmans, 2002.

Smith, Mark and Wayne Pitard. *The Ugaritic Baal Cycle. Introduction with Text, Translation and Commentary of KTU/CAT 1.3–1.4*. Vol. II. VTSup 114. Leiden: Brill, 2009.

Sng, Bobby E. K. *In His Good Time: The Story of the Church in Singapore 1819–2002*. 3rd edition. Singapore: Bible Society of Singapore, 2003.

Snyman, S. D. *Nahum, Habakkuk and Zephaniah: An Introduction and Commentary*. Edited by David G. Firth and Tremper Longman III. TOTC 27. Downers Grove: IVP Academic, 2020.

Steussy, Marti J. *Samuel and His God*. Columbia: University of South Carolina Press, 2010.

Sung, Winnie and Philosophy Documentation Center. "Xin: Being Trustworthy." *International Philosophical Quarterly* 60, no. 3 (2020): 271–286.

Sweeney, Marvin A. "Form and Eschatology in the Book of the Twelve Prophets." In *The Book of Twelve & The New Form Criticism*. Edited by Mark J. Boda, Michael H. Floyd, and Colin M. Toffelmire. ANEM 10. Atlanta: SBL Press, 2015.

———. "Sequence and Interpretation in the Book of the Twelve." In *Reading and Hearing the Book of the Twelve*. Edited by James D. Nogalski and Marvin A. Sweeney. SBL Symposium Series 15. Atlanta: Society of Biblical Literature, 2000.

———. "Structure, Genre, and Intent in the Book of Habakkuk." *VT* 41, no. 1 (1991): 63–83.

———. *Zephaniah: A Commentary*. Edited by Paul D. Hanson. Hermeneia. Minneapolis: Fortress, 2003.

Taylor, John B. *Ezekiel: An Introduction and Commentary*. Edited by Donald J. Wiseman. TOTC 22. London: Tyndale, 1971.

"The Presbyterian Church in Singapore – History." https://www.presbyterian.org.sg/history.htm.

Thomas, Winton D., trans. *Documents from Old Testament Times*. London: Thomas Nelson and Sons, 1958.

Tiwald, Justin. "Song-Ming Confucianism." In *The Stanford Encyclopedia of Philosophy*. Edited by Edward N. Zalta. Summer 2020. Metaphysics Research Lab, Stanford University, 2020.

Toffelmire, Colin M. "Sitz Im What? Context and the Prophetic Book of Obadiah." In *The Book of Twelve & The New Form Criticism*. Edited by Mark

J. Boda, Michael H. Floyd, and Colin M. Toffelmire. ANEM 10. Atlanta: SBL Press, 2015.

Troxel, Ronald L. "The Problem of Time in Joel." *JBL* 132, no. 1 (2013): 77–96.

Tsai, C. C., ed. *The Analects: An Illustrated Edition*. Translated by Brian Bruya, vol. 4. The Illustrated Library of Chinese Classics. Princeton: Princeton University Press, 2018.

Tuell, Steven S. "The Psalm in Habakkuk 3." In *Partners with God*. Edited by Shelley L. Birdsong and Serge Frolov. Claremont Studies in Hebrew Bible and Septuagint. Claremont: Claremont Press, 2017.

Tully, Eric J. *Reading the Prophets as Christian Scripture: A Literary, Canonical, and Theological Introduction*. Grand Rapids: Baker Academic, 2022.

UN News. "Ukraine: More than 14,000 Casualties to Date but 'actual Numbers Are Likely Considerably Higher'," September 9, 2022. https://news.un.org/en/story/2022/09/1126391.

Veen, Pieter Gert van der and Dr. Robert Deutsch. "The Bulla of #39; Amaryahu Son of the King, the Ancestor of the Prophet Zephaniah?" In *Bible et Proche-Orient. Mélanges André Lemaire*. Edited by J. Elayi and J. M. Durand. *Transeu* 46. Paris: Gabalda, 2014.

Veldhuis, Niek. *Religion, Literature, and Scholarship: The Sumerian Composition of Nanése and the Birds, with a Catalogue of Sumerian Bird Names*. CM 22. Leiden: Brill, 2004.

Walker, H. H. and N. W. Lund. "The Literary Structure of the Book of Habakkuk." *JBL* 53, no. 4 (1934): 355–370.

Waltke, Bruce K. "Superscripts, Postscripts, or Both." *JBL* 110, no. 4 (1991): 583–596.

Watts, James W. and Paul R. House, eds. *Forming Prophetic Literature: Essays on Isaiah and the Twelve in Honor of John D. W. Watts*. JSOTSup 235. Sheffield: Sheffield Academic, 1996.

Watts, John D. W. *Isaiah 1–33*. WBC 24. Waco: Word Books, 1985.

Weis, Richard D. *A Definition of the Genre "Massa" in the Hebrew Bible*, 1986.

Weiss, Bari. "The Story Behind a 2,600-Year-Old Seal." *The New York Times*, March 30, 2019, Sunday Review. https://www.nytimes.com/2019/03/30/opinion/sunday/bible-josiah-david-seal.html.

Wendland, Ernst R. "'The Righteous Live by Their Faith' in a Holy God: Complementary Compositional Forces and Habakkuk's Dialogue with the Lord." *JETS* 42, no. 4 (1999): 591–628.

Wenzel, Heiko and Georg Fischer, eds. *The Book of the Twelve: An Anthology of Prophetic Books or the Result of Complex Redactional Processes? Osnabrücker Studien Zur Jüdischen Und Christlichen Bibel 4*. Göttingen: V&R Unipress, 2018.

Selected Bibliography

Westermann, Claus. *Basic Forms of Prophetic Speech*. Philadelphia: Westminster, 1967.

Weyde, K. W. "Once Again the Term Maśśā' in Zechariah 9:1; 12:1 and in Malachi 1:1: What Is Its Significance?" *AcT* (2018): 251–267.

Wijaya, Philip. "What Does It Mean That Our Security Is in the Lord?" Christianity.com. https://www.christianity.com/wiki/salvation/what-does-it-mean-that-our-security-is-in-the-lord.html.

Yip, Brandon Zhen Yuan. "Understanding the Four Critiques of Singapore's Meritocracy." TODAY, April 29, 2019. https://www.todayonline.com/commentary/understanding-four-critiques-singapores-meritocracy.

Yoder, Tyler R. "Fishing for Fish and Fishing for Men: Fishing Imagery in the Hebrew Bible and the Ancient Near East." PhD Dissertation, The Ohio State University, 2015.

Zvi, Ehud Ben. "The Concept of Prophetic Books and Its Historical Setting." In *The Production of Prophecy: Constructing Prophecy and Prophets in Yehud*. Edited by Diana Vikander Edelman and Ehud Ben Zvi. London: Routledge, 2014.

Asia Theological Association
54 Scout Madriñan St. Quezon City 1103, Philippines
Email: ataasia@gmail.com Telefax: (632) 410 0312

OUR MISSION

The Asia Theological Association (ATA) is a body of theological institutions, committed to evangelical faith and scholarship, networking together to serve the Church in equipping the people of God for the mission of the Lord Jesus Christ.

OUR COMMITMENT

The ATA is committed to serving its members in the development of evangelical, biblical theology by strengthening interaction, enhancing scholarship, promoting academic excellence, fostering spiritual and ministerial formation and mobilizing resources to fulfill God's global mission within diverse Asian cultures.

OUR TASK

Affirming our mission and commitment, ATA seeks to:

- **Strengthen** interaction through inter-institutional fellowship and programs, regional and continental activities, faculty and student exchange programs.
- **Enhance** scholarship through consultations, workshops, seminars, publications, and research fellowships.
- **Promote** academic excellence through accreditation standards, faculty and curriculum development.
- **Foster** spiritual and ministerial formation by providing mentor models, encouraging the development of ministerial skills and a Christian ethos.
- **Mobilize** resources through library development, information technology and infra-structural development.

To learn more about ATA, visit www.ataasia.com or facebook.com/AsiaTheologicalAssociation

Langham Literature, along with its publishing work, is a ministry of Langham Partnership.

Langham Partnership is a global fellowship working in pursuit of the vision God entrusted to its founder John Stott –

> *to facilitate the growth of the church in maturity and Christ-likeness through raising the standards of biblical preaching and teaching.*

Our vision is to see churches in the Majority World equipped for mission and growing to maturity in Christ through the ministry of pastors and leaders who believe, teach and live by the word of God.

Our mission is to strengthen the ministry of the word of God through:
- nurturing national movements for biblical preaching
- fostering the creation and distribution of evangelical literature
- enhancing evangelical theological education

especially in countries where churches are under-resourced.

Our ministry

Langham Preaching partners with national leaders to nurture indigenous biblical preaching movements for pastors and lay preachers all around the world. With the support of a team of trainers from many countries, a multi-level programme of seminars provides practical training, and is followed by a programme for training local facilitators. Local preachers' groups and national and regional networks ensure continuity and ongoing development, seeking to build vigorous movements committed to Bible exposition.

Langham Literature provides Majority World preachers, scholars and seminary libraries with evangelical books and electronic resources through publishing and distribution, grants and discounts. The programme also fosters the creation of indigenous evangelical books in many languages, through writer's grants, strengthening local evangelical publishing houses, and investment in major regional literature projects, such as one volume Bible commentaries like the *Africa Bible Commentary* and the *South Asia Bible Commentary*.

Langham Scholars provides financial support for evangelical doctoral students from the Majority World so that, when they return home, they may train pastors and other Christian leaders with sound, biblical and theological teaching. This programme equips those who equip others. Langham Scholars also works in partnership with Majority World seminaries in strengthening evangelical theological education. A growing number of Langham Scholars study in high quality doctoral programmes in the Majority World itself. As well as teaching the next generation of pastors, graduated Langham Scholars exercise significant influence through their writing and leadership.

To learn more about Langham Partnership and the work we do visit **langham.org**

www.ingramcontent.com/pod-product-compliance
Lightning Source LLC
Chambersburg PA
CBHW070535170426
43200CB00011B/2428